AN INDEPENDENT F
CHALLENGES AND C

Edited by Brian Bow and Patrick Lennox

In 1968, with the United States increasingly involved in Vietnam, questions were raised in Canada about America's international leadership and about Canada's own foreign policy goals. Forty years later, faced with seemingly intractable wars in Iraq and Afghanistan, Canada must ask similar questions: could Canada pursue a genuinely independent foreign policy? Does Canada have the capacity and the political will to chart its own course in the world?

This collection of essays by a new generation of scholars considers the question of Canada's foreign policy independence in historical and theoretical perspective, with attention to issues including defence and security, Arctic sovereignty, trade, culture, and environmental policy. Accessible and insightful, *An Independent Foreign Policy for Canada?* represents a provocative and long-overdue reassessment of Canada's foreign policy challenges and choices in the twenty-first century.

BRIAN BOW is an assistant professor of Political Science at Dalhousie University.
PATRICK LENNOX is a postdoctoral fellow at the Centre for Military and Strategic Studies at the University of Calgary.

An Independent Foreign Policy for Canada?

Challenges and Choices for the Future

Edited by Brian Bow and Patrick Lennox

UNIVERSITY OF TORONTO PRESS
Toronto Buffalo London

© University of Toronto Press Incorporated 2008
Toronto Buffalo London
www.utppublishing.com
Printed in Canada

ISBN 978-0-8020-9690-6 (cloth)
ISBN 978-0-8020-9634-0 (paper)

Printed on acid-free paper

Library and Archives Canada Cataloguing in Publication

An independent foreign policy for Canada? : challenges and choices for
the future / edited by Brian Bow and Patrick Lennox.

Includes bibliographical references.
ISBN 978-0-8020-9690-6 (bound). – ISBN 978-0-8020-9634-0 (pbk.)

1. Canada – Foreign relations – 21st century.   2. Canada – Foreign
relations – 1945–.   I. Bow, Brian J.   II. Lennox, Patrick

FC242.I65 2008   327.71   C2008-905520-9

University of Toronto Press acknowledges the financial assistance to its
publishing program of the Canada Council for the Arts and the Ontario
Arts Council.

University of Toronto Press acknowledges the financial support for its
publishing activities of the Government of Canada through the Book
Publishing Industry Development Program (BPIDP).

Contents

Foreword

STEPHEN CLARKSON

It is a distinct honour to be asked to greet the readers of this timely volume of well-written and well-argued essays with a few of my own words. It is also gratifying to have my first published book resurface as an *agent provocateur* for a new generation of scholars working on the empirical and normative dilemmas raised in a rapidly changing world by their country's being joined at the hip to the United States.

In the forty years that have elapsed since the debate I edited for the University League for Social Reform was published as *An Independent Foreign Policy for Canada?* – during Pierre Trudeau's campaign for the Liberal party's leadership – much has changed both at home and abroad.

Abroad, the tripolar world – in which the non-aligned bloc played the United States off against the Soviet Union in the two superpowers' nuclear-armed standoff – has been reconfigured. The former military, economic, and cultural hegemon of the West quickly morphed by 1995 into the economic hegemon of the World thanks to Washington's stunning success in negotiating its transnational corporations' wish list into the World Trade Organization's new rules. A decade later, however, its folly in trying to impose its will coercively in the Middle East has undermined its military supremacy and shattered its moral leadership. These seismic shifts in U.S. power might be expected to raise Canada's relative power and so give it more international room for manoeuvre, were it not for Canada's relative decline on the global stage given the greater role being played there by China, India, and even Brazil, South Africa, and Mexico.

On the North American continent, equally significant transformations have occurred. The power disparity between the United States and

Canada, which formed the realpolitik background for my colleagues' ruminations four decades ago, was deepened and entrenched by Ottawa having negotiated away numerous powers through the Canada–United States and then the North American Free Trade Agreements. When complemented by the World Trade Organization, these treaties' market-liberating norms, rules, rights, and institutions created a new external constitution that significantly restricted the domestic autonomy of Canada's federal, provincial, and municipal governments. In exchange for these concessions, the government of Canada – on behalf of its transnational corporations operating outside the country – calculated that it had gained external capacity in the economies of the other states that had taken on the same obligations when they signed these treaties. This increased capacity was supposed to reduce the asymmetry between the two neighbours, but U.S. reluctance to comply with adverse dispute-settlement rulings has largely vitiated this putative levelling of the economic playing field.

NAFTA's provisions had not all come into effect before its border-erasing paradigm was displaced following an Islamic terrorist group's sensational attack on New York and Washington on 11 September 2001. While Washington's resulting security obsession required Ottawa to adjust its border security, anti-terrorism intelligence, and immigration policies, the United States' new dependence on its neighbour's security processes arguably increased Canada's continental strength.

On the home front, Canadian liberalism reached its apogee in 1982 with the patriation of a constitution that was enriched by Pierre Trudeau's long-fought-for Charter of Rights and Freedoms. While the Charter helped integrate millions of the country's new immigrants, Canadian political and economic elites were already following their British and American counterparts in their switch from a socially generous Keynesianism to a budget-cutting neoconservativism whose most notorious victims, as far as Canadian diplomacy was concerned, were the country's foreign-aid funding and foreign affairs department. Thus, while the country's external challenges increased in complexity, its diplomatic capacity abroad was steadily constrained by budgetary cutbacks at home.

In such a fundamentally modified context of external forces and internal doctrines, the pertinence of the fresh, realistic, and careful thinking offered in this volume is obvious. The question I will address is how much this new work shows that Canadian foreign policy discourse has altered and how much it has remained constant. I will organize this brief overview in terms of the book's concepts, findings, norms, and emotions.

Concepts

The best example of change in the conceptual basis of this book's new foreign policy discourse is Patrick Lennox's brilliant transcendence of much sterile international-relations theory by his linking the question of global 'anarchy' with what he calls the U.S.-Canada hierarchy. Supporting his powerful argument that Canadian independence is an illusion, Adam Chapnick dismisses the notion as analytically misleading. Chapnick has a good point if he means that the concept can include quite different phenomena. Independence may refer both to the Canadian government's ability to pass domestic laws in the face of American resistance and to its capacity to pursue a particular foreign policy despite U.S. opposition. To distinguish these two distinct issues, I prefer to reserve 'autonomy' for a political jurisdiction's ability to achieve what it wants within its territory and to employ 'capacity' to refer to a government's ability to achieve what it wants outside its territory. The related notion of sovereignty has quite precise meanings for international jurists: a country's sovereignty is largely determined through its recognition by other states as a legitimate political entity. It is also what is given up when states sign treaties with other states, each exchanging part of its sovereignty to achieve some collective good. In common discourse, 'sovereignty' is appropriated by public-interest activists for whom it has a powerfully emotional resonance. All that being said, readers may be surprised to find that most of the other authors consider independence to be a valid and useful starting point for their analysis. It is a term that continues as a central focus of public debates surrounding questions of Canadian foreign policy.

A recent week in Mexico City spent interviewing diplomats and international relations scholars brought home to me how Canadians are not unique in their interest in foreign policy independence. As a middle power similarly attached along a lengthy border to the world's only superpower, Mexico also has difficulty building an independent foreign policy. It participates actively in the United Nations to escape the power asymmetry of its bilateral relationship with Washington. While its diplomacy has been much more stridently and publicly confrontational with the United States – particularly regarding Cuba in the 1960s and in opposing Ronald Reagan's militarization of Central America's conflicts in the 1980s – it has been more pragmatic than other Latin countries because of the need to cooperate with its neighbour to the north. Just as Canada offered itself as a mediator between the United States and Great Britain, Mexico saw itself as a bridge between the hegemon and the hemisphere. As with Canada too, the era of 'free trade' represents a historical sea change. Signing on to NAFTA was a device used by neo-conservative elites to 'lock in' changes to the Mexican state that future social democrats could not reverse. Joining NAFTA also required Mexico to resign from the G-77 group of developing countries, whose agenda of resistance to U.S. economic domination it had long championed. Ottawa's negotiation of trade and investment agreements with Washington did not represent so radical a rupture with its foreign-policy tradition, but it found itself having fewer contacts with like-minded countries across the Atlantic because the European Union's common foreign and security policy reduced its members' capacity to work directly with Canada. With both members of the North American periphery looking for new international partners, the two countries have discovered each other. Under the umbrella of the Security and Prosperity Partnership (SSP) North America, Mexico City and Ottawa are developing a new bilateral partnership that deals with issues of common interest, including asserting independence from their often imperious neighbour.

Another apparent change in concepts concerns the debate between 'quiet diplomacy' and 'public diplomacy,' which was central to my authors' concerns in 1967. In their conclusion, the editors here deem that distinction to be a false dichotomy. Chapnick inveighs against the term as well, but for normative reasons: he rightly objects – as did I forty years ago – to the idea that Canadian diplomats should be noisy just to seem different from their American counterparts. But the distinction is not simply one of style; it involves substance. Most of this book's authors favour Canada asserting its separate positions and pursuing them with vigour. And Stephanie Golob uses 'quiet diplomacy' as the conceptual core in her analysis of Ottawa's strategy towards the SPP. Given the prominence in the media of Allan Gotlieb's 'Mr. Ambassador' argument that Canadian diplomats should ingratiate themselves with the White House by quietly supporting U.S. positions, the old dichotomy seems alive and well.

Findings

These authors provide plenty of evidence that much has changed since 1968. The SPP itself is an institutional deepening of the then-undreamed-of continental free trade agreement, and Golob's finding – that Ottawa is quietly using this trilateral agreement to re-establish its special relationship with Washington to Mexico's disadvantage will raise a number of eyebrows. Christopher Sands's discussion of border security and defence speaks to both change and continuity: whereas the characteristics of Canada's military integration with the Pentagon remain largely similar to those of the Cold War, *mutatis mutandis*, present levels of semi-militarized border security would have shocked my colleagues forty years ago. Using my terms, the border security conundrum appears to have reduced Canadian autonomy (since Ottawa was obliged to make countless policy changes in response to Washington's paranoia about terrorism) but increased Canadian capacity (since the various border agreements made U.S. security more dependent on the Canadian government's willing cooperation).

Chris Kukucha's analysis of provincial engagement with trade policy shows how far globalization has impacted sub-central governments. Although he does not make the point explicitly, his findings also suggest that greater provincial autonomy in the many policy fields affected by the new generation of economic treaties has increased Canada's negotiating capacity. Just as US negotiators can claim that, however much they might like to agree with their foreign counterparts' position, their hands are tied by Congress, Canadian diplomats can protest that provincial politics or provincial constitutional jurisdictions do not allow them to make certain concessions. As the book's last two chapters show, there are major new additions to the international agenda, including the environment with Kyoto (Heather Smith) and culture at the WTO (Patricia Goff).

There are two other findings that might make this book's analysis seem very familiar to those who remember the arguments in mine. To start with, a number of authors agree that in many cases, Canada's apparent dependence on the United States is actually self-inflicted, resulting less from U.S. dominance than from Ottawa's inability or unwillingness to act in its own long-term interests, Arctic sovereignty and Kyoto being the most salient instances. Second, as Brian Bow explains in his chapter, the fear of U.S. retribution in response to actions that do not toe the White House's line is greatly exaggerated. More often than not, the threat of retaliation is conjured up by those Canadians who want Ottawa to fall into step with Washington – for instance, conservative military historian Jack Granatstein argued in 2002 that Canada should join the United States in its war on Iraq to avoid being punished by Uncle Sam.

Emotions

Although most of their authors are liberal internationalists, the editors have done well to create an internal debate within the volume by recruiting contributors with a more conservative, anti-nationalist bent. Standing in for Peyton Lyon's somewhat intemperate defence of quiet diplomacy in my book is Adam Chapnick's historical attack on my own and my fellow authors' concern for independence. He criticizes us for a 'passionate emotionalism' bereft of empirical evidence, our 'obsession' with optics displacing 'hard policy choices' – charges that space does not permit me to refute. Standing in for my book's conservative economists Wynne Plumptre and A.E. Safarian is Geoffrey Hale, who brings a much-needed political-economy content to the collection, arguing that Ottawa has demonstrated considerable macro-economic autonomy in managing external pressures, while provinces have strengthened their autonomy, notably in energy matters.

Still, I couldn't help but be surprised at the degree to which Hale's argument degenerated into an ad hominem attack. When Peyton Lyon uncorked his blockbuster attacks on those colleagues who questioned the virtues of quiet diplomacy, he managed to flail their ideas but not their persons. Hale's setting me up as the straw man of Toronto-centred nationalism implies a geographical and ideational determinism that would only make sense if he could show me to be an organic intellectual defending specific economic, social, or regional interests. Apparently my positions reflect 'persistent insecurities.' Hale presumes to know that I 'would respond in dismay' to current trends in the capital markets. In fact, capital markets are the subject of one of the nineteen case studies in my next book, *Does North America Exist?* which addresses the complexities of transborder governance in North America – issues that are not so much causes for my dismay as they are objects for my analysis. In his last sentence he lumps me in with an unspecified cabal: 'Clarkson and many of his ideological soulmates,' he writes, are unwilling to admit that Canada's governments and citizens are 'up to the task' – which raises the normative issues that are as central to this volume as they were to my own.

Norms: Up to What Task?

Bow and Lennox conclude their book on a hortatory note. Canada 'must pursue' a 'national purpose' supported by an increased public awareness. Since, in my callow editorial youth, I, too, ended my collection with a call for public involvement, I am the last to take issue with their call for increased democratic engagement. But we know enough about Canada's gaping democratic deficits to be less than optimistic. Since interests are socially constructed, it is far from obvious that agreement about a single national purpose would emerge from more consultation. Consistent with their long history governing this outpost of three successive imperiums, Canada's principal economic players want the closest possible economic relations with their current Rome. A genuinely participatory public debate in which market forces took part alongside civil society would not likely yield the results that these liberal-internationalist editors wish.

Adam Chapnick chastises my book for having provoked a 'nationally divisive' debate, but I could not wish any better fate for this volume than to merit similar opprobrium. Democratic engagement is inconceivable without debate, and debate is necessarily divisive. The fact is that there *is* a wide normative difference between the intellectual tradition identifying with the imperial centre and that which advocates autonomy because it is both ethically and effectively preferable. Hale is obviously right that Canada's governments are up to the task – as defined by recent Canadian government leaders. Yet an important role for scholars is to question how that task is constructed. Is it, as Smith points out in her analysis of Ottawa's lamentable performance on global warming, to adopt an independent, environmentally activist posture while obstructing action that might forestall ecological catastrophe? Is it timorously to support whatever the Washington administration of the moment decides is in the United States' interests? Or is it, as many argue in these chapters, to think for ourselves and invest the necessary resources in achieving what we believe needs to be done?

I trust that many Canadians will have their values and ideas sharpened by this book's rich material and that, forty years from now, a new generation of sceptics will take aim at the independent thinking of my 'ideological soul-mates.'

Preface

Not many countries have spent as much time as Canada has arguing about whether and to what effect they can pursue an 'independent' foreign policy. And though the concept of foreign policy independence may have fallen out of fashion somewhat among academic specialists, it still echoes in our political debates today, and still resonates with the general public. Revisiting the idea of 'independence' now struck us as the right thing to do, as many of the same kinds of international and domestic pressures that sparked the great 'independence' debate of the 1960s are again stirring up disagreements about what foreign policy direction Canada should take in a post-NAFTA, post-9/11 world.

Forty years ago, some of this country's brightest intellectuals took direct aim at answering the independence question in a series of debates at the University of Toronto, and their arguments were brought together in a volume edited by Stephen Clarkson, fittingly entitled *An Independent Foreign Policy for Canada?* In one of the early reviews of the collection, James Eayrs was harshly critical of the way the debate had been framed, but nevertheless predicted it would become 'a landmark in the intellectual history of Canada.' Eayrs, unsurprisingly, was on the mark. The terminology has changed a little, but many of our foreign policy debates today still seem to reflect the same dividing line, between proponents of 'quiet diplomacy' and advocates of 'independence,' that Clarkson drew back in 1968.

In a world characterized by unparalleled American power, the pressures of economic globalization, and the emergence of multiple, overlapping structures of global governance, one would be hard pressed to make the argument that *any* state can pursue a genuinely 'independent' foreign policy – particularly a relatively small one like Canada. Perhaps the general apathy about Canadian foreign policy these days can be traced back to unattainable expectations set by the independence debates. We believe that the time has come to take aim not at *answering* the independence question, but rather at the independence question itself. By getting beyond independence, we hope to open up the terrain for a meaningful and mature discussion of our place in the world – one that focuses on matching means and ends, and recognizes different challenges in different issue areas. We felt that this was a task that was uniquely suited to an emerging generation of Canadian foreign policy scholars, which might find cohesion and shared purpose through this common enterprise. We thank Adam Chapnick, Patricia Goff, Stephanie Golob, Geoffrey Hale, Rob Huebert, Christopher Kukucha, Christopher Sands, and Heather Smith for their fine contributions to this volume.

We also hope that our volume, which recognizes all that has changed over the last forty years, but which holds on to the legacy of past scholarship, will catalyse inter-generational dialogue on these issues. In that spirit, we are also grateful to Kim Richard Nossal and Denis Stairs for their advice and encouragement in the early stages, and particularly to Stephen Clarkson for agreeing to write the foreword. Finally, we would like to express our sincere appreciation to the organizations that supported the publication of this volume: the Centre for Foreign Policy Studies at Dalhousie University, the Canadian Forces College, and the Centre for Military and Strategic Studies at the University of Calgary.

Brian Bow   Patrick Lennox
Halifax, Nova Scotia   Calgary, Alberta

AN INDEPENDENT FOREIGN POLICY FOR CANADA?
CHALLENGES AND CHOICES FOR THE FUTURE

Introduction: The Question of Independence, Then and Now

BRIAN BOW AND PATRICK LENNOX

In 1968 the University League for Social Reform published a collection of essays under the title *An Independent Foreign Policy for Canada?* (hereafter *IFPC?*).[1] The culmination of a year's worth of debates at the University of Toronto, featuring a diverse group of academics and former policy-makers, the collection effectively captured the intense feelings of uncertainty, frustration, and even excitement about foreign policy that swept the country at the end of that turbulent decade. This relatively unheralded volume, edited by a junior scholar named Stephen Clarkson, has since come to be recognized as a substantial work in the field, and it continues to influence the way Canadians – on both the left and right of the political spectrum – think about the question of foreign policy autonomy.

The debate in 1968, as Clarkson characterized it, was between proponents of 'quiet diplomacy,' on the one hand, and advocates of an 'independent' foreign policy for Canada, on the other.

The 'quiet diplomacy' view, reflected most clearly in Peyton Lyon's contribution to the original volume, was a rationalization of the basic approach that had generally been pursued by successive Canadian governments since 1945. Lyon argued that Canada simply was not powerful enough, acting alone, to have a real impact on the course of world affairs. If Canada were going to be successful in promoting a stable, rule-governed international order, then it would be through the leveraging of its influence in Washington, and through (U.S.-led) multilateral institutions such as the United Nations and NATO. Canadian policy-makers were therefore advised to put a high priority on the management of the bilateral relationship, assessing any given policy option in terms not only of Canada's interest in the particular issue at stake, but also of its effect on the 'special relationship.' Canadian leaders could disagree with their American counterparts on foreign policy issues, but they ought to do so privately, behind the scenes. Public criticism of the United States might score some political points at home, by playing to the anti-American impulses in some segments of the Canadian public, but it would only undercut Canada's leverage in Washington, and ultimately weaken Canada's position on the world stage.

The proponents of 'independence,' on the other hand, were sceptical of the 'quiet diplomacy' argument that Canada's self-restraint actually secured much influence in Washington, and more optimistic about what Canada could achieve on its own. This position was most clearly reflected in the chapter by Charles Hanly, and in Clarkson's conclusions to the volume. Their argument was not that Canadian policy-makers should take every opportunity to thumb the Americans in the eye, but rather that they ought to weigh their options objectively, and be prepared to take a different road from the United States when doing so was more consistent with Canadian interests and values. In other words, the impulse to go along quietly with the flow of American foreign policy should and indeed could be resisted, if only policy-makers were willing to break old habits, master their fear of American retaliation, and work hard to develop a clear sense of national purpose.

The 'quiet diplomacy' versus 'independentist' dichotomy effectively captured something essential in the foreign policy debates of that time. And, for better or worse, it continues to resonate today, shaping the way we think about the range of choice for Canadian foreign policy. There are, however, at least three important reasons to question this dualistic way of thinking about what is at stake, and the choices to be made.

First, like all efforts to identify the essential dividing lines in a complex policy debate, the 'quiet diplomacy' versus 'independentist' dichotomy compressed and simplified a much more subtly varied landscape of ideas. Many people at that time – including some of the contributors to the original volume – held views that did not fit neatly into either of the two rival camps. Denis Stairs, for example, supported the independentists' claim that Canadians tended to overestimate the danger of American retaliation, but rejected their argument that this meant Canadians should expect their government to make a much bigger mark on the world.[2] At the same time, Stairs questioned the premises of 'quiet diplomacy,' particularly the expectation that a compliant Canada could have significant influence over American foreign policy decisions.

Authors on both sides of the *IFPC?* divide argue for a foreign policy driven by 'national interest,' as if that in itself might clear up the differences between them. But of course 'national interest' is a notoriously malleable concept; if it is of any use in policy debates, then it is probably only when made more 'concrete' within the context of specific policy issues and challenges.

The proponents of independence suggested that there was also a normative divide. Hanly and Clarkson argued for a conception of national interest explicitly informed by normative commitments to international peace, justice, and development. It is true that proponents of 'quiet diplomacy' did not have the same moral compass that Hanly and Clarkson did, but that doesn't mean that there wasn't a normative component to their arguments. Lyon in particular makes the case that working closely with the United States is best for Canada, both in terms of serving its interests and in terms of pursuing its ideals. But Lyon's view was anything but idealistic, reflecting the classical realist argument that it is immoral for a policy-maker to be too moralistic: as representatives of the public trust, political leaders should do right when they can, but ultimately they have a responsibility to put the national interest ahead of their own moral impulses.[3]

The bottom line here is that, while the 'quiet diplomacy' versus 'independentist' dichotomy did reflect a crucial axis of debate, there is actually a lot of room for perspectives and priorities that fall 'in between' the two hostile camps. Indeed, it is our contention that moving beyond this dichotomous position will open up an intellectual space into which a mature discussion of the future of Canadian foreign policy can move.

Second, Clarkson's framing of the debate looks for the limits on Canada's foreign policy autonomy in terms of whether or when the United States might be prepared to retaliate against provocative Canadian policies. Given that Stairs and others find that the United States is either unwilling or unable to pursue retaliation, Clarkson argues that this shows Canada has room to pursue policies that are at odds with its neighbour's. But there are other ways in which being out of step with the United States might have negative consequences for Canada, and these ought to be included in our weighing of foreign policy options. Lyon, for example, draws our attention to the way conflict with the United States can entail not only potential direct costs, but also opportunity costs, in the sense that it can undercut Canada's capacity for influence on American policies.

The bilateral relationship with the United States, moreover, is not the only kind of possible limit on Canada's freedom of choice. Clarkson and some of the other contributors recognize the way that *domestic* political cleavages might interfere with foreign policy-making. Specifically, Quebec's challenge to the federal structure was a focus of the original *IFPC?* volume. As Clarkson himself has emphasized in most of his subsequent work, the federal government is embedded in an increasingly complex political environment, constrained from within by municipalities, provinces, business associations, and NGOs, and from without by international institutions, complex legal structures, and global markets.[4] Constraints abound, and indeed may be becoming more abundant as the domestic and international systems in which the Canadian state must operate continue to become more densely layered. The complex nature of these constraints is easily glossed over by the false dichotomous choice of an 'independent' or a 'quiet' foreign policy course.

And third, whereas the 'independentist' versus 'quiet diplomacy' dichotomy focuses our attention on the calculation of the benefits from supporting the United States and the costs of defying it, we might be better off to start by thinking about what Canada is willing and able to do independently. It is one thing to sort out whether or not there is 'room' for Canada to pursue a more autonomous foreign policy; but it is another thing altogether for Canada to develop a clear sense of its purpose as an international actor as well as the resources and political determination to act upon that sense of purpose.

We believe the time is right to revisit the question of Canada's foreign policy independence, not simply because forty years have passed since the publication of Clarkson's original volume, but because looking back from our own time to the late 1960s stirs up a profound sense of *déjà vu*.

The same three historical developments that provoked the debate   in the original *IFPC?* volume have come together again in our post-NAFTA, post-9/11 world. Once again they set the stage for renewed debate over Canada's foreign policy. Then, as now, a disastrous war abroad and political turbulence at home raised profound questions about the nature and quality of America's global leadership. Then, as now, a sense of uncertainty and fluidity in international political alignments encouraged Canadians to think about new international partnerships and opportunities. Then, as now, recent diplomatic and commercial successes for the federal government, and upheaval within the federal system, created an electrified political landscape within Canada, with a heightened sense of national vitality, but also renewed anxieties about national cohesion.

In the next section of this introductory chapter, we explore these historical parallels in order to set down a contextual foundation for the more focused and concrete considerations of the independence question in the chapters that follow. We then outline the main ways in which we think the world has changed over the last forty years, and consider the impact of these changes on the 'independence' debate. We wrap up with some brief reflections on the differences between the original volume and our own, and some thoughts on what we hope this new volume will achieve, in both academic and political terms.

Historical Parallels ...

The State of the 'Special Relationship'

In the late 1960s the Canadian government was under fire for what many considered its complicity in America's involvement in Vietnam. Instead of working as an agent for peace in Indochina (as it had agreed to do on behalf of the international community at the Geneva Convention of 1954), Canada was seen to have taken on the role of an American accomplice in an endless, atrocity-ridden war that was doing severe damage to the image of the United States, both at home and abroad. Through the Defence Production Sharing Agreement, which the Diefenbaker government had signed with the United States in 1958, Canada was producing and selling to Washington large quantities of arms and equipment in support of the American war effort. And through a diplomatic back-channel developed out of its long-time service on the International Control and Supervisory Commission, Canada was delivering the ultimatums that were escalating the war against Ho Chi Minh's communist regime in the north.[5]

Anti-war rallies from Vancouver to Halifax reflected a deepening distrust of the United States as leader of the western alliance, and a growing desire to see Canada distinguish its voice in the world from that of its neighbour. Canadians wanted their government to 'do something' about the Vietnam War, but there was little to be done.[6] In a speech at Temple University in Philadelphia in 1965, Prime Minister Lester Pearson suggested that a pause in the 'rolling thunder' bombing campaign might help in 'injecting some flexibility' into the communist regime's position.[7] Pearson's foreign minister, Paul Martin, then came up with the idea to send Chester Ronning to Hanoi in an effort to broker a cease-fire. But neither initiative bore fruit. Both only succeeded in annoying Washington and diminishing whatever influence Canadian diplomats might have had over the direction of the war.

Perhaps for the first time, Canadians began to seriously question the implications of their 'special relationship' with the United States. Was the catastrophic failure of American foreign policy in Vietnam a sign that Canada had no choice but to go its own way? Was it even possible to define a place for Canada in the world outside the shadow of American power? As it turned out, however, Vietnam was the tragic exception, not the rule, for American global leadership throughout the Cold War. Canada and the other NATO countries maintained their close ties to the United States, and rode through the rough patches until the Soviet Union's collapse in 1991.

During the golden decade that followed the end of the Cold War, Canadians were for the most part content to see their economic ties to the United States tighten, as their capabilities to contribute abroad withered under the fiscal constraints of a neoliberal economic creed enforced by global finance. Canadians were evidently prepared to reap the benefits of U.S.-led economic globalization at home, while chipping in occasionally abroad by playing a variety of supporting roles, and they saw little need to find an independent direction for Canada to take in the world. On occasion a foreign minister would take on a high-profile initiative, as Lloyd Axworthy did with the International Campaign to Ban Landmines, at least partly as an affirmation that Canada could still operate in the world without the backing – direct or indirect – of the United States. Such efforts, derided by some as 'pulpit diplomacy,'[8] seemed to satisfy the instinctive Canadian need to contribute in some distinctive fashion to the flow of foreign affairs, but they could only partially obscure Canada's long-term retreat from internationalism into what Kim Richard Nossal called 'pinchpenny diplomacy.'[9]

After the 9/11 terrorist attacks, however, the relative complacency of the post–Cold War era has given rise to a new anxiety about Canada's place in the world. Under President George W. Bush the United States turned towards confrontational unilateralism, and turned its back on many of the international institutions it had renewed (with Canadian support) in the early post–Cold War years.

Scepticism about the current tenor of America's global leadership is in the air in Canada and indeed across much of the western world. And again there is uncertainty and doubt, at least in some circles, about the nature and effects of the so-called 'special relationship.' Canadians are confronted with difficult choices that seem to echo those of the late 1960s. Just as in the debates over Vietnam, today some argue that American unilateralism forces Canada to strike out on its own, while others argue that Canada must try to get closer to the United States, in order to pursue what Denis Stairs once called the 'diplomacy of constraint.'[10]

The Search for New Partners and New Opportunities

While the war in Vietnam raised troubling questions about the wisdom and benevolence of America's international leadership, the increasing integration of the Canadian and American economies raised questions about how far Canada could go down a 'continentalist' path without compromising its political sovereignty and foreign policy independence. American investment in the Canadian economy was a source of anxiety for many, particularly after the Gordon Commission study in 1968. Foreign investment had fuelled Canada's impressive growth after 1945, but many worried that dependence on U.S. direct investment would create a stunted, 'branch plant' economy, and make Canada vulnerable to economic blackmail.[11] Given these developments, and the charged nationalist rhetoric swirling around them, it is not surprising that many in Canada were inclined to look for economic and political 'counterweights' to the bilateral relationship with the United States.

Most Canadians had no reservations about Canada's dependence on Britain in the first half of the twentieth century. Canada was after all a dominion of the British Empire. The shift of economic activity from Britain to the United States after 1945 likewise caused little anxiety, at least at first, precisely because it was still seen to be a matter of 'balance' between different (friendly) centres of power. As the balance shifted decisively towards the United States in the second half of the century, however, there was a new interest in preventing all of Canada's economic eggs from ending up in the American basket.

Some hoped for a turn towards a milder version of 'National Policy' autarkism, and others for a renewal of commercial ties with Britain, and by extension with the resurgent economies of the emerging European Economic Community. Still others recognized the formation in the 1960s of new centres of economic opportunity in Japan, China, and India, and – as decolonization gained momentum – across the developing world more generally. But it was not until after the 'Nixon shocks' of August 1971 that Canadian policy-makers became genuinely alarmed about the prospect of being bound to a self-centred and unpredictable United States. It was at this point that the argument emerged that Canada should buy some diplomatic insurance, by building up new 'counterweights' overseas. The idea found its fullest expression rhetorically in the Trudeau government's Third Option statement of 1972, and politically in the negotiation of the 'contractual link' with Europe in 1976. The contractual link came to nothing, and the counterweight argument was seen by most to have been thoroughly discredited by the early 1980s.[12] But the original 1968 impulse to prevent overdependence on the United States, and the vague sense that there might be other partners out there, has persisted.

The Chrétien government was the most ambitious seeker of counterweights in recent years – though of course not under that rubric – particularly in its relentless pursuit of new trade opportunities in Asia. The Asian Financial Crisis took most of the steam out of these efforts, but there were plenty of signs that Ottawa was already well aware that 'Team Canada' missions to Asia could never hope to have anything more than marginal effects on Canada's overall trade portfolio. The Martin government actively sought out trade opportunities with China, and seemed to encourage speculation about Chinese investment in the Alberta oil sands, at least in part to cultivate the impression that Canada might have alternatives to American finance. Again, there was no reference to 'counterweights' per se, but support for this idea was certainly reminiscent of the old impulse to economic diversification for political effect.

The current Conservative government of Stephen Harper seems to have moved away from the Chrétien-era focus on trade with China – if only in being willing to criticize Chinese policies, even at the risk of losing Chinese investment opportunities.[13] Instead, Harper has followed up on and extended Paul Martin's support for the idea of greater involvement in Latin America. But there is room for debate about whether Harper's attention to 'hemispheric' ties is driven by a perceived need to cut a separate and distinct international profile, or rather to be seen to be relevant to, and supportive of, U.S. policies in this part of the world.

National Confidence, National Crisis

The late 1960s are often seen as the high-water mark for Canadian nationalism.[14] Those on the right were learning to let go of the imperial tie to Britain, while those on the left were beginning to build up the idea of a developmental model at odds with the American one. Lester Pearson's successful diplomatic intervention in the Suez Crisis – and the invention of 'peace-keeping' – had a lasting effect on Canadians' sense of their power and purposes internationally, and successive governments were continually trying to renew that feeling through an active, values-driven foreign policy. There was also growing confidence in the federal government more generally, as it had effectively intervened to keep the economy running smoothly, build the country's infrastructure, and establish a popular and effective universal health and social welfare system. The Canadian economy struggled in the early 1960s, but overall it had grown rapidly and steadily since the end of the war, and Canada looked to be making the jump from a backward 'hewer of wood and drawer of water' to a modern, industrial society. Centenary celebrations and the 1967 World Exposition in Montreal encouraged Canadians to think positively about their national accomplishments and their place in the world, and the election the following year of the youthful and charismatic Pierre Trudeau cemented a feeling of renewal and vitality.

In the midst of this new confidence there were also reasons for concern about national unity and coherence. Canadians have of course always been worried about regional fragmentation and the relative weakness of their collective national self-identification. But these fears were intensified in the late 1960s by the emergent separatist movement in Quebec and by renewed anxiety about 'Americanization.' Ottawa had been hard-pressed through the 1960s to try to contain Quebec's efforts to use independent action abroad to bolster claims to sovereignty at home, and national unity anxieties were further intensified by French president de Gaulle's 1967 'Vive le Québec libre' speech. At the same time, a series of studies highlighted the scale of Canada's reliance on American investment capital and its appetite for American popular culture and products, prompting widespread anxiety about gradual 'absorption' into the United States.[15] This, in combination with the rejection of American involvement in Vietnam, triggered an outpouring of anti-Americanism, and catalysed a new interest – particularly, but not only, on the political left – in charting a separate path for Canada.

Today, there is nothing like the intensity of national feeling in Canada in the late 1960s, but there is a certain sense of quiet confidence. The 1990s were a time of impressive economic growth in Canada, just as they were in the United States, but whereas the American economy cooled abruptly and has been unsteady ever since, the Canadian economy has kept humming along. The fact that the dollar has recently been at or above par with its U.S. counterpart for the first time since the mid-1970s may worry Canadian exporters, but it is a source of pride and confidence for the general public.[16] At the same time, there is growing anxiety that deepening economic troubles in the United States will inevitably find their way to Canada.

Many Canadians were excited by the 'aggressive multilateralism' of the Chrétien/Axworthy years, and opinion polls suggest that many supported the decisions to opt out of the war in Iraq and the U.S. missile defence initiative. The scope and nature of Canada's involvement in Afghanistan has prompted some criticism, but on the whole it seems to have bolstered Canadians' sense of the country's international importance and raised hopes of closing the long-standing gap between rhetorical commitments and concrete capabilities. The political polarization and sense of impasse in the United States over the last few years has tended to reinforce a sense that the Canadian way of doing things is separate and different from – and, for many at least, better than – the American model.[17] Popular dissatisfaction with the Liberals' management of the Canada–U.S. relationship and Harper's turn back toward a more 'pragmatic' approach suggest that the nationalist/anti-American fever is cooling. Opinion polls indicate that Canadians have gone back to being generally positive and optimistic about the bilateral relationship, but there is still a deep reservoir of ambivalence about the United States, which seems likely to persist even after George W. Bush is out of office.[18]

As in the late 1960s, today's confidence is tempered by a profound uncertainty about the future. Anxiety about the Quebec separatist challenge has subsided since the 1995 referendum, but it remains a political time bomb, which many Canadians worry will never be defused. The national unity problem has become much more complex after the constitutional-reform struggles of the 1980s, as 'western alienation' and other forms of regional discord threaten the federal structure and hinder the building of a coherent national identity. The resulting sense of national crisis is further reinforced by long-running trends to political disengagement, social atomization, and the continuing displacement of distinctively Canadian culture by American products and ideas.

... and Profound Changes

There are, then, parallels between 1968 and 2008 that go far beyond Vietnam's echoes in Iraq. Historical parallels like these can help us get at what is essential and enduring about foreign policy, but they can only take us so far. 'History doesn't really repeat itself,' as Mark Twain once said, 'at best it rhymes.' One could readily identify dozens of ways in which the world has changed since the publication of *An Independent Foreign Policy for Canada?* Each one of them might be another good reason to revisit the original volume's central questions (and its contributors' various answers). Here we outline three major historical developments that ought to figure into any conversation about foreign policy independence.

First, and perhaps most obvious, is the shift from the rigid bipolar structure of the international system during the Cold War to a much more complex and ambiguous distribution of power today. The Cold War confrontation made clear for most Canadians what side of the fence they were on, but in the post–Cold War world there are many fence-lines, and conflicting signals about where Canada fits in. World politics today could be looked upon as a clash of civilizations, in which the modern liberal democracies of the West are locked in an existential conflict with the religious authoritarian traditionalism of the Islamic world. Or it could be seen as poised on the threshold of a new bipolarity, in which the United States and its traditional allies will square off against an emerging China, a resurgent Russia, or perhaps both together.[19] Most have tended to see the post–Cold War world as a unipolar one,[20] with the United States cast either as a hegemonic leader[21] or as the centre of a global empire,[22] depending on one's view of American foreign policy. A more nuanced interpretation might see the system as a 'uni-multipolarity,' in which the United States outstrips all the other major powers in virtually every measure state capability, yet continues to depend on the political support of lesser powers (or at least their acquiescence) to achieve its foreign policy aims.[23] The fact that there is such a wide range of plausible interpretations out there suggests that the strategic environment within which Canadian foreign policy-makers operate today is significantly more complex than it was in 1968.

During the Cold War Canada sought both to establish its own 'special relationship' with the United States and to try to work with other countries to harness (or at least contain) American power through multilateral organizations like NATO, the GATT, and the OECD. But America's post–Cold War primacy has brought a new impulse to unilateralism and ad hoc coalition-building, which weakens the hand of smaller allies and supporters like Canada. Some have argued that this breakdown of old bargains might create opportunities for Canada to create some new ones, and to establish counterweights to the United States that might enhance its foreign policy autonomy; but there is not much evidence to suggest this is happening, and the Harper government seems instead to be struggling to hold on that much tighter to the traditional partnership.

These international ambiguities aside, Patrick Lennox argues in chapter 2 that the key to understanding Canada's foreign policy choices is actually found at home. The country's dependent relationship with the United States, he argues, drives it to pursue a strategy of 'specialization' in its foreign policy, which satisfies both the need to be supportive of American initiatives abroad and the political impulse to cast those policies as 'independent' at home. In line with Lennox's reasoning on the connection between Canada's relations at home in North America and abroad in the world, Christopher Sands, in chapter 5, argues that Canada's failure to make meaningful contributions to continental defence and other security policy initiatives in recent years has seriously undercut its influence on the broader American global agenda. Canada may be able to pursue policies at odds with the United States, he argues, but doing so has actually undercut its capacity to govern its own defence at home, and to make a meaningful mark on security issues abroad. In chapter 6 Rob Huebert considers the northern dimension of Canadian–American security relations. Finding common ground with Sands, Huebert argues that Canada's claims to Arctic sovereignty and its influence 'North of 60' have both been significantly diminished by its consistent failure to invest in the military resources necessary to patrol the vast territory and to assert its sovereign presence to the world.

The second major historical development is the profound broadening and deepening over the last forty years of the extraordinary economic interdependence between Canada and the United States. Canada's dependence on the American market has gone from about 65 per cent of total exports in 1968 to about 85 per cent today. Reliance on American direct and indirect investment, which had reached a high point of about 75 per cent in the late 1960s and then declined through the 1970s, began to rise again rapidly in the late 1980s, and has recently surpassed 1960s levels.[24] This intensification of bilateral interdependence between Canada and the United States has taken place within a broader deepening of interdependence among all the industrial economies, and, against the backdrop of the globalization of production and finance, has raised profound questions about how much autonomy *any* country can have over its own domestic economic policies. Since the late 1960s there has been much greater awareness of the variety of different development strategies within the advanced capitalist economies, both as a basis for adaptation and growth and as a source of diplomatic frictions. More recently, however, there have been intense debates over whether the market pressures associated with globalization are pushing countries towards convergence on a particular model – in most minds, the American model – that may not be well suited to dealing with Canada's particular social and political challenges.[25] In chapter 7, Geoffrey Hale looks more closely at the mechanisms of interdependence, and their implications for the Canadian government's capacity to develop effective and autonomous policies designed to have a meaningful and specific effect on the lives of its citizens.

This economic interdependence has been reinforced by the creation and strengthening of formal, integrative institutions. In the bilateral/regional context, this is of course exemplified by the 1987 Canada-U.S. Free Trade Agreement (CUSFTA) and the 1993 North American Free Trade Agreement (NAFTA). At the global level, it is represented by the hardening of the GATT process into the World Trade Organization, and its binding dispute-resolution mechanisms. On the one hand, this institutional architecture imposes new legal and political obstacles to the exercise of some foreign economic-policy instruments. Clarkson has in recent work argued that it amounts to a 'super-constitution' that strictly limits state autonomy and undercuts democracy.[26] On the other hand, these agreements also impose limits on what other countries – most importantly the United States – can do, which might open up new space for Canada to exercise autonomy. This latter argument is of course not a new one, as it was the key premise behind Canada's initial, enthusiastic involvement in the GATT and the Bretton Woods institutions,[27] as well as in the decision to give up a measure of sovereignty through CUSFTA and NAFTA. The strategic logic is still the same, but the context is much more complicated today, bringing in a much broader array of countries, locking up a much longer list of policy instruments, and making the whole process more transparent and 'automatic' through formal legal standards and procedures. In chapter 4, Stephanie Golob reviews Canada's approach to regional integration after 9/11, with particular focus on the Security and Prosperity Partnership (SPP) initiative of 2005. She argues that the government has reverted to a 'quiet diplomacy' approach, and the resulting secrecy and exclusiveness are pushing the process towards a weak and unequal institutional structure, and provoking public opposition.

The third and final historical development to be noted here is the increased complexity in the context of foreign policy decision-making, with a variety of newly empowered actors and complex new connections between issues. There was of course never a time when foreign policy–making was as simple and straightforward as it often appears in international relations textbooks. But foreign policy decision-making in Canada and the United States during the early Cold War decades was limited to a much narrower array of actors, and it was more hierarchical and streamlined than it is today.

There have been a number of important institutional changes within both countries. In both Canada and the United States, the political leadership has increased and consolidated its control over key aspects of foreign policy decision-making, including the management of public perceptions thereof.[28] At the same time, however, we have seen fragmentation within the foreign policy bureaucracy in both countries, and the acceleration of distinctive patterns of decentralization, with power devolving to the provinces in Canada and to Congress in the United States. In chapter 8, Chris Kukucha looks at the Canadian provinces' capacity to pursue their own autonomous foreign policies, and the interaction between provincial and international pressures on federal policy-making. In chapter 3, Brian Bow considers the fragmentation of power within the American system, and its effects on the management of the Canada–U.S. relationship. He argues that these and other developments have had an impact on the United States' willingness and ability to pursue retaliatory linkages vis-à-vis Canada, but that the overall effects on Canada's capacity to 'get away with' provocative policies are complex and ambiguous.

On the other hand, governments have had to accept the increasing relevance of other kinds of actors in the foreign policy arena. Globalization in the world economy – as noted above – has reconfigured the relationship between states and transnational corporations, giving the latter greater influence over the means and ends of state economic policies. The consolidation of international institutions and new communications technologies has empowered an emerging universe of nongovernmental organizations, which are able to put pressure on states to change policies and even shift their political priorities.

These same technological developments have also fostered what Robert Keohane has called the 'globalization of informal violence' – the empowerment of a new generation of transnational terrorist organizations, which challenge the Canadian government both directly and indirectly, through their effects on American priorities and strategies.[29]

The terrorist attacks of 9/11, and the American reaction to them, have effectively broken down conceptual and practical barriers between commerce, transportation, and security. Canada is thus confronted with the need to find ways to satisfy a United States that is 'hardening' the border against terrorist threats, while seeking ways to 'soften' it for trans-boundary trade and investment.

One aspect of this new complexity is an 'internationalization' of policy issues that had previously been seen as exclusively domestic, as Hale describes in chapter 7. Another is the new prominence of a number of foreign policy issues that were not even 'on the radar' in the late 1960s. In chapter 9, Patricia Goff reviews the foreign policy aspects of Canada's cultural policy, and the 'culture' component of its foreign policy. She finds that 'international developments are constraining the range of motion of cultural policy-makers at home and domestic choices are limiting the effectiveness of cultural diplomacy abroad.' In the volume's final chapter, Heather Smith considers the question of foreign policy 'independence' in the context of Canada's approach to global climate change, and the Kyoto Protocol regime in particular. She argues that Canada's decision to ratify the protocol when the United States did not might be seen as a sign of foreign policy independence, but it should be understood in the context of a larger pattern of diplomatic cooperation with the United States, and of the subsequent failure to live up to Canada's Kyoto commitments.

Possibilities and Pessimism

The implications of the preceding developments for the question of foreign policy 'independence' are complex and contradictory. The same trends and transformations that seem to undermine Canada's foreign policy autonomy may also be seen to open up new opportunities or create new capabilities. Any given development, moreover, is likely to have different kinds of effects across the broad spectrum of foreign policy issues. Careful thinking about the meaning and measure of foreign policy independence, in other words, can only happen in the context of specific policy problems or contexts, and that is the direction in which we turn in the chapters that follow.

This volume was inspired by the 1968 original, but it was not designed to reproduce it. There are important differences in the way that this new volume was put together, which should inform the reader's consideration of the arguments presented here.

Like the original *IFPC?* volume, this new collection showcases the original research and insights of a new generation of experts on Canadian foreign policy. But, whereas the 1968 volume featured a strikingly diverse collection of contributors, with academics from several different disciplines and a handful of former government officials, all but one of the contributors to our new volume are academics trained in political science. Our one historian, Adam Chapnick, has sharpened our perspective on what is genuinely 'new' – and what is not – in the evolving policy context and concurrent policy debates. The new volume's contributors are nevertheless a fairly diverse group, in terms of their theoretical perspectives, empirical referents, and research methods. And, as noted above, our volume addresses a wider variety of different policy areas, including traditional subjects like defence and diplomacy, but also gives more extensive attention to economic integration and 'new' issues like cultural policy and environmental conservation.

The 1968 volume – like the broader University League for Social Reform movement – was very much concerned with fostering public debate, and can be credited with helping to catalyse the 'opening' of the foreign policy–making process to non-government actors that has developed since then. (Whether the forms of public involvement that have emerged over the last forty years would do much to satisfy those proponents of 'public input' is of course another matter.) This new volume is not paired with extensive efforts to facilitate open forums for debate or to gather public input on foreign policy issues in the way that the original was, but we are concerned with generating the broadest possible debate on Canadian foreign policy. We are particularly interested in fostering (and fuelling) interest in these issues among younger Canadians, and in catalysing an inter-generational debate on the 'independence' question that highlights both the continuing relevance of the classic works of the 1960s and 1970s and new perspectives on what has changed in the post–Cold War, post-NAFTA, post-9/11 world.

As was the case with the original Clarkson volume, we do not see it as the purpose of this volume to *resolve* the 'independence' debate, but rather to bring together diverse viewpoints, refine the terms of the debate, and identify pathways by which it might be carried on. This is in keeping with the overall editorial approach behind the volume, in which the individual contributors were deliberately left to sort out for themselves what lessons to draw from the original volume, how best to understand foreign policy independence, and how it might be assessed and accounted for. The result of this approach, as one might expect, is that our contributors have interpreted our initial questions in different ways and come up with different kinds of answers, both explanatory and prescriptive. And yet, as will be evident across the following pages, strong commonalities exist across their contributions. There is a clear, nearly unanimous desire throughout this volume to take the analysis and discussion of Canadian foreign policy beyond the independence debate. A sense of resignation to the reality of Canadian dependency on the United States pervades the chapters, but it does so in a way that is fundamentally optimistic and hopeful about the country's future in foreign affairs. It is our hope that readers will be inspired (or provoked) by these contributions, and by the agreements and disagreements that run through the volume, to make up their own minds about what Canada can and cannot achieve in the international arena, and to bring those convictions into a renewed national dialogue on Canadian foreign policy.

NOTES

1 Stephen Clarkson, ed., *An Independent Foreign Policy for Canada?* (Toronto: McClelland & Stewart [for the University League for Social Reform], 1968).

2 Denis Stairs, 'Confronting Uncle Sam: Cuba and Korea,' in *An Independent Foreign Policy for Canada?* 68.

3 Hans J. Morgenthau, *Politics among Nations*, 4th ed. (New York: Knopf, 1985), 12.

4 See, for example, S. Clarkson, *Uncle Sam and Us: Globalization, Neoconservatism, and the Canadian State* (Toronto: University of Toronto Press, 2002). See also the discussion in Hale, this volume.

5 James Eayrs, *In Defence of Canada*, vol. 5, *Indochina: Roots of Complicity* (Toronto: University of Toronto Press, 1983).

6 Robert Bothwell, *The Big Chill: Canada and the Cold War* (Toronto: Canadian Institute for International Affairs / Irwin, 1998), 68.

7 Lester B. Pearson, *Mike: The Memoirs of the Right Honourable Lester B. Pearson*, vol. 3, *1957–1968*, ed. John A. Munro and Alex I. Inglis (Toronto: University of Toronto Press, 1975), 138.

8 See Fen O. Hampson and Dean F. Oliver, 'Pulpit Diplomacy: A Critical Assessment of the Axworthy Doctrine,' *International Journal* 53 (Summer 1998): 379–406.

9 Kim Richard Nossal, 'Pinchpenny Diplomacy: The Decline of "Good Inter-

national Citizenship" in Canadian Foreign Policy,' *International Journal* 54 (Winter 1998–9): 89–105.

10 Denis Stairs, *The Diplomacy of Constraint: Canada, the Korean War, and the United States* (Toronto: University of Toronto Press, 1974).

11 George Grant, *Lament for a Nation: The Defeat of Canadian Nationalism* (Toronto: Macmillan, 1965), esp. chap. 2.

12 Edelgard E. Mahant, 'Canada and the European Community: The First Twenty Years,' *Journal of European Integration* 4 (1981): 263–79.

13 'Canada Won't Appease China on Human Rights: Harper,' *CTV News*, 15 November 2007. Accessed 1 October 2007 at http://www.ctv.ca/servlet/ArticleNews/story/CTVNews/20061115 /china_snub_061114?s_name =&no_ads=.

14 Stephen Azzi, *Walter Gordon and the Rise of Canadian Nationalism* (Montreal and Kingston: McGill-Queen's University Press, 1999).

15 See, for example, Kari Levitt, *Silent Surrender: The Multinational Corporation in Canada* (Toronto: Macmillan, 1970; new edition, Montreal and Kingston: McGill-Queen's University Press, 2002).

16 Eric Beauchesne, 'Canadians Having a "Parity Party," Says Poll,' *CanWest News Service*, 21 September 2007.

17 Michael Adams, *Fire and Ice: The United States, Canada and the Myth of Converging Values* (Toronto: Penguin Canada, 2004).

18 Brian Bow, 'Anti-Americanism in Canada, before and after Iraq,' *American Review of Canadian Studies* 38, no. 3 (Fall 2008): 141–59.

19 Russia and China have cooperated on security issues through the recently formed Shanghai Cooperation Organization, in conjunction with Kazakhstan, Uzbekistan, Kyrgyzstan, and Tajikistan.

20 Charles Krauthammer, 'The Unipolar Moment,' *Foreign Affairs* 70, no. 1 (1991): 23–33; cf. Christopher Layne, 'The Unipolar Illusion: Why New Great Powers Will Arise,' *International Security* 17, no. 1 (1993): 5–51.

21 G. John Ikenberry, 'Liberal Hegemony and the Future of American Postwar Order,' in *International Order and the Future of World Politics*, ed. T.V. Paul and John Hall (Cambridge: Cambridge University Press, 1999)

22 Andrew Bacevich, *American Empire: The Realities and Consequences of U.S. Diplomacy* (Boston: Harvard University Press, 2002); Benjamin Barber, *Fear's Empire: War, Terrorism, and Democracy* (New York: Norton, 2003); see also *Hegemony or Empire? The Redefinition of US Power under George W. Bush*, ed. Charles Philippe David and David Grondin (Burlington, VT: Ashgate, 2006).

23 Samuel Huntington, 'The Lonely Superpower,' *Foreign Affairs* 78, no. 2 (1999): 35–49.

24 Statistics Canada, 'Study: Trends in Foreign Investment,' *The Daily* [report], 18 November 2005. Accessed at 11 August 2007 http://www.statcan.ca/Daily/English/051118/d051118b.htm.

25 For example, Suzanne Berger and Ronald Dore, eds., *National Diversity and Global Capitalism* (Ithaca: Cornell University Press, 1996).

26 *Uncle Sam and Us: Globalization, Neoconservatism, and the Canadian State.*

27 A.F.W. Plumptre, 'Tit for Tat,' in *An Independent Foreign Policy for Canada?* 44–5.

28 Donald Savoie, *Governing from the Centre: The Concentration of Power in Canadian Politics* (Toronto: University of Toronto Press, 1999); Paul E. Peterson, 'The President's Dominance in Foreign Policy-Making,' *Political Science Quarterly* 102 (February 1994): 215–34.

29 'The Globalization of Informal Violence, Theories of World Politics and the "Liberalism of Fear,"' *Dialog-IO*, Spring 2002: 29–43.

PART ONE

Continuities and Discontinuities, Structure and Choice

This part of the volume features two very different kinds of arguments about what Denis Stairs once referred to as 'will and circumstance' – that is, the question of where the weight of circumstances leaves off and the policy-maker's capacity to choose (and be held accountable) begins. One takes a broader historical perspective, and reflects on the evolution of Canadian attitudes towards foreign policy 'independence.' The other looks under the surface of day-to-day policy choices to make an argument about the deep structural forces that drove Canadian foreign policy through the twentieth century, and will continue to drive it in the twenty-first. Both see particular choices as shaped by enduring circumstances and reflective of recurring tendencies, but both emphasize that there is still room for Canada to make its own foreign policy choices.

The volume as a whole is predicated on the idea that there are thought-provoking parallels to be made between 1968 and 2008. Adam Chapnick's chapter turns our attention back to the time before 1968, and to the different problems and perceptions that animated the 'independence' debates of prior eras. There are obvious differences, he notes, such as the shift from isolationism to internationalism in the mid-twentieth century. But there are also important continuities, such as the temptation for political elites to let foreign policy be driven by what Charles de Gaulle called 'the politics of gesture,' even at the expense of sensible calculations of national interest. Chapnick concludes with a plea for a more pragmatic approach to foreign policy, which would de-emphasize independence for its own sake and shift the focus to concrete policy objectives.

Patrick Lennox's chapter also tries to see the 'bigger picture,' by applying theoretical ideas from the study of international relations to broad patterns in Canadian foreign policy. He argues that the international relations conception of the international system as an 'anarchic' one (i.e., one without government) ignores the prevalence of hierarchy and its implications for the foreign policies of smaller, subordinate states. Canada, he argues, is one of these subordinate states, and its dependency on the United States in the continental context compels it to pursue a strategy of 'specialization' in the broader international context. By pursuing a specialized foreign policy – that is, by acting as a mediator, advocate, and problem solver – Canada is able to support the United States abroad and contribute to the maintenance of international order and stability, while creating the illusion of foreign policy independence.

1 Running in Circles: The Canadian Independence Debate in History

ADAM CHAPNICK[1]

Independence is hardly a Canadian word. It cannot be found in the original British North America Act, in the 1982 Constitutional Act (including the Charter of Rights and Freedoms), or even in the national anthem. Nonetheless, this idea of freedom from external pressures or influence has been one of the history of Canadian foreign policy's dominant themes, one that has existed since well before the time of Confederation and continues to resonate today. The intensity of the argument over the extent of Canada's so-called independence in world affairs probably reached its peak around the time of the publication of Stephen Clarkson's collection *An Independent Foreign Policy for Canada?* in 1968. Looking back forty years later, this landmark work is now most notable not so much for having enriched the debate as for having changed it. Those advocating greater Canadian independence in the 1960s assumed, largely ahistorically, that economic integration was antithetical to foreign policy creativity. In doing so, they helped to launch, or indeed relaunch, a nation-wide debate over Canada's place in the world that was focused on style as much as it was on substance. That debate still echoes intermittently today, evidence of a Canadian approach to world affairs that has largely stagnated. And until the political and intellectual leadership shift their focus beyond the immediate gratification that comes from 'independent' initiatives, it is unlikely that the people of the country will see any real changes.[1]

The political culture of the modern Canadian state was founded on a proud and forthright dismissal of the concept of independence. During the American Revolution, thousands of self-proclaimed Loyalists rejected calls to break free from the Empire and instead declared their full allegiance to Great Britain, their mother country. No longer comfortable in what became the United States, they immigrated to British North

America, bringing with them a passionate devotion to imperialism and the British way of life. To them, independence was anathema to national greatness, and it was their escape from it that demonstrated their moral superiority over their southern neighbours.[2]

Through the early nineteenth century, this outright rejection of independence gradually evolved into a less passionate ambivalence. An imperial statute in 1846 allowing the British North American colonies to establish their own customs laws went virtually unnoticed by the general public. There was no sense at the time that economic freedom had any impact on foreign policy formulation. Similarly, the onset of responsible government in 1847 was not looked upon by the Baldwin-Lafontaine administration as anything more than progress towards greater national self-rule. The end of reciprocity with the United States in 1866 was seen by some Canadians as more problematic, but it caused the country to turn to Britain for support as much as it generated calls for greater economic self-sufficiency. Even Confederation itself in 1867 was a domestic event, with few, if any, members of the political elite making mention of greater independence in world affairs. At the time, not only did the leadership in Ottawa not need a foreign policy, it did not want to have one either.[3]

It was only closer to twenty years into the establishment of the Dominion of Canada that foreign affairs in the traditional sense began to play a role in the national discourse. Even then, however, the ultimate goal was much different than the ideas brandished today. Independence, certainly, but independence *from* external responsibilities was the real aim. The first significant incident to reveal the growing Canadian desire to be free from global obligations arose in 1884 when a British imperial adventure into Egypt created problems in neighbouring Sudan. As London struggled to evacuate its troops from the besieged province of Khartoum, Governor General Lord Lansdowne asked Canadian prime minister Sir John A. Macdonald for military support. Macdonald responded that he would not stand in the way of Canadian troops who wished to sail off to Africa, so long as they did so at Britain's expense. Historian C.P. Stacey has called the 386-person Canadian Voyageur Contingent 'Canada's first small contribution to a British overseas war,' but the government in Ottawa would have seen things differently. These were British subjects on a British mission being paid in British pounds. The Dominion of Canada had not been a participant at all. If any independent decision had been made, it was not to make a national contribution.[4]

Macdonald's approach to foreign policy was based on a rational calculation of the benefits that could accrue to Canada through its continued commitment to imperialism. In the 1907 words of the noted scholar Stephen Leacock:

> Nor is it ever possible or desirable that we in Canada can form an independent country. The little cry that here and there goes up among us is but the symptom of an aspiring discontent, that will not let our people longer be colonials. 'Tis but a cry forced out by what a wise man has called the growing pains of a nation's progress. Independent, we could not survive a decade.

> Not independence then, not annexation, not stagnation ... Find for us something other than mere colonial stagnation, something sounder than independence, nobler than annexation, greater in purpose than a Little Canada ... Build us a plan, that shall make us, in all hope at least, an Empire Permanent and Indivisible.[5]

Certainly, Leacock's sentiments were not shared by all. Fellow academic J.S. Ewart believed that by 1911 Canada had achieved complete practical independence; this simply had not been acknowledged yet by Great Britain. He maintained that legal independence in all aspects of Canadian life was necessary to place his country's 'war-relationship [with Great Britain] upon known and reasonable footing.' Ewart was never at ease with Canada's binding commitment to the Empire in times of crisis, particularly since he did not feel comfortable relying on the government in London to come to Ottawa's aid in its moments of need.[6] Ewart's was also an independence *from* international obligations.

So too was the independence advocated by Quebec journalist and politician Henri Bourassa. 'In the sphere of external relations,' he argued in 1916, 'in all issues of peace and war, Canada, once freed from the intricacies of Imperial politics, would be much safer than she is now. Menaces to her peace, if any, would be much fewer and far less redoubtable ... An independent Canada would have to deal only with her own foes,' and Canada had none.[7] Bourassa abandoned the Liberal party during the South African crisis of 1899 when Prime Minister Sir Wilfrid Laurier responded to another British request for military support similarly to the way that Macdonald had fifteen years earlier. To Bourassa, allowing Canadians to fight the Boers in South Africa was an indication of a colonial allegiance to Great Britain that was unbecoming of a sovereign dominion. His attitude towards the overwhelming Canadian commitment to the First World War, and to the call for compulsory military service in particular, was even more fervently confrontational.

But Bourassa's campaign failed. Prime Minister Sir Robert Borden did impose conscription, a decision that served as a turning point in the path towards independence. It was under his leadership that a new stage in the debate began, one best called, to paraphrase a future Canadian prime minister, 'independence if necessary, but not necessarily independence.' Borden himself was a proud imperialist. He had brought Canada into the First World War not only because of its legal obligation as a British dominion, but also because he sincerely believed that an attack against one part of the Empire was an attack against all of it. The war was a battle for freedom worldwide, one that would have to continue until a clear victory had been achieved. Nevertheless, British prime minister Herbert Asquith's mismanagement of the Allies' military strategy and refusal to keep Canada fully informed of any progress, or lack thereof, made the Canadian prime minister increasingly frustrated. Over time, his initial reluctance was replaced by a new conviction that his country would have to pursue a more independent position in world affairs. This was not, it must be noted, because of any great interest in shaping the future world order; rather, it was to protect the lives of Canadian soldiers from the dangers posed by poor British leadership in the field.

That Borden's motivation for independence was much closer to arch-rival Bourassa's than it was to the conceptions of today was most evident in his attitude towards the League of Nations. Certainly, Canada insisted on signing the Treaty of Versailles in 1919 and thereby joining the League independently,[8] but Borden also campaigned actively to reduce, if not eliminate completely, the commitment of League members to the concept of collective security. The obstructionist approach to article 10 of the League's covenant that continued in the following years was consistent with this hesitancy. Canada took a leadership role in attempting to reduce League members' international obligations. Independence, it seemed, was needed as security against unnecessary external commitments. Successive Canadian governments showed no interest in leveraging that independence into influence on the world stage.[9]

It is therefore hardly surprising that the constitutional path towards complete Canadian autonomy in world affairs was pursued only halfheartedly during the interwar period. Although, in his frustration, Borden had insisted in 1917 that after the Great War ended the members of the British Commonwealth would have to re-evaluate their constitutional relationship so that future negotiations among them would be based on 'a full recognition of the Dominions as autonomous nations of an Imperial Commonwealth ... [with the right to] an adequate voice in foreign policy and foreign relations,'[10] neither he nor successor Arthur Meighen objected when the idea was put off to deal with a crisis with Japan in 1921. Nor did the new Liberal leader, William Lyon Mackenzie King, force the issue during his first term in government. In fact, it was only in 1926, when the nationalist Prime Minister J.B.M. Hertzog of South Africa threatened to secede from the Commonwealth if the situation did not change to his liking that Canada participated in a multilateral process meant to re-evaluate its dominion status. Five years later, when the British government adopted the Statute of Westminster granting the dominions the option of assuming complete independence, the government in Ottawa did not take full advantage. Prime Minister King did demonstrate a degree of independence when parliament declared war on its own in September 1939 (a declaration, it is worth noting, that came just one week after a British decision to act similarly), but Canadians continued to be British citizens at   birth until 1946, and legal appeals beyond the Supreme Court to London's Privy Council remained possible until 1949. As for the BNA Act, amendments to it would continue to be passed by the British parliament until 1982.[11]

The real breakthrough, or the emergence of the Canadian commitment to a modern conception of national independence in foreign affairs, took place during the Second World War. Much of the credit should be given to a group of budding internationalists in the public sector. A January 1942 memorandum from the leading idealist in the Department of External Affairs, Escott Reid, was one of the first signs of change. Frustrated with his country's lack of worldly initiative, Reid urged his department to become 'a planning, thinking, creative body,' a unit that contemplated foreign policy strategically and independently.[12] It took eighteen months, but eventually, in late July 1943; Canada's under-secretary of state for external affairs, Norman Robertson, set in motion a process that resulted in the first two foreign policy planning groups in Canadian history: a strategic and advisory body called the post-hostilities committee, and a smaller working committee on post-hostilities problems that assumed responsibility for more detailed, practical discussions.[13] The committees represented the earliest formal mechanisms within the government bureaucracy designed specifically to formulate independent foreign policy ideas.

Also in January 1942, Canada's minister-counsellor in Washington and one of the Department of External Affairs' leading strategic thinkers, Hume Wrong, became fed up with the ever-increasing disconnect between Canada's military and economic contribution to the Allied cause in Europe and its corresponding lack of influence in wartime policy. Unlike Borden, Wrong was not as concerned with the battles themselves; he was thinking more specifically about how the wartime precedent would affect peace-making negotiations that would inevitably follow. It was here, he believed strongly, that Canada had a duty to play a meaningful role.

His proposed solution, borrowed in part from the American philosophy of 'no taxation without representation' and in part from the writings of a young British foreign service officer, became known as the functional principle: countries should have influence in world affairs commensurate with their contribution to the individual event in question. When Prime Minister Mackenzie King echoed this thinking in a speech to the House of Commons in the summer of 1943, the functional principle became the first clear articulation of an activist independent Canadian approach to foreign policy. Finally, the political establishment demanded independence *for* something: influence in world affairs.[14]

King led the country in a direction that seemed to conflict strongly with the isolationist inclinations that had been so evident in his previous actions and comments because, politically, he did not have a choice.[15] By mid-1943, the Canadian public had bought into the internationalist world view and had transformed itself from a generally uninterested, passive observer of world affairs into an increasingly proud and demanding voice for leadership in the construction of a new global order. In retrospect, the movement began in the bureaucracy, the nongovernmental community, and select media outlets in the early 1940s and then quickly shifted to the political realm. By 1943, members of all of Canada's major parties were advocating greater international involvement. And by that November, according to the Canadian Institute of Public Opinion, 78 per cent of adults across the country, including typically isolationist Quebec, believed that after the war Canada would have an international obligation to send forces abroad to help keep the peace.[16] In 1943 a majority still believed that Canada should make the commitment as a part of the Commonwealth, but by the end of the war, Canadians were almost fully in favour of complete independence in foreign policy.[17]

The shift in attitudes, it is worth noting, was much greater than the corresponding political impact. In 1939 Canadian independence in world affairs was limited by the country's almost non-existent military capacity, its lack of foreign intelligence capability, and the perception of the vast majority of the international community that it remained a British colony. Although Canada's hard power capabilities increased significantly throughout the early 1940s, policy planners generally remained dependent on British briefs for their background material, Canada was excluded from the combined chiefs of staff that prosecuted the war, and a significant proportion of the country remained at least instinctively committed to rebuilding the British-led Commonwealth as a major international power when the conflict ended.

The decline of Great Britain in the immediate postwar era changed the national context. With ties to the old Empire – both political and economic – waning, Canadians came to view the United States as the only power capable of negating their capacity for independent action on the world stage. Moreover, as Canadians began to take greater pride in their contributions to the shaping of the new world order – the founding of the GATT, the establishment of NATO, a foreign aid program for the Commonwealth, a UN-mandated war in Korea – the insecurity that naturally accompanied the new sense of internationalism that had been developing since the early 1940s came to be expressed antagonistically. A 1954 editorial in *Maclean's* exposed the problem. 'We all enjoy criticizing our hefty neighbours,' it maintained,

> but most of us are furiously indignant if they ever criticize us. Let an American tourist so much as make a face at the coffee he's been served in some roadside stand, and he is tartly told that if he doesn't like the way Canadians do things he better go back home. This is known as sturdy Canadian independence.

The article concluded with a warning:

> For a small country lying alongside a big powerful country the problem of maintaining independence is always real. No Canadian wants our government tamely to follow Washington's lead in everything ... We have a right and a duty to speak for ourselves.

But maybe we all ought to remember that we can be independent without making a virtue of being unpleasant.[18]

Unfortunately, the advice was not heeded particularly well. By the early 1960s, there was evidence of a new and indeed bitter independence debate, this time focused exclusively on the Canadian–American relationship.

Although the discussion would not become particularly intense until close to five years later, the signs of trouble were evident in 1961. That June, the Canadian Institute of International Affairs (CIIA), the leading non-partisan think tank on foreign policy in Canada, held its annual study conference in Montreal to discuss what it called 'problems of Canadian independence.' In the words of the graduate student who was tasked with summarizing the results of the dialogue, 'The fundamental problem confronting participants in the conference was that of reconciling the desire of Canadians for independence in the political sphere with what most of them considered to be the reality of interdependence between Canada and the entire Western community in the spheres of military security, economic welfare and moral values.' The so-called Western community, it turned out, referred primarily to the United States, and the greatest fear expressed by conference participants was that American economic penetration of the Canadian economy would jeopardize national freedom in other aspects of external relations.[19]

What would soon become a feud between those who felt that Canada had to break free from its commitments to what is now North American Aerospace Defence Command (NORAD) and the North Atlantic Treaty Organization (NATO), and those who saw involvement in such bilateral and multilateral security institutions as crucial to the maintenance of Canadian influence in world affairs, heated up quickly. Academic Peyton Lyon, who himself attended the CIIA conference, wrote an article shortly afterwards attacking the neutralists as naive and misguided. They were not genuinely interested in independence, he claimed, but rather in protecting a wistful interpretation of the national identity based upon an alleged Canadian moral righteousness in world affairs; moreover, their approach was less than helpful. 'We not only want merely to be independent,' he complained, 'but to be recognized as such, and also to be applauded for bold initiative. This demand leads to posturing, which fools no one but ourselves – to steps designed to demonstrate our independence regardless of the cost in diplomatic credit among our friends ... Like so many other immature nations,' he added, 'we prefer to be abused rather than ignored.' Canada had to learn to 'become more concerned about having something worth saying rather than clamouring for the right to be heard in the councils of the world.'[20]

Lyon's reasoning underlay the general foreign policy approach of the federal Liberal government under Prime Minister Lester B. Pearson from 1963 through 1968. Canada and the United States were permanently bound by geography and shared a number of mutual interests based on their similar cultures and political ideals. There would certainly be times when the two countries would disagree, and they had every right to, but it would be in both states' best interests to resolve the vast majority of these disputes cooperatively, through what came to be known as quiet diplomacy. Canada could be independent while still agreeing with American foreign policy decisions that did not conflict with its own national interests. It could also exercise its independence in disagreeing without necessarily embarrassing the government in Washington on the world stage. Being diplomatic, foreign minister Paul Martin maintained, did not imply subservience. Rather, it reflected a conscious effort to consider Canada's long-term needs ahead of any hollow desire to feel important or to humour a restless general public.[21]

Initially, Martin's most vocal detractors came largely from the school of political economy. Walter Gordon, a successful accountant and businessperson, had chaired a royal commission on Canada's economic prospects from 1955 through 1957 that had concluded that his country was in danger of being dominated economically by the United States. Six years later, having been one of Lester Pearson's key supporters throughout the 1963 election, Gordon was offered the position of minister of finance. After his first budget, which included take-over taxes and other measures designed to discourage American investment, had to be withdrawn because of criticism from both within and outside the party, Gordon's influence in the cabinet waned. He resigned in 1965 and did not return to cabinet until 1967.

As a backbench member of parliament, Gordon had greater freedom to speak his mind. In 1966 he published a short, controversial text, *A Choice for Canada: Independence or Colonial Status*, in which he reiterated the argument that Canadians were succumbing to American economic imperialism. If change did not come soon, if his country did not reassert its independence, its standing in the world would be permanently diminished. Just as Canada had once been a colony of Great Britain, it was on its way to becoming a colonial dependency of America.[22] For Gordon, the world had changed dramatically since the Second World

War. The nuclearization of the East-West conflict, for example, meant that Canada's conventional military strength was no longer particularly relevant to its ability to maintain an independent position in the world. While he did not argue in favour of renouncing international commitments to NATO and NORAD, Gordon did promote a gradual reduction in expenditures on defence.

It was here, in the fusion of foreign and economic policy, that Gordon contributed to a rather unhelpful shift in the independence debate. The argument in *A Choice for Canada* was one of the first efforts in the postwar period to link increasing U.S. control of the North American economy to Canada's capacity to pursue its own interests at the security level. This implicit and unyielding faith in the primacy of economics in continental affairs would also be found in the Clarkson text, which was published less than two years later. Although the latter did not claim to put forth a unanimous view – indeed Peyton Lyon himself contributed what could only be considered a dissenting chapter – the underlying definition of independence put forth by the editor had little to do with the traditional conceptions of security that had typically dominated the independence debate to that point, and thus transformed the discourse rather than advancing it.

Independence, according to Clarkson, meant 'being able to control one's own socio-economic environment.'[23] Certainly, the members of the University League for Social Reform who contributed to his collection identified all sorts of non-economic problems in Canadian external relations – the government was too willing to compromise its ideals, both domestic and international, in favour of consensus; the policy process was elitist and did not reflect the views and interests of the general public; the national approach to world affairs was no longer grounded in an ethical philosophy that could make Canadians proud – but underneath it all was a clear belief that the gradual takeover of the Canadian economy by American corporate interests had made the government in Ottawa increasingly vulnerable to pressures from Washington on security issues. It was this same attitude that underlay the campaign of the Committee for an Independent Canada, founded not much later by Gordon, writer Peter Newman, and scholar Abraham Rotstein.[24]

For the critics, the combination of the 1965 Merchant-Heeney report, a bi-national government-sponsored investigation into the state of the Canadian–American relationship that advocated quiet diplomacy, and the Canadian government's unwillingness, or inability, to stop national businesses from supplying the American military with armaments and munitions during the Vietnam War[25] was simply too much to take. Not surprisingly, their black-and-white approach to foreign policy, made clearest by philosopher Charles Hanly's assertion of a dichotomy between affiliation and independence, was grounded largely in well-intentioned and indeed passionate emotionalism as opposed to empirical evidence. As a result, it lacked the nuance necessary to have a genuine long-term impact.[26] It was a debate over foreign policy conducted, in the words of sympathetic critic Leonard Beaton, 'in the context of an obsession with the United States,'[27] one that would fluctuate over the years in response to external trends and incidents outside of Canada's direct control.

As part of the nationally divisive fall-out from the release of the Clarkson text, senior commentators such as John Holmes sought to find a middle ground. He and others used history to demonstrate that American economic investment in Canada had not resulted in undue U.S. influence in the Canadian foreign policy decision-making process. At the same time, however, Canada's economic dependence on the United States created a problematic situation that politicians could not simply ignore.[28] Others reminded the critics that there was no longer any such thing as complete independence in world affairs. Canada was a member of a world order. Its success and prosperity hinged on maximizing the benefits of the series of interdependent relationships that resulted from that order.[29]

What was most notable about the allegedly new dialogue was its lack of originality. The Loyalists of the eighteenth century had brought with them to British North America a fervent, if not arrogant, belief in their superiority to the citizens of the United States and in the need to differentiate themselves at every opportunity. As one former president of the Royal Society later explained, they saw themselves as 'the very cream of the Thirteen Colonies. They represented in very large measure the learning, the piety, the gentle birth, and wealth and good citizenship of the British race in America.'[30] Similarly, fears of an American economic takeover of Canada have existed since the late nineteenth century; they in many ways inspired Sir John A. Macdonald's national policy. Later, Robert Borden came to power on the back of a movement that argued, with reference to freer trade with the United States, that 'Canadian nationality is now threatened with a more serious blow than any it has heretofore met.'[31] The concept of global interdependence is also hardly new. This very argument was presented to the Canada Club by William L. Grant in 1912: 'The fallacy is the belief that in this modern world there is any such thing as independence. In this new world,' he said, 'every state is bound to every other state by filaments as impalpable yet as real and as numerous as those which thrill the instruments of Marconi.'[32]

What the independence debate of the 1960s did do was entrench a misleading analytical framework that has dominated strategic discussions of Canadian foreign policy ever since. Put simply, there are now two debates. The first is rhetorical, focused on a disagreement over the value of quiet diplomacy. Both sides see what is said, and indeed what is not said, as a critical determinant of a country's ability to promote its own interests on the world stage. The second debate revolves around the meaning of independence. On one side stand those who believe that Canada can best demonstrate its international freedom by pursuing policies that differentiate it from the United States. Others counter that a mature, independent country uses the resources available to it, and those include a generally healthy and cooperative relationship with a powerful neighbour, to its advantage in promoting its strategic aims.

Ironically, neither side believes in true independence. Critics of the United States rarely advocate unilateralism or even multilateral initiatives in which Canada dictates the policy for the group. They prefer that their country work in conjunction with other like-minded states and within international frameworks that necessarily require compromises and concessions. The alternative, it seems, is closer collaboration with just one country, which implies the same thing. In the words of a successful former secretary of state for external affairs who revisited the independence debate in the mid-1980s, '"Going it alone" is never ruled out, but is usually less productive for a country in Canada's circumstances.'[33]

Whether independence is even possible in the twenty-first-century world should hardly matter to a country like Canada. Too small to engineer a revolution in global politics on its own, and too closely reliant – both economically and militarily – on the international community to try, Canada has little to gain from academic discussions about the extent of its freedom. For internationalists, the independence debate should have ended during the Second World War when the goals of the Canadian approach to international engagement shifted from avoiding commitments to maximizing opportunities for them. For those less inclined to activism, the nature of Canada's activities on the world stage should be relatively unimportant. Any adventure, 'independent' or not, consumes resources that might be used more effectively at home. As scholar Charles Pentland explained so eloquently in 1970, 'the concept of "independence" provides us neither with criteria for judging existing policies nor with a fixed principle from which to deduce desirable policies in the issues now being debated. What it does provide, unfortunately, is a way of polarizing the debate so that the arguments are liable to dwell less on substance of policy than on questions of style and status.'[34]

Why, then, does this debate persist? In 1968 Leonard Beaton suggested that the emphasis on independence was 'a considerable substitute for hard work and real responsibilities.' 'Anything more than posturing will cost money and effort,' he said. 'It is a hard thing for politicians under pressure to decide to do unless they can see the promise of tangible results. That is why in the final analysis Canada remains a large small power rather t5an a small large power. Changing this will take ambition and effort.'[34] Forty years later, it is difficult to conclude that there has been much of either. Meanwhile, the dreaded and long-promised hostile takeover of Canadian society by U.S. corporate interests has yet to occur and Canada's admittedly always limited ability to go its own way in foreign policy has not been lost. At the same time, the overwhelming Canadian obsession with the optics of its approach to world affairs continues to overwhelm any strategic interest in maximizing the national impact on desired outcomes. The focus on independence remains a convenient alternative to hard policy choices. Looking forward to the rest of the twenty-first century, Canada can and should do better.

NOTES

1 The author thanks Margo Horosko for able research assistance, and Walter Eisenbeis for retrieving a particularly hard-to-find article.
2 On these ideas, see Leonard W. Labaree, 'The Loyalist as Conservative,' J.H. Coyne, 'Loyalty and Empire II,' and George Taylor Denison, 'The Superiority of the Loyalists,' in *The United Empire Loyalists: Men and Myths*, ed. L.S.F. Upton (Toronto: Copp Clark Publishing, 1967).
3 The Canada First movement that followed immediately on the heels of Confederation was not sufficiently united in its commitment to greater independence in foreign policy to merit inclusion here. See D.K. Farrell, . 'The Canada First Movement and Canadian Political Thought,' *Journal of Canadian Studies* 4, no. 4 (November 1969): 16–26.

4 C.P. Stacey, *Canada and the Age of Conflict*, vol. 1, *1867–1921* (Toronto: University of Toronto Press, [1977] 1984), 42.

5 Stephen Leacock, *Greater Canada: An Appeal – Let Us No Longer Be a Colony* (Montreal: Montreal News Co. Ltd, 1907), 8–10.

6 J.S. Ewart, 'The Kingdom of Canada,' in *Imperialism and Nationalism, 1884–1914: A Conflict in Canadian Thought*, ed. Carl Berger (Toronto: Copp Clark, 1969), 82–4.

7 Henri Bourassa, 'Future Anglo-Canadian Relations: Independence or Imperial Partnership,' in *Henri Bourassa on Imperialism and Biculturalism, 1900–1918*, ed. Joseph Levitt (Toronto: Copp Clark, 1970), 94–5.

8 Admittedly, that signature had no legal significance since it followed one from Britain on behalf of the entire Empire.

9 Hector Mackenzie, 'Canada's Nationalist Internationalism: From League of Nations to the United Nations,' in *Canadas of the Mind: The Making and Unmaking of Canadian Nationalisms in the Twentieth Century*, ed. Norman Hillmer and Adam Chapnick (Montreal and Kingston: McGill-Queen's University Press, 2007), 90.

10 Resolution IX of the Imperial War Conference of 1917, quoted in Stacey, *Canada and the Age of Conflict*, vol. 1, 213.

11 On these issues, see Maurice Ollivier, *Problems of Canadian Sovereignty from the British North America Act, 1867 to the Statute of Westminster* (Toronto: Canadian Law Book Co., 1945).

12 Escott Reid, 'The United States and Canada: Dominion, Co-operation, Absorption,' 12 January 1942, in Library and Archives Canada [hereafter LAC], Escott Reid Papers, MG31 E46, vol. 30, United States and Canada, 1942–5.

13 The most thorough discussion of the committees can be found in Don Munton and Don Page, 'Planning in the East Block: The Post-Hostilities Problems Committees in Canada, 1943–5,' *International Journal* 32, no. 4 (Autumn 1977): 677–726.

14 Adam Chapnick, *The Middle Power Project: Canada and the Founding of the United Nations* (Vancouver and Toronto: UBC Press, 2005), 23, 46, 47.

15 On 27 March 1943, for example, King received the results of a private public opinion survey that concluded his government, which was slumping in the polls, would improve its image dramatically if it promoted Canada's past and potential achievements in foreign policy more aggressively. See Wartime Information Board Survey 7, 27 March 1943, in LAC, W.L.M. King Papers, MG26 J2, vol. 379, file W-319-2, War-W.I.B. Surveys, 1943.

16 Canadian Institute of Public Opinion poll, 20 November 1943, in *Public Opinion Quarterly* 8, no. 1 (Spring 1944): 160.

17 This theme is dealt with in detail in Chapnick, *The Middle Power Project*.
18 'Being Independent Doesn't Mean Being Rude,' *Maclean's* 67 (1 April 1954):
    2.
19 Paul C. Noble, 'Problems of Canadian Independence,' *CIIA Notes* 2, no. 2
    (August 1961), 1. An early, book-length discussion of the issues can be found
    in Hugh G.J. Aitken, *American Capital and Canadian Resources* (Cambridge,
    MA: Harvard University Press, 1961).
20 Peyton V. Lyon, 'Problems of Canadian Independence,' *International Journal*
    16, no. 3 (Summer 1961): 257, 259. See also R.J. Sutherland, 'A Defence Strat-
    egist Examines the Realities,' in *Canadian Foreign Policy since 1945: Middle
    Power or Satellite?* ed. J.L. Granatstein (Toronto: Copp Clark Publishing,
    1969), 21–9. Aitken made the point less confrontationally: 'The danger is
    that resistance to economic integration may engender in Canada a narrow,
    introspective nationalism which, by its insistence on defense against exter-
    nal threats, may stultify the very sources that should be encouraged.' See
    Aitken, *American Capitalism and Canadian Resources*, 193.
21 Paul Martin, 'An Independent Foreign Policy,' in *Statements and Speeches*
    66, no. 3 (Ottawa: Department of External Affairs Information Division,
    1966). The speech was given to the Canadian Club in Toronto on 31 January
    1966.
22 Walter L. Gordon, *A Choice for Canada: Independence or Colonial Status* (Tor-
    onto and Montreal: McClelland and Stewart, 1966), 124. See also Stephen
    Azzi, *Walter Gordon and the Rise of Canadian Nationalism* (Montreal and King-
    ston: McGill-Queen's University Press, 1999).
23 Stephen Clarkson, 'The Choice to Be Made,' in *An Independent Foreign Policy
    for Canada?* (Toronto: McClelland & Stewart, 1968), 255.
24 See, for example, Abraham Rotstein and Gary Lax, eds, *Independence: The
    Canadian Challenge* (Toronto: Committee for an Independent Canada, 1972).
25 The Canadian government's hands were tied by the Defence Production
    Sharing Agreement of the late 1950s.
26 Charles Hanly, 'The Ethics of Independence,' in *An Independent Foreign Pol-
    icy for Canada?* 22.
27 Leonard Beaton, 'Declaration of Independence,' *Canadian Forum* 48 (April
    1968): 1. See also an outstanding analysis by Charles Pentland, 'Mandarins
    and Manicheans: The "Independence" Debate on Canadian Foreign Policy,'
    Queen's Quarterly 77 (Spring 1970): 99–103.
28 John W. Holmes, 'Interdependence: Political Aspects,' *Canadian Forum* 48
    (February 1969): 245–6.
29 A.D.P. Heeney, 'Independence and Partnership: The Search for Principles,'
    International Journal 27, no. 2 (Spring 1972): 159–71; Desmond Morton, 'In-

dependence: It Won't Be Easy,' *Canadian Forum* 52 (April 1972): 20–1, 47; Douglas J. Gibson, 'Canada's Declaration of Less Independence,' *Harvard Business Review* 51 (September/October 1973): 69–79; and Grant L. Reber, 'Canadian Independence in an Asymmetrical World Community: A National Riddle,' *International Journal* 29, no. 4 (Autumn 1974): 535–56.

30 J.H. Coyne, 'Loyalty and Empire, II,' in *The United Empire Loyalists*, 13.

31 J.L. Granatstein, *Yankee Go Home? Canadians and Anti-Americanism* (Toronto: HarperCollins, 1996), 40.

32 William L. Grant, 'The Impossibility of Isolationism,' in *Imperialism and Nationalism*, 61.

33 Joe Clark, *Canada's International Relations: Response of the Government of Canada to the Report of the Special Joint Committee of the Senate and the House of Commons* (Ottawa: Minister of Supply and Services Canada, 1986), 5.

34 Pentland, 'Mandarins and Manicheans,' 102.

35 Beaton, 'Declaration of Independence,' 3.

2 The Illusion of Independence

PATRICK LENNOX

A foreign policy independent from the pre-eminent international power is difficult to achieve unless one is a rogue or a rival state. Of course there will be opportunities for middle powers to pursue initiatives of international importance independent from what the United States happens to be doing in the world, but those will likely be few and far between, and, to the extent that they can be achieved without at least the tacit backing of the superpower, are likely to have minimal impact on the grand scheme of world politics. The fact of the matter is that Canada inhabits an international system constructed largely in the American mould and on the basis of American power.[1] For the most part, when the foreign policies coming out of Washington have been generally well received in the rest of the international system since 1945, this has proved a very fortunate situation indeed. Occasionally, American foreign policy has taken a turn in an unfortunate direction, and Canada has found itself in the awkward position of having either to go along against the better judgment of its officials in Ottawa and public opinion more generally, or to find a way to distinguish Canada's voice and separate its role in the world from the United States.

At least this is the way it would *appear* in times such as our own, and in the period surrounding the publication of Stephen Clarkson's *An Independent Foreign Policy for Canada?* Appearances in times of crisis, however, can be deceiving if one is not attuned to the possibility of their revealing a deeper reality about the normal ebb and flow of events.

The Crisis Reveals the Normal

The war in Vietnam then and the war in Iraq now both had disquieting effects on the so-called special relationship. Among other factors mentioned in the introduction to this volume, this discomfort inspired a seemingly new desire to see Canada venture out independently into the world. In the context of Vietnam abroad and the race riots much closer to home, this desire to distinguish the Canadian polity from the American one amplified to an audible level an otherwise discrete tendency in Canada's approach to world affairs, one that has had a determining effect on the patterns of its foreign policy since the end of the Second World War.

This tendency was first articulated on the world stage in the form of a principle by the Canadian delegates to the San Francisco Conference in the spring of 1945. Tasked with the monumental responsibility of drafting a charter for the United Nations out of the proposals brought forth by the great-power authors of the Dumbarton Oaks proposals, and struggling to find a role for Canada in the emergent world order, Prime Minister Mackenzie King and key members of the Department of External Affairs maintained the position that the responsibility for the establishment and preservation of stability in the system not be left entirely to the great powers themselves. An emergent class of middle powers (of which Canada was one) should be involved in aspects of systemic maintenance in which they could be expected to make important contributions. Moreover, they should be represented in the decisions leading to such involvement. The Charter and the organization to which it would give birth must create this space for non-great-power involvement in the major movements of international affairs, or risk isolating the middle powers entirely. Such an outcome would create a top-heavy and unstable postwar order, prone to toppling back into systemic chaos.

What came to be known as the functional principle of representation was eventually embedded in the UN charter in a number of ways.[2] But the principle was not solely a way of creating a space for the involvement of non-great powers in the play of international politics. Contained within the logic of the principle was a clear sense of what aspects of international politics were outside the ambit of middle powers. In particular, the Canadian delegation had no objection to the permanent place of the great powers on the Security Council, or to their individual wielding of veto power over the decisions of the Council. Matters of high security were predominantly the domain of the great powers.[3] It was in the other, more specialized aspects of international affairs that middle powers could have an influence.

The principle of functional representation, in other words, contained within its logic a strategy for Canada's future involvement in international politics. To separate at a conceptual level the strategy from the principle, we might label the strategy dimension 'specialization.' The driving forces behind the strategy are not altogether separate from the realities that inspired the invention of the principle, but they do require separate analysis, as they can only be recognized at a deeper level of abstraction.

Specialization, as this chapter will demonstrate, is a strategy pursued in the world out of a necessity born of Canada's position in North America. It amounts to a prolonged sleight of hand trick designed to maintain the illusion of Canada's independence from the United States for audiences both at home and abroad. The trick works because the Canadian public, the United States, and the rest of the international community all have an interest in not seeing through the illusion. This essay explains the necessity behind the illusion of independence created by Canada's pursuit of specialized roles within the international system.

The Illusory Dichotomy

As was noted in the introduction to this volume, a stark dichotomy formed the axis of the 1968 version of *IFPC*? On the one hand, Canada's best strategy was thought by the proponents of quiet diplomacy to be one of close affiliation with the United States. Content to be a degree of separation removed from the real action, Canada should go along quietly with the United States and attempt to have influence in world affairs by gently steering Washington in the right direction. On the other hand, it was thought by the 'independentists' that Canada's best shot at international sway was to strike out on its own course. Regardless of the often exaggerated potential consequences that might follow from an angered or slighted United States, an independent course for Canadian foreign policy, steered by national interests and values (as well as utilitarian calculations of the greater good of international society), provided the clearest path to international influence. Those in search of a middle ground between these two positions were left wanting by the conclusions drawn by Clarkson, and perhaps a bit suspicious that such a starkly drawn debate may in fact have been a false one.

Peyton Lyon's contribution, entitled 'Quiet Diplomacy Revisited,' asserted that the most influence Canada could hope to wield in world affairs was through its close relationship with the United States. The relationship was seen to facilitate the occasional critical instance where

Canada could emerge quietly from the wings to guide America's foreign policy away from the sorts of irresponsible and tragic blunders to which Washington was prone. Canadian 'sanity' and 'wisdom' in such cases, combined with special access to the levers of American power granted to only the best of Uncle Sam's friends, were seen by Lyon to be the country's best hope of achieving influence in the world. Lyon contrasted this diplomatic tact with what he described as 'raucous diplomacy': a movement to break ranks with the U.S. alliance structure; to declare Canada a neutral state; and to shun our relationship with Washington in favour of closer ties to other capitals, all in the name of Canadian independence.

Yet, in his brief chapter Lyon alluded to the logic of what would otherwise be a truly independent (though perhaps less than raucous) foreign policy for Canada. As Lyon recommended: 'A more promising approach is to adopt policies that point up the different characteristics and roles of Canada and the United States, without causing serious friction between Ottawa and Washington.'[4] Such a strategy is something quite apart from maintaining a quiet proximity to power in Washington in the hopes of being allowed at the crucial moment to make a critical suggestion that somehow alters the course of world politics. Such a strategy, on the contrary, carves out for Canada an independent set of roles – distinct from those of the United States – and yet ultimately in service to the same basic ends: (1) the general aim of system stability defined in terms of the absence of general war; and (2) a generally rules-based system in which both disputes and cooperative enterprises between states are initiated and seen through on the basis of mutually agreed upon laws (as opposed to that of who has the upper hand in material capability).

On the other side of the 1968 debate, Charles Hanley advocated an independent approach to world affairs based on 'the utilitarian imperative,' which, as he saw it, compelled Canadian decision-makers to calibrate their foreign policy movements on the basis of rational evaluations of Canada's national interests, as well as 'the interests and aspirations' of the other peoples who would be affected by Canada's foreign policies. Hanley contrasted this independence strategy with that which he felt Canada had tended to pursue to that point: the strategy of affiliation. By placing itself in basic agreement with the major foreign policy decisions of first Britain and then the United States, Canadian governments had undersold their country's ability to have an independent impact on the course of world affairs. Such an ideological impulse towards affiliation with Canada's more powerful allies created, in Hanley's view, 'a major obstacle to following an ethical foreign policy' (18). It was 'regressive' and 'futile' in his estimation, and impeded a clear view of a complex international system in which Canada had a duty to position itself independently in order to act both ethically and effectively according to the basic principle of utilitarianism.

To dispense with the affiliation strategy and move on to a strategy of independence, however, required more than any Canadian government would have been capable of: it would have required, by Hanley's own admission, the staking out of a non-aligned position in the Cold War.[5] Such a position then, as now, would have completely neutralized any possibility of Canada having an influence on the trajectory of world affairs. More seriously, it would have dealt a devastating blow to the Canada–U.S. relationship, and done much to jeopardize the country's internal cohesion.

Thus, the stark dichotomy that formed the basis of the 1968 debate was set up on both sides – as most debates are – in a manner far too polarized to have any sound bearing on reality. The real choice that lay before Canadian foreign policy-makers then (as now) was to be found somewhere in the middle ground. Between a raucous independence and a quiet affiliation is found a set of specialized and distinct roles suited to Canada, which if cultivated and pursued with skill and resources can contribute not only to the amelioration of the international system, but to its progress, and not only to Canada's improved relations with the United States, but to improved relations across the regional divisions that exist within Canada itself.

Indeed, it has been through the strategy of specialization that Canadian governments, over the last half-century, have (knowingly or unknowingly) had the most success in maintaining the illusion of independence. The tendency to want to break more forcefully with the direction of American foreign policy that arises in times such as our own and those of the mid-to-late nineteen-sixties, if acted upon will paradoxically have the effect of shattering the illusion and revealing the reality of Canadian dependency. The current combat mission that the Canadian Forces find themselves fighting in Kandahar, Afghanistan, provides a striking contemporary example of this paradox, which we will return to analyse in the concluding section of this essay. To understand how this case exemplifies the dangers of breaking with the strategy of specialization, and how the strategy of specialization works to maintain the illusion of independence, we must first come to grips with the underlying structural factors that both enable and indeed compel its pursuit.

The Invisible Connection

The analogy between the state of nature imagined by well-known liberal political philosophers such as Thomas Hobbes, Immanuel Kant, and Jean-Jacques Rousseau and the realm of international politics, which is without an overarching government, capable of presiding over a common body of law, has been drawn not only by the philosophers themselves,[6] but by modern international relations theorists as well.[7] This insight, that the realm of international politics is anarchic (meaning without government), has (however strangely) in fact become the foundational insight from which much of mainstream international relations theory has derived.[8]

From this precept that the anarchic structure of the international system had its own causal weight two further insights were derived. First, specialization in particular aspects of international politics could not be expected to be a general pattern followed by states in the anarchic international system. This was thought to be the case since the flip side of specialization is (inter)dependency, which in an anarchic realm is a strategy thought to be tantamount to suicide. Second, hierarchy – the dichotomous ordering principle – would not be possible within the realm unless either a world government or a global empire were to be established by either agreement or the force of one dominant state.[9]

A growing number of international relations scholars have come to view the anarchy insight with scepticism.[10] Jack Donnelly, for one, is of the belief that the anarchy insight is in fact 'a conceptual error that significantly impedes understanding the nature of international inequalities. Rather than thinking of anarchy *or* hierarchy we should attend to hierarchy *in* anarchy.'[11] Coming to grips with this seemingly contradictory notion that within an anarchic international system hierarchical inter-state relationships can and do form is the first step in understanding why the illusion of Canadian foreign policy independence is necessary, and through what methods it is created.

Looking, for example, at the basic structure of the Canada–U.S. relationship at home, we can see clearly that it does not operate according to the competitive, self-help logic imposed on rival states by the otherwise anarchic structure of the international system. On the contrary,

Canada is engaged in a dependent relationship with the United States in terms of both its economic and physical security. Consider as evidence of this the overwhelming trade dependency that sees 80 per cent of Canadian exports headed south into the American marketplace, and over two-thirds of its imports coming from that same market. A border closure might pose significant costs to the U.S. economy; but such an event would send the Canadian economy into depression. Consider also NORAD as an institution representative of how the material asymmetry between the two countries has shaped their defence relationship. NORAD headquarters were built into an American part of the Rocky Mountain range. It was agreed that the commander-in-chief of NORAD would always be an American, and that his deputy commander-in-chief, a Canadian, would take decision-making power only when the commander was absent. Today, over 94 percent of NORAD's personnel are American, and over 84 percent of NORAD's budget is paid for with American funds. And while Canada supplies the remainder of the staff and budget, the practical imbalance in this symbolic institution remains an obvious reflection of the hierarchy in the continental relationship.

We can say then that Canada finds itself on the subordinate end of an inter-state hierarchy that has formed within the broader international anarchy: both states retain and cling jealously to their formal legal sovereignty, and yet one is very much dependent upon the other for its physical and economic survival. This is – to those who are familiar with the literature on Canada–U.S. relations with all of its talk of asymmetry and dependency – an old insight in new packaging. But in this case, the conceptual packaging makes a big difference, since it allows us to finally resolve the theoretical puzzle that lurked at the heart of the original *IFPC?* volume: how does the hierarchy at home affect Canada's place in the world abroad?

The Strategy of Specialization

Reasoning by analogy and abstracting from the immediate example of Canada for the moment: if hierarchy is the permissive or generative cause of specialization, then just as the individual in domestic society must specialize in some trade or vocation in order to make him or herself necessary to that society as a means of ensuring his or her survival and well-being, so too must a subordinate state in the international system find a way to make itself necessary to the superordinate state and to the broader international society in order to ensure its survival and well-being. This necessity provides the impulse for the subordinate state to specialize, playing particular roles in the international system that remain distinct from those most suited to great powers.

Specialization in the international system is related to the internal functional differentiation allowed to the subordinate state by virtue of its position within the hierarchical sub-system. When, by virtue of its dependency on another sovereign state for its physical and economic security, a state is permitted to become less of a typical Westphalian warfare state – to channel more of its resources into education, or health care, or infrastructure as opposed to defence spending – in other words, when subordinate states become internally functionally differentiated, then they take on the characteristics that permit them to become externally functionally differentiated.

A direct and immediate connection might exist between a particular subordinate state's internal functional differentiation and its external functional differentiation – for example, state emphasis on health care might provide the domestic background expertise and material capability for specialization in preventing and combating the transnational spread of infectious disease. But more generally it is the movement away from the maintenance of an independent war-fighting capability that both permits and compels the pursuit of specialization as an alternative mode of maintaining sovereignty in the international system. A state's movement away from maintaining an independent warfare capability negates the threat it poses to other states, thus creating the internal preconditions for that state to take on a benign, as opposed to potentially malignant, external posture. To use an analogy from microeconomics, this gives the subordinate state a comparative advantage in the performance of roles unsuited to great powers who maintain an independent war-fighting capacity, and thus the power to impose their will through coercive force on other states in the system.

To return to the Canadian case momentarily, practitioner and scholar of Canadian foreign policy John Holmes hinted at this very notion in his collection of essays *The Better Part of Valour*. He explained that the 'precarious state of the world after 1945 required the forceful intervention in far corners of a benevolent great power like the United States. It turned out also that the preservation of order often required the services of middle powers whose principal value was their very incapacity to threaten or command.' Holmes further noted that, in the postwar era of international politics, Canada had shed its reluctance to be useful. 'Canadians coveted [international] responsibilities, and Canadian diplomatic missions multiplied from seven in 1939 to sixty-five in 1962.'[12]

Compelled to work towards ensuring their survival through means other than material-power accumulation, and power balancing – the strategies recommended by the otherwise anarchic structure of the international system – subordinate states can be expected to exploit their comparative advantage in the performance of roles in the international system not suited to their superordinate partners. The performance of these roles will contribute to the preservation of their external and internal sovereignty through the construction of a recognizable and distinct international identity, which will serve as a reminder to audiences both at home and abroad of the necessity and relevance of the subordinate state to the proper functioning of the status quo international system. The performance of a given specialized role on the part of a subordinate state is thus determined by a triad of constraints imposed by the dual structural pressures of hierarchy and anarchy.

First, since the subordinate state comes to derive a portion of its internal cohesion from its external functions, internal constraints from its own domestic society will play a role in determining its specialized behaviour in the international system. The dominant ideas about the state's place in world politics formed within its society as a result of pre-existing patterns of the state's behaviour in the international system will come to set the parameters of legitimate state action in this realm. For example, after having cultivated a reputation as a peacekeeper, Canadian governments have recently found themselves hard pressed to justify the combative posture into which they have put the Canadian Forces in the south of Afghanistan to certain segments of the Canadian public. These parameters of legitimate behaviour act as both constraining and compelling internal structural pressures bearing down on the state: they limit what the state can and cannot do in the external sphere with the broad-based support of its population; and they suggest what the state ought to do when presented with certain opportunities or perceived obligations to engage in world affairs.

Second, since the permissive cause of the subordinate state's ability to specialize in the international system is located in its position in the inter-state hierarchy, the requirements and needs of the superordinate state will factor in determining the specialized behaviour of the subordinate state in the international system. In the performance of roles in which it has a comparative advantage over its superordinate partner the subordinate state will be expected to carry its share of the burden of status quo systemic management. Consider, as an example, Canada's involvement in supervising the 2005 Iraqi elections. The country's reputation as a reliable mediator/supervisor, combined with its lack of formal involvement in the regime change that was initiated by the United States in 2003, allowed and compelled its performance of this specialized role. The interests of the superordinate state will always, therefore, be a structuring influence on the particular modes of behaviour pursued by the subordinate state in the international system.

Finally, the specialized behaviour of the subordinate state must be of some utility to the functioning of the status quo international system. Specialization is thus generated in part by the demand for non-great power intervention in a complex international system that requires more to remain functional and stable than great power leadership and direction alone. States with specialized capabilities carry out functions unsuited to great powers in an effort to ameliorate potential systemic ruptures and to serve as a buffer between those states that benefit and those states that struggle under the status quo world political and economic system.

The following roles conform to the triad of structural pressures bearing down on subordinate state specialization in the international system. An operational definition of each role is followed by Canadian case examples. These examples are suggestive of the Canadian tendency to perform in a specialized capacity as an alternative means of persevering as a sovereign state in the international system. They do not constitute a systematic test of the theorized connection between Canada's place in North America and its place in the world.

Mediator/Supervisor: In the aftermath of inter-state, or civil war, states with neither the capacity for nor the inclination towards imperialism are necessary to separate combatants and prisoners of war, to establish stability, to help implement peace treaties, and then to withdraw. The term associated with this mode of behaviour is peacekeeping. The mediation and supervision of post-combat situations is of high significance for the ability of the international system to maintain order and stability. Disorder and conflict in one part of the complex interdependent international political system can easily spread to create disorder and conflict in other parts of the system.

Great powers, of course, have the military and diplomatic capability to perform the services of mediation and supervision. However, their subordinate partners have a comparative advantage over them in the performance of such services to the international system, thanks to their internal functional differentiation, which gives them an unthreatening external posture particularly suited to mediation/supervision roles.

Examples of Canada's performance of variations on the mediator/supervisor role are numerous, but perhaps most famously they can be seen in its service to the International Commissions for Supervision and Control (ICSC) in Vietnam, Cambodia, and Laos during the period of 1954 to 1973; the United Nations Emergency Force in Suez, 1956; the United Nations Congo Force, 1960; the United Nations Peacekeeping Force in Cyprus, 1963–93; the UN Protection Force in Yugoslavia, 1992–present; Lloyd Axworthy's efforts with the OAS in helping to democratize Peru in 2000; and Canada's leading role in supervising the Iraqi parliamentary elections in 2005.

Messenger: In situations when communication breaks down between states in conflict or about to be in conflict, it becomes necessary for a third party to play an interlocutor role. By passing messages faithfully back and forth between the two parties, the messenger state works towards a resolution to a potential combat or crisis situation. Such a role can be of great consequence in a complex international political system in which language barriers, surveillance technology, fear, and paranoia can combine to tip the balance in crisis situations towards instability and armed conflict.

Great powers, however, either because they are on one side or the other of these situations, or because they have a perceived myopic self-interest in the outcome, are uniquely unsuited to the performance of such a messenger role. This gives the comparative advantage to subordinate states in this important aspect of international politics, thus creating the necessity for both their continued sovereign existence and their maintenance and cultivation of this advantage in the performance of such a service to the international system.

For example, Canada served in this capacity during the war in Vietnam, as its commissioner on the ICSC, Blair Seaborn, was used repeatedly as an interlocutor between Washington and Hanoi in 1964;[13] prior to this, during the Cuban missile crisis, Dean Rusk, President Kennedy's defence secretary, suggested that Canada's ambassador in Havana be used to try to explain to Fidel Castro that Cuba was being victimized in the conflict.[14]

Advocate: Raising awareness of a problem or issue, generating interstate cooperation for resolution of the problem or issue, and defending a particular position (i.e., West vs East) on a problem or issue are advocacy roles that fall to specialized states. The conventional political term employed in describing of this type of behaviour is multilateralism. Because of their superior material capabilities great powers are uniquely inclined towards unilateralism. This inclination can be staved off by the work of dynamic political leaders and statesmen, but it nevertheless is an underlying tendency associated with great power. Yet the need for multilateralism or advocacy to collectively work towards resolutions to otherwise intractable international problems and towards what Stanley Hoffman referred to as 'peaceful change' remains.[15]

A comparative advantage in the performance of such an advocacy role exists for subordinate states that, without the ability to 'go it alone,' have a genuine interest in generating multilateral action towards collective measures as a means to resolving the unique problems presented in an interdependent, anarchic system of sovereign states.

Again, there are numerous examples of Canada working in such a capacity at the international level. In this volume alone, Heather Smith describes how Canada, under the leadership of the Mulroney government, was the first to recognize global climate change as an issue requiring a multilateral solution. The organization of the Toronto conference on the implications of the changing atmosphere for global security in 1988 thus provides an example of Canada's propensity for advocacy in the international system. Patricia Goff's contribution here provides us with a second example. Leading the process that culminated in 2007 with the ratification of the UNESCO Convention on the Protection and Promotion of the Diversity of Cultural Expressions, Canada, in Goff's words 'led a movement that, in record time, created a widely supported and innovative multilateral solution to a pressing global governance challenge.' Canada's innovation of the so-called Ottawa Process in the campaign to ban anti-personnel landmines is perhaps the most seminal contemporary example of Canada's advocacy efforts in the international system.

Problem solver: Seemingly intractable international problems create opportunities for the ingenuity and initiative of a specialized power for their resolution. The political term for this behaviour, at least in the Canadian context, is, of course, 'helpful fixing.' Such behaviour is particularly suited to subordinate states because they are, for the most part, 'outside the box' of great-power politics. They are thus more able to see the modes of conflict resolution, methods of crisis aversion, and courses of action towards the resolution of problems that have eluded the great powers themselves. Indeed, this ability, should it be proved repeatedly, will come to be depended upon by the great powers in charge of managing the major movements of world affairs, thus creating a bond of interdependence between the system and the continued sovereign survival of the subordinate state.

Notable examples of such behaviour on Canada's part include Escott Reid's suggestion at the Couchiching Conference of the Canadian Institute of Public Affairs in 1947 of a regional security organization open to any Western country (what would later become NATO) in response to the problem created by the Soviet Union's abuse of its Security Council veto power; Lester B. Pearson's efforts to diffuse the Suez crisis in 1956 through the innovative concept of UN-led peacekeeping; Mitchell Sharp's development of what came to be known as the 'Canadian formula' for recognizing Mao's China, while only taking note of its claims over Chiang Kai-shek's Taiwan; Pierre Trudeau's peace initiative to de-escalate the Cold War in 1983; Brian Mulroney's efforts with the Bush administration to ensure the first Gulf War was fought under a multilateral banner; and, most recently, the efforts of Paul Heinbecker and Jean Chrétien in 2002 to generate a second UN resolution to win Security Council support for the impending war against Iraq.

Intelligence gatherer: Uncertainty and misperception are constant and potentially deadly factors in international politics. Occasions repeatedly arise when non-principal powers will be granted access to crucial information the principals are not privy to. The accurate gathering and communication of that information thus becomes a specialization suited to subordinate states.

Blair Seaborn was instructed by the Johnson administration to play this role during his missions to Hanoi in 1964; throughout the Cold War (and to this day) Canada supplies the United States with information from within Castro's (first Fidel's, now Raul's) Cuba through its continued diplomatic contacts with his regime; and a major part of Canada's ongoing mission in the south of Afghanistan involves intelligence gathering on behalf of the United States.[16]

Canada can be expected to fill one of these functions when at least two of the structural imperatives to do so coincide with an opportunity. For example, if the internal pressures emanating from lagging or faltering internal cohesion and the hierarchical pressures emanating from a needy United States combine with an opportunity to fill a mediator/supervisor role, then Canada can be expected to do so. If only one of the structural pressures is present, then Canada can be expected to reject the opportunity to pursue a specialized role in the international system. Take the following as a hypothetical case in point: if the opportunity to act as an intelligence gatherer on behalf of the United States exists, but there is no domestic support for the mission, and the balance of the international community appears opposed to the American initiative, it can be expected that sovereignty concerns would trump concerns for good relations with Washington. In this case Canada would expectedly remain uninvolved, since only one (as opposed to the necessary two) of the three structural pressures to perform in a specialized capacity is present.

Shattered Illusion

In early 2003 Prime Minister Jean Chrétien stood in the House of Commons and denounced the American-led invasion of Iraq. Canada, he said, would have no part in the 'unnecessary' war. The announcement was very popular at home, as 70 per cent of Canadians supported the government's decision.[17] It may, in fact, have turned the tide in a crucial provincial election in Quebec, which saw Jean Charest's Parti libéral du Québec come from behind in the polls to defeat Bernard Landry's incumbent Parti Québécois. The turnaround in the polls corresponded in time with the prime minister's decision to maintain Canada's symbolic independence from the Coalition of the Willing. In the closing days of his leadership, Chrétien was thus able to boast at his final fundraiser, 'My friends, in all modesty, I think that we can state without hesitation that when it comes to the important file of national unity, we can say, "Mission accomplished."'[18] The ironic reference to George W. Bush's famous declaration on the flight deck of the USS *Abraham Lincoln* of 2 May 2003 (during which he prematurely announced the end of all major combat operations in Iraq) can be read as an acknowledgment of how important to Canada's national unity Chrétien viewed the decision to maintain Canada's symbolic independence from the Iraq invasion.

Yet Canada (indirectly) contributed more to the invasion of Iraq than most members of the Coalition of the Willing (only the United States, Australia, and Britain contributed more). Canada was even formally thanked for its efforts in a report issued on 30 April 2003 by U.S. Air Force lieutenant general T. Michael Moseley. In the report, which dealt exclusively with the war in Iraq, Moseley listed thirty-one Canadian troops in a table entitled 'Deployed Personnel for OIF [Operation Iraq Freedom]' and went on to acknowledge the input of Canadian and allied officers in their 'collection and collation' of the data contained in the unclassified document.[19]

Indeed, the notion that Canada would stand independently aside from the Iraq War was illusory from the start. The HMCS *Halifax* and the HMCS *Winnipeg* were put on patrol in the Arabian Sea, and Canada had taken up command of a naval task force in that region in the prelude to the Shock and Awe campaign. Canadian military planners were sent to a U.S. command post in Qatar to participate in the development of strategy for the impending war on Iraq under American General Tommy Franks.[20] The HMCS *Iroquois*, a destroyer out of Halifax, was sent to the Gulf of Oman on a mission that the minister of national defence, John McCallum, admitted could become 'double-hatted' if U.S. naval forces needed support during a war in Iraq.[21] And one hundred Canadian officers remained on exchange with their British and American counterparts in the Iraqi theatre of operations.[22]

The illusory nature of Canada's independent stance on the Iraq war is made all the more evident by the fact that the decision to send a significant number of troops to Afghanistan was made almost as soon as it became clear that the war against Saddam Hussein's regime would commence without UN approval. Defence Minister John McCallum's announcement that between 1500 and 2000 troops would deploy for Afghanistan just one month before the Iraq War began precluded the possibility of any substantial Canadian involvement on the second front of the War on Terror. The Canadian Forces were already overstretched. Indeed, in late 2002, the Senate Standing Committee on Defence and Security issued a report recommending that all of Canada's troops posted overseas be returned home for a rest period of two years. And when questioned about sending a significant number of troops back to Afghanistan the commander of Canada's army at the time, Lieutenant General Mike Jeffrey, advised the Chrétien government against the possibility.[23]

The announcement of the Canadian deployment to Afghanistan therefore carried with it a greater significance. With the prospect of participating in a non-UN-sanctioned war of choice being politically untenable at home, and the prospect of being symbolically uninvolved in either front of the War on Terror being political untenable in terms of Ottawa's relations with Washington, the Chrétien government was compelled to find a way back into Afghanistan. Defence Minister McCallum pitched the possibility to Donald Rumsfeld and received favourable response from the Secretary of Defense, who was well aware of the fact that it would free up American forces for Operation Iraqi Freedom.[24] To compensate for the Iraq decision, Canada had to make a significant contribution to the Afghanistan front of the War on Terror.

That contribution became even more significant and even more outside of Canada's bounded array of specialized roles once it became clear that the Paul Martin government would have to disappoint the Bush administration yet again by declining to participate in (and thus symbolically endorse) its Ballistic Missile Defense project. The decision was made to move forces from the relative stability of Kabul to the dangerously unstable province of Kandahar to set up a Provincial Reconstruction Team (PRT). The PRT of some 220 members from different government agencies – CIDA, DFAIT (Department of Foreign Affairs and International Trade), DND, RCMP – would be supported by a robust 2000-member battle group, which would be engaging in what David S. McDonough describes as 'force protection and combat/counterinsurgency operations against neo-Taliban adversaries.'[25] Added to this sizable contribution would be a small and specialized Strategic Advisory Team that would be embedded with the Karzai government, working to assist it in the implementation of the Afghanistan National Development Strategy.

Saying 'yes' to making the move from Kabul to Kandahar was made in an effort to compensate for saying 'no' to first Iraq, and then BMD. Both of these no's were regarded by officials in DND and DFAIT as a serious threat to the smooth functioning of Canada–U.S. relations.[26] But this 'yes' has come at a significant cost in terms of blood, treasure, and the image of Canada as a peaceable kingdom both at home and abroad.

Having taken on a significant task that is outside its realm of expertise, Canada currently finds itself involved in a mission that is proving difficult to sustain at both the political and operational levels. Politically, the current Afghan mission runs the risk of re-igniting the separatist movement in Quebec, particularly as the francophone regiment that has taken centre stage in Kandahar becomes the focus of the Taliban attacks, but more generally because Quebeckers have (from the start) viewed the deployment with considerably more scepticism than other Canadians. The mission is thus a threat to Canada's internal sovereignty. Internationally, the mission is an odd fit for Canada, as it contrasts sharply with the country's reputation for serving in other more specialized capacities, namely as a mediator/supervisor of post-conflict situations. Canada thus puts at risk its reputation to participate in international politics in precise and reserved ways each time it must decline a role to which it is more suited as a result of its commitment to Afghanistan. The 26,000-strong UN peacekeeping force being sent to stem the genocide in Darfur that was announced in August of 2007 stands out as an immediate example, considering that both France and Denmark committed to contributing to the mainly African force.

At the operational level, evidence that the mission in Kandahar might not be one that will be easily handled by a Canadian Forces beleaguered by decades of financial cutbacks that have only very recently been reversed is seen most clearly in the fact of the 98 Canadian soldiers who have been killed in Afghanistan. Over 90 per cent of these battle deaths have come in the last three years (2005–2008). Not surprisingly, all these deaths have come since the bulk of Canada's operations in Afghanistan moved from what were predominantly peacekeeping duties in Kabul to what are now predominantly counterinsurgency duties in Kandahar being fought on behalf of the American-led Operation Enduring Freedom. The growing instability in Kandahar province is by no means the fault of the CF, but it highlights some of the tensions created when Canada steps outside its bounded array of specialized roles to play a part in international politics that may prove to be tragically beyond its capabilities.

The authors of the *Independent Panel Report on Canada's Future Role in Afghanistan* (known popularly as the Manley Report) were clearly aware of this reality. The report predicted chaos in Kandahar and dark days ahead for NATO should Canada choose to end its combat operations in the region. Accordingly, the panel recommended that Canada prolong its combat role beyond the slated 2009 end point. However, this extension of the mission was contingent primarily on Canada receiving a significant helping hand with the effort: 1000 extra International Security Assistance Force (ISAF) troops.[27] Considering that the total number of Canadian troops in Kandahar is approximately 2500, this would suggest that Canada is a significant percentage shy of being able to play the part of a principal military power in the international system, and has gotten itself in well beyond its depth in the south of Afghanistan. As an organization, NATO will have to help bail Canada out in Kandahar, or risk having to bail itself out of a future credibility crisis. The recently announced, massive influx of U.S. troops (and the smaller, but significant, French contribution) will lift much weight from Canadian shoulders. But it will not lift away questions about whether Kandahar is the right kind of mission for Canada.

Conclusion

It should be clear from the above that the illusion of Canada's independence must be maintained, and that specializing in an array of roles
unsuited to the United States is an effective way of carrying off the
sleight-of-hand trick that is behind much of what Canada has accomplished in the world.

Suggesting that decision-makers go mechanically about selecting
and performing such roles on the basis of Canada's internal unity
needs, the needs of the United States, and these of the broader international system, however, implies that there is no artistry behind the
maintenance of the illusion. This, of course, is far from the case; and as
James Eayrs has maintained, government and foreign policy in Canada
is very much 'the art of the possible.'

That being said, grasping the basic mechanics of the sleight-of-hand
trick (knowing what is possible) is as important to being able to ele-
gantly (and consistently) execute the trick as having the magician's
artistic touch. Understanding from a theoretical perspective these basic
mechanics – the internal, continental (hierarchical), and international
(anarchical) structural pressures that bear down on Canada as it engages abroad – might help foreign policy-makers grasp intellectually
what they have most often appeared to understand intuitively about
how to maintain the illusion of Canada's foreign policy independence.

NOTES

1 G. John Ikenberry, 'Liberalism and Empire: Logics of Order in the American
   Unipolar Age,' *Review of International Studies* 30 (2004): 620–4.
2 Most prominently this can be seen in the form of article 23, which outlines
   the criteria to be considered for nomination as a non-permanent member
   of the Security Council; and in article 44, which guarantees that any state
   asked to participate in the application of force for the re-establishment of
   order be involved in the decisions of the Security Council leading to that
   application. Since Canada was a trading state with a strong economy, the
   Canadian delegates also placed a strong emphasis on the development of
   the Economic and Social Council, in which they foresaw significant involvement for Canada.
3 F.H. Soward and Edgar McInnis, 'Forming the United Nations, 1945,' in

Canadian Foreign Policy: Selected Cases, ed. Don Munton and John Kirton (Scarborough, ON: Prentice-Hall, 1992), 13.

4 Peyton Lyon, 'Quiet Diplomacy Revisited,' in *An Independent Foreign Policy for Canada?* ed. Stephen Clarkson (Toronto: McClelland & Stewart, 1968), 29–43.

5 Charles Hanley, 'The Ethics of Independence,' in *An Independent Foreign Policy for Canada?* 17–29.

6 Thomas Hobbes, *Leviathan* (New York: Penguin, 1981), 120; Immanuel Kant, 'Perpetual Peace: A Philosophical Sketch,' in *Kant's Political Writings*, ed. Hans Reiss, trans. H.B. Nisbet (Cambridge: Cambridge University Press, 1970), 103; Jean-Jacques Rousseau, *Project of Perpetual Peace: Rousseau's Essay*, trans. Edith M. Nuttall, intro. G. Lowes Dickinson (London: Richard Cobden-Sanderson, 1927), 7.

7 See, most importantly, Kenneth Waltz, *Man, The State, and War: A Theoretical Analysis* (New York: Columbia University Press, 1954).

8 Brian C. Schmidt, *The Political Discourse of Anarchy: A Disciplinary History of International Relations* (Albany, NY: SUNY Press, 1998).

9 See, for example, the seminal work of Kenneth Waltz, *Theory of International Politics* (Don Mills, ON: Addison-Wesley, 1979).

10 See, for example, David A. Lake, 'Escape from the State of Nature: Authority and Hierarchy in World Politics,' *International Security* 32, no. 1 (Summer 2007): 47–79; Katja Weber, *Hierarchy amidst Anarchy: Transaction Costs and Institutional Choice* (Albany, NY: SUNY Press, 2000); and Alexander Wendt and Daniel Friedheim, 'Hierarchy under Anarchy: Informal Empire and the East German State,' *International Organization* 49, no. 4 (Autumn 1995): 689–721.

11 Jack Donnelly, 'Sovereign Inequalities and Hierarchy in Anarchy: American Power and International Society,' *European Journal of International Relations* 12, no. 2 (2006): 141.

12 John Holmes, *The Better Part of Valour: Essays on Canadian Diplomacy* (Toronto: McClelland & Stewart, 1970), 6.

13 J. Blair Seaborn, 'Mission to Hanoi: The Canadian Channel, May 1964–November 1965,' in *Canadian Peacekeepers in Indochina, 1954–1973*, ed. Arthur E. Blanchette (Ottawa: Golden Dog, 2002), 92.

14 Timothy Naftali and Philip Zelikow, eds, *The Presidential Recordings, John F. Kennedy: The Great Crises*, vol. 2 (New York: Norton, 2001), 405.

15 Stanley Hoffman, *Gulliver's Troubles* (New York: McGraw-Hill, 1968), 371.

16 Col. Alain Tremblay, 'The Canadian Experience in Afghanistan,' in *The New World of Robust International Peacekeeping Operations: What Roles for NATO*

and Canada? ed. Brian S. MacDonald and David S. McDonough (Toronto: Royal Canadian Military Institute, 2005), 49.

17 Cited in Donald Barry, 'Chretien, Bush, and the War in Iraq,' *American Review of Canadian Studies* 35, no.2 (Summer 2005): 229.

18 Lawrence Martin, *Iron Man: The Defiant Reign of Jean Chrétien*, vol. 2 (Toronto: Viking, 2003), 420.

19 T. Michael Moseley, Lt. Gen. USAF, Commander, *Operation Iraqi Freedom – By the Numbers* (30 April 2003), 3, 16. Available at http://www.globalsecurity.org/military/library/report/2003/u scentaf_oif_report_30apr2003.pdf.

20 Paul Samyn, 'Planners in Mideast a Prelude to War?' *Winnipeg Free Press*, 12 February 2003, A12.

21 Sheldon Alberts, 'Saddam Should Have Weeks, Not Months,' *National Post*, 25 February 2003, A11.

22 The most senior of those officers was Brigadier General Walt Natynczuk. According to Janice Stein and Eugene Lang, Natynczuk 'was directly involved in planning the invasion of Iraq from the American headquarters in Kuwait.' He ended up moving with the mobile American headquarters unit into Iraq once the war had begun. This raises the issue of whether Canada was actually a belligerent in the war. See Stein and Lang, *The Unexpected War: Canada in Kandahar* (Toronto: Viking, 2007), 88.

23 'Chretien Government Rejected Military's Advice on Afghan Deployment: Ex-Army Chief,' *CBC News*, 18 October 2006. Available at http://www.cbc.ca/canada/story/2006/10/18/afghan-military-advice.html.

24 Barry, 'Chretien, Bush, and the War in Iraq,' 224.

25 David S. McDonough, 'The Paradox of Afghanistan: Stability Operations and the Renewal of Canada's International Security Policy?' *International Journal* 62 (Summer 2007): 626.

26 Stein and Lang, *The Unexpected War*, 181–2.

27 Independent Panel on Canada's Future Role in Afghanistan (January 2008): 38; accessed 6 February 2008. Available at http://www.independent-panel-independant.ca/pdf/Afghan_Report_web_e.pdf.

PART TWO

Dealing with Uncle

In this section Brian Bow and Stephanie Golob consider the evolution of Canada's strategic approach to managing relations with the United States. Bow returns to one of the key questions of the original *IFPC?* debate: whether or not American retaliation, or the anticipation of retaliation, sets strict limits on Canada's independence. This, he argues, is more complicated than is commonly understood. The United States has been prepared to employ direct, 'tit-for-tat' linkages to force other countries to change their policies, but the historical record suggests that it has not been prepared to do so with Canada. That does not mean, however, that Canada can push ahead with whatever policy it likes, without taking the American reaction into account. Provocative Canadian policies can trigger more indirect and diffuse forms of linkage ('grudges'). Canada is therefore in a position to pursue policies that are at odds with those of the United States, but it must recognize there will likely be a price to be paid in other aspects of the bilateral relationship.

In her chapter, Golob weighs the costs and benefits of Canada's 'quiet diplomacy' approach to continental integration after 9/11. She focuses on the controversial Security and Prosperity Partnership with the United States and Mexico. Taking the negotiations 'underground' has made it possible to insulate them against domestic political pressures today – which may be a high priority for governments with more pressing problems abroad (United States) or a shaky mandate at home (Canada, Mexico) – but it is likely to undercut the process in the long run. The resort to 'quiet diplomacy' has provoked concerns about a secret agenda, and stirred up scepticism and opposition in the general public. And it represents a missed opportunity to shape the future progress of North America towards a more democratically transparent and developmentally equal society of states that is more in tune with Canada's traditional values.

On the one hand, Bow's analysis seems to make room for Golob's policy prescriptions: Washington might hold a grudge if Ottawa brings the back-room dealings of the SPP out into the open, but this may in the end be a meaningful way of spending 'diplomatic capital.' On the other hand, his analysis might also suggest that the 'two-speed,' 'double-bilateral' approach to continental integration that favors Canada over México in negotiations within the American orbit might be jeopardized if Golob's prescriptions were followed.

3 Rethinking 'Retaliation' in Canada–U.S. Relations

BRIAN BOW

Given the overall asymmetry of the Canada–United States relationship, and the sheer scope of Canada's strategic and economic dependency on the United States, how much room is there for Canada to pursue policies that are at odds with those of its southern neighbour? When and where is it deterred or forced back by the threat of American retaliation? These are crucial questions for both the study and the practice of Canada's relations with the United States, and its foreign policy more generally. Much has been said and written on the question of retaliation, but very little of it is satisfying. Government officials from both sides of the border assure us that ours is a 'special relationship,' where problems are resolved without recourse to primitive forms of coercive diplomacy. Many of their critics, on the other hand, are certain that the United States twists Canada's arms all the time, or at least that the threat of retaliation terrifies Canadian policy-makers into obedience. The truth, most of us suspect, is probably somewhere in between. But where, exactly? And what does that tell us about where and how Canada can pursue a genuinely 'independent' foreign policy?

Media coverage and popular-history accounts of particular disputes often speculate about actual past or potential future acts of cross-issue retaliation. But most of the 'bigger-picture' accounts of the bilateral relationship over time tend to agree that retaliation has never – or virtually never – been a factor in Canada–U.S. relations. Indeed, all seem to agree that the absence of retaliation is the key to the supposed 'special relationship.'

Those who think that Canada's foreign policy is best served by close collaboration with the United States – the original proponents of 'quiet diplomacy' and their descendents – have argued that there is no retaliation in order to mitigate the fear that closer ties only make Canada more vulnerable to American political pressure. (Yet they also some-times hint that retaliation might be possible in order to highlight the potential costs of breaking with the United States.) Those who think that Canada should distance itself from the United States – the 'inde-pendentists' of the 1960s and their descendents – have also argued that there is no retaliation, in order to make the argument that Canada can 'get away with' charting its own course. (Yet they have also hinted that retaliation might be possible in order to paint a picture of American bullying and capriciousness.)

There are three main kinds of arguments made about why the United States might be unwilling or unable to pursue retaliatory linkages against Canada. Some have argued that the institutional structure of foreign policy decision-making in the United States severely undercuts its capacity to make linkages vis-à-vis not only Canada, but all coun-tries. A number of observers have argued that the separation of powers (and other kinds of fragmentation of authority) in the American system have paralysed U.S. foreign policy, often in ways that have increased Canada's autonomy, but sometimes in ways that have severely dam-aged Canadian interests.[1] Michael Mastanduno, however, has made the case that the American system is not so self-confining, as the executive branch has often found ways to work through – or around – the system, and still get things done.[2]

Others have argued that the exceptional breadth and depth of inter-dependence between Canada and the United States make it virtually impossible for the United States to retaliate against Canada without injuring itself in the process. Robert Keohane and Joseph Nye, for example, argued that the interpenetration of the two societies had cre-ated a network of transnational and transgovernmental coalitions with a stake in the larger relationship, and that these groups would consis-tently intervene to 'block' retaliatory linkages.[3]

Still others have argued that the United States might be able to pur-sue retaliation against Canada, but it would not be willing to do so, because coercive linkages are ruled out as part of a larger framework of bargaining norms – what we might call a distinctive 'diplomatic cul-ture' joining the two countries. The norm against retaliatory linkages was so deeply embedded in the day-to-day management of the bilat-eral relationship, in fact, that former Canadian ambassador Allan Got-lieb once identified it as one of the 'ten commandments' governing Canada–United States relations.[4]

Each of these three arguments is an important part of the story. The diplomatic culture was most important during the early Cold War decades, but it still has some weight today. Since the 1970s, the fragmentation of American institutions and the implications of interdependence have done most of the work in explaining the absence of retaliation. But their effects are more complex than is usually recognized; each of them works to create both pressures for retaliation and obstacles to it.

The problem with most of what has been written on retaliation is not that it is wrong, but rather that it tends to miss the point, because it thinks in simple yes-or-no terms: either retaliation happens or it doesn't. In fact, retaliation itself is much more complicated, and so are its implications for Canadian foreign policy autonomy. To get started on thinking about these questions in a more subtle and complex way, we have to go back in time to the classic debates of the 1960s.

One of the most sophisticated treatments of the problem of retaliation that we have is the roundtable discussion in the original *An Independent Foreign Policy for Canada?*[5] Its four participants – A.F.W. Plumptre, A.E. Safarian, Pauline Jewett, and Abraham Rotstein – generally agreed that the usual 'tit-for-tat' way of thinking about retaliation was not very useful for describing the application (and anticipation) of diplomatic pressure in the Canada–U.S. relationship. But they also agreed that there was a sense in which Canadian policies sometimes provoked a 'reaction' in the United States, and that this reaction – and the anticipation of it – was an important part of the way that political power is exercised within the Canada–U.S. relationship.

Here, I want to develop two main ideas: first, Plumptre and the other members of the roundtable hit on the most important element in thinking about 'retaliation' in the Canada–U.S. context – both in the 1960s and today – by shifting the focus from direct retaliation to more indirect and diffuse reactions to Canadian policies. And second, both the rules of the game and the shape of the playing field have gone through several kinds of changes over the last forty years. The net result of these cross-cutting developments has not been either a clear-cut intensification or a relaxation of diplomatic constraints on Canada, but rather the emergence of an increasingly complex and unpredictable political landscape, in which the shadow of American pressure flickers and bends from one issue to another, and from one moment to the next.

How Retaliation Works, or Doesn't

It is worth pausing to clarify what 'retaliation' is supposed to refer to, and how it relates to other kinds of diplomacy. Retaliation is one of several kinds of issue-linkage – that is, one kind of signal that one's position on a given issue is contingent on the resolution of another, unrelated issue. First and most obviously, retaliation refers to coercive linkages, rather than cooperative ones. Second, retaliation refers to damaging policy shifts that are made *after* the target country has gone ahead with an unwelcome policy, rather than in anticipation of such a policy. It is, in other words, usually understood in terms of revenge, rather than coercion. And third, retaliation usually refers to negative linkages that are made in a straightforward, direct way, as opposed to more indirect and diffuse negative reactions. The aggrieved party 'hits back' in a way that is carefully designed to make clear to the target that this is a response to a specific, previous provocation, but also to send a clear signal about the retaliating state's broader expectations about how the relationship is supposed to work.

This last distinction is especially important here. Building on the ideas developed in the *IFPC?* roundtable (especially by Plumptre and Safarian), I want to distinguish here between clear-cut 'retaliation' and what I will call 'grudge' linkages. In true retaliation, the negative linkage is immediate, direct, and carefully chosen to make the right kind of impression. The purpose of the retaliatory linkage is to inflict harm on the target in a way that makes it as clear as possible that the move was made in response to the target's unacceptable policy, and to send the signal that future provocations will draw more of the same. To that end, it generally involves an active change of policy whose effects on the target are readily observed and unmistakably negative. Grudges, by contrast, normally take the form of a malign passivity, and the relevant linkages between issues are often indirect and diffuse. Retaliation, as defined here, has historically been far less salient to the process and outcomes of bilateral bargaining in the Canada–U.S. relationship than in other international relationships. But, at least partly because that is so, grudges have been much more important.

Retaliation's Dark Shadow

As mentioned above, the editorial pages, airwaves, and cyberspace are packed with speculation about American arm-twisting – past, present, and future. In fact, there probably hasn't been a single high-level bilateral dispute over the last sixty years that did not provoke at least some speculation about retaliation. It isn't hard to figure out why. The image of an angry American colossus taking a backhanded swipe at its northern neighbour injects drama and intrigue into what might otherwise be mundane, technically complex negotiations over food safety regulations, lumber subsidies, or border security procedures. We see this same kind of hype in other parts of the world as well. But apprehension about American retaliation is more pervasive and more profound in Canada, because it taps directly into one of the country's defining existential anxieties: given the extent and the asymmetry of the interdependence between Canada and the United States, if the United States is willing and able to 'strike back' at Canada for pursuing policies that it doesn't like, then Canada's policy autonomy (both foreign and domestic) is not limited just by broad structural forces like the balance of power or globalization, but also more immediately and concretely by the interests and purposes of the United States.

So the question of retaliation is directly related to the broader question of Canada's sovereign independence. Canadians are therefore naturally preoccupied with the question of retaliation, acutely sensitive to even the vaguest hints that it is in the works, and inclined to associate it with all kinds of threatening intentions and circumstances.

With this much smoke, we might conclude that there must be some fire as well. It is hard to say for certain, but it is striking how little solid evidence there is of *any* clear-cut retaliation over the last sixty years. It turns out, in fact, that much of the popular conventional wisdom about retaliation is debatable at best.

Much of the media speculation has been driven by public statements by U.S. officials. American foreign policy bureaucrats and military officers make unauthorized statements to the press all the time, sometimes to raise the stakes for a foreign government, but more often to put pressure on their own. It is quite likely that some of these statements have been permitted or encouraged by the political leadership in order to send signals about the seriousness with which many in Washington oppose a proposed Canadian policy, and to highlight the 'availability' of various retaliation options. But even where we could trace these threatening comments back to the White House, it is not clear that threats of retaliation are in play as a meaningful diplomatic move.[6] To be tactically effective, a threat to retaliate would have to be explicit and direct enough that it left no doubt about the threatener's willingness and ability to follow through on the commitment if certain expectations were not satisfied. An anonymous quote in the newspaper may trigger anxiety among Canadian policy-makers, but it will also leave them wondering about whether the source really reflects the true American position, and therefore whether or not to take the threat itself seriously.

Some academic studies have made the case that the United States explicitly threatened retaliation or actually pursued it in particular bilateral disputes. Knowlton Nash, for example, wrote that the Kennedy administration threatened to restrict imports of Canadian oil as part of its effort to pressure Diefenbaker's government into deploying nuclear weapons on Canadian soil.[7] Edgar Dosman argued that the Nixon administration cut Canada's share of the U.S. oil import quota in 1970 to punish the Trudeau government for pushing ahead with its claim to jurisdiction over the Northwest Passage.[8] Stephen Clarkson maintained that the Reagan administration threatened to have Canada kicked out of upcoming G8 meetings in order to force Trudeau to dismantle the National Energy Program.[9] In all these cases, the authors based their accounts on government documents or interviews with well-placed Canadian politicians or officials, and there is no reason to doubt that at least some high-ranking Canadian officials believed that retaliatory linkages were being seriously considered in Washington.

Yet there are at least two kinds of reasons to be cautious about thinking that retaliation – as we have defined it above – was really in play in all these episodes.[10] First, the archival record for the older disputes does not support it. U.S. records for the nuclear weapons dispute, for example, indicate that the Kennedy administration was at wit's end about what to do with Diefenbaker, but there is not the slightest trace of evidence that anyone in Washington seriously considered retaliatory linkages. Without concrete evidence that any given linkage scenario was actually studied by at least some component of the U.S. government, it is probably better to treat free-floating hints at retaliatory linkages – even those made by cabinet-level officials – as eruptions of raw frustration, rather than meaningful bargaining moves.

Second, this hunch is often confirmed by objective assessment of the conjectured linkage scenarios, which frequently leads to the conclusion that, if American policy-makers had seriously considered these options, they would almost certainly have rejected them out of hand. The Nixon administration's decision on the oil import quota, for example, doesn't make much sense as an attempt at retaliation. Eliminating the 'overland' exemption from the quota, or even radically cutting back Canada's quota share, would have seriously damaged the Canadian oil industry. But the Nixon administration made its decision on the quota *before* it was clear what Canada's Arctic waters legislation would look like, and it ultimately made only minor changes to Canada's quota share.[11] In fact, the quota reduction was so small, relative to what U.S. domestic producers and the Venezuelan government had demanded, that it looks more like a favour to Canada than a punishment.

The Absence of Retaliation – Explanations and Implications

Most 'insider' accounts categorically reject the idea that direct retaliation has played an important part in Canada–U.S. relations. Plumptre, a well-placed former senior civil servant and negotiator, reflected that he 'could only remember two or three occasions, in regard to rather specific issues, on which either the word or the concept of "retaliation" against Canada entered into consideration.'[12]

If retaliation seems not to have played an important role in Canada–U.S. relations, why might that be? One possibility is that there actually *has* been quite a bit of retaliation, but it has been covered up very thoroughly. It is not particularly surprising that, in spite of decades of thorough research on postwar Canada–U.S. relations, no one has found any 'smoking-gun' evidence of retaliation. But it *is* surprising that no one has yet turned up any compelling *circumstantial* evidence of retaliation being pursued, of retaliatory threats being made, or even of threats of retaliation being seriously considered in Washington. Given the number and variety of other kinds of skeletons found in the archival closet – including several instances of profoundly undiplomatic diplomacy – it is hard to believe that officials on both sides could have done that good a job of cleaning up after themselves.

Another possible explanation is that Canada has never done anything sufficiently provocative to bring about American retaliation. Each of the four contributors to the *IFPC?* roundtable saw this as an important part of the story, and disagreed mainly over whether this was because Canadian interests generally coincided with American ones (Safarian), or because Canadian policy-makers shied away from pursuing divergent interests and purposes (Jewett, Rotstein). There have undoubtedly been times, as Pauline Jewett remembered, when anxiety about U.S. retaliation had a 'mesmerizing effect' on Canadian policy-makers, and they backed down when they might have pushed farther.[13] Her account of the magazine-tax confrontation in the mid-1960s seems a good example.[14]

But there were also a number of episodes in the 1950s and 1960s where Canada severely tested U.S. self-restraint. In the disputes over the expansion of UN membership and nuclear weapons, Canada broke with the United States on important diplomatic and strategic questions. In the early phases of the auto-production dispute and in the Mercantile Bank affair, Canada put the bite on powerful American corporations and challenged the core premises of U.S. foreign economic policies.[15] It wasn't easy for American policy-makers to be forbearing with Canada in these episodes because the stakes were high within the bilateral context, but also because Canadian policies set dangerous precedents that might be (and sometimes were) followed by others. Since the late 1960s, Canada has from time to time pursued foreign and domestic policies at odds with those of the United States, including ongoing circumvention of the U.S. blockade of Cuba, the National Energy Program and Trudeau's 'peace initiative,' the public break over relations with South Africa, aggressive support for the landmine ban treaty and the International Criminal Court, and the more recent decisions to opt out of the war in Iraq and the ballistic missile defense program (BMD).

The most popular explanation for American restraint is economic interdependence. The two countries are so extensively inter-penetrated that just about anything the United States might do to hurt Canada would 'bounce back' and hurt the United States as well. The crucial question though is not whether a linkage would set up high costs for the United States in absolute terms, but rather whether those costs would outweigh the costs of doing nothing – that is, accepting a provocative Canadian policy, and the diplomatic precedent that would go with it. In general, then, we ought to expect the United States to be cautious about pursuing retaliation against Canada, but still inclined to do so when the stakes are very high.

The breadth and complexity of the Canada–U.S. relationship means there are always literally hundreds of possible linkage scenarios 'available' to American negotiators at any given time. But only a small number of these involve policies over which the executive branch is actually able to exercise the kind of direct, timely control that would be necessary to make an effective retaliatory linkage. The most obvious and distinctive limit on the United States' capacity to make linkages between issues is the constitutional separation of powers, which sometimes gets in the way by setting up formal limits on executive decision-making, but more often does so by making secret negotiations public and enabling bureaucratic and societal interests that oppose linkages. The United States is a formidable international power, but it is a 'weak' state in terms of the institutional structure of foreign policy-making, and is in that sense not well equipped to play the retaliation game.[16]

As Keohane and Nye argued, the extensive interdependence between the two societies fostered the growth of political coalitions with a stake in maintaining both the overall health of the bilateral relationship and their own particular interests. These groups monitor bilateral relations closely, and intervene to prevent their interests from being traded off in potential issue linkages. In some cases, such as the long-running speculation about an attack on the Auto Pact in various disputes during the 1970s, mobilized domestic actors in the United States actively lobbied to derail potential retaliatory linkages. More often, it is the anticipation of this kind of domestic opposition that steers the White House away from particular linkage options.[17]

In addition to these political and strategic reasons, the United States is generally reluctant to pursue retaliation, and especially so with Canada, for normative reasons. Because this kind of coercive diplomacy is inherently provocative, all states are cautious about engaging in it, particularly with close allies and partners. This is especially true for the United States, because blackmail and retaliation conflict with the country's sense of exceptionalism.[18] Of course, the United States doesn't always live up to its high ideals, but they are there nonetheless, and they do set limits on what American diplomats can say and do. This normatively grounded sense of self-restraint is even more pronounced when it comes to disputes with Canada, because the close, almost familial relationship between the two countries sets it up as a crucial test case for America's foreign policy virtues. Canada and the United States have gradually developed their own distinctive 'diplomatic culture,' in which – as Kal Holsti explained it – 'conflicts of interest ... are essentially "problems" to be solved rather than ... confrontations to be won at all costs,' and there is a deeply rooted, shared norm against coercive issue-linkage.[19]

Of course, none of these bases for U.S. restraint are absolute, and there can be no doubt that if Canada were to push hard enough, the United States would eventually feel compelled to retaliate.[20] Still, the number and weight of barriers against direct retaliation outlined above would seem to open up quite a bit of space for Canada to 'get away with' policies at odds with those of the United States. But, as the contributors to the *IFPC?* roundtable recognized, and as Canadian negotiators have always known, there are other ways in which provocative Canadian policies can trigger a negative response from the United States, and these less-direct forms of diplomatic counter-pressure are the most important mechanism of external constraint on Canada's foreign policy independence.

Grudges and Goodwill

Not all American 'reactions' are best understood as retaliation. Some changes to U.S. policies are better understood as essentially automatic adjustments to choices made, or not made, in Ottawa. One way to think about this is through the chess-match metaphor introduced by Plumptre and refined by Safarian: 'Each move takes into account all previous moves made by *both* players, and their possible future moves,' and every move is driven by the desire to improve future options, not to take revenge for previous upsets.[21] American officials' frustration at the Martin government's decision not to formally participate in the BMD initiative, for example, probably has coloured their handling of bilateral defence cooperation. But the decision to shift some aerospace defence decision-making from NORAD to NorthCom, and to change information-sharing protocols within NORAD, was driven primarily by the need to adapt to Canada's non-involvement in this aspect of continental defence.[22] These post-BMD changes are likely to undercut the benefits Canada derives from its participation in NORAD, and probably NORAD itself, but it is misleading to think of them as 'retaliation.'

More interesting and more consequential here are 'grudge' linkages. As noted above, grudge linkages usually take the form of malevolent inaction, rather than active coercion. The Canada–U.S. relationship requires perpetual care from bureaucratic managers and occasional attention from the political leadership, in order to prevent mobilized bureaucratic and societal interests from attacking and destabilizing the vast and complex latticework of bilateral agreements and informal trade-offs. The absence of this kind of care and attention can hurt the interests of both countries, but it usually hurts Canada much more, and so the United States is in a position to signal its unhappiness with Canada, and even inflict harm on it, just by neglecting it. As Plumptre explained:

There can hardly be a day, and never a week, in Washington when some US official is not taking action to ensure that some Canadian interests under this treaty, or that agreement, or some non-recorded but gentlemanly understanding, are being protected. In Washington, as indeed in Ottawa and in every capital, the erosive rats are always nibbling away. However, there are always borderline cases, matters for judgment. And in those cases the judgment may be affected by whether the wind is, at the moment, blowing in favour of Canada or in the opposite direction.[23]

Thus – to add just one more metaphor – the management of Canada's relationship with the United States depends in part on the getting and spending of what could be called 'diplomatic capital.' When Canada's stock of goodwill in Washington is abundant, it can expect the political leadership there to be more inclined to put its own political capital at risk in order to support policy outcomes that help Canada, and to derail those hurt it. When Canada pursues policies that are at odds with core U.S. priorities – particularly when it does so in a confrontational way – its stock of accumulated diplomatic capital is 'burned up,'[24] and the political leadership will be less inclined to pay costs or take risks to keep the relationship running smoothly. Of course, no U.S. administration is going to risk domestic political disaster just to do Canada a favour (or to do it harm), but most can be expected to lean in Canada's favour (or against it) at the margin.

The accounting for this kind of diplomatic capital is definitely not an exact science. Whether the wind inside the Washington beltway is blowing in favour of Canada or against it does not depend on objective and detailed assessments of the vast inventory of Canadian policies, but rather on impressionistic judgments about whether or not Canada has been – and therefore is likely in the future to be – a helpful, reliable, and trustworthy partner.[25] And, while the amount of weight that the administration is prepared to put behind an issue based on its effects on Canada will depend in part on the weight of current goodwill or grudges, it will also depend on other conditions over which Canada has no control, such as the president's approval rating, the balance of votes in Congress, the electoral calendar, and the number and importance of other international issues crowding the White House agenda.

As with more direct forms of retaliation, the identification and confirmation of grudge effects is always ultimately based on counterfactuals that cannot be readily tested empirically. But grudge linkages are even harder to find than instances of 'tit for tat' retaliation, because – by definition – the cause-and-effect connection between the original Canadian provocation and the American reaction is indirect and diffuse, and the expected effects on U.S. policy are marginal. There have nevertheless been a number of episodes in Canada–U.S. relations in which we can see what look to be fairly clear-cut grudge effects.

One example, which highlights both the absence of direct retaliation and the salience of grudge linkages, is the previously mentioned confrontation over nuclear weapons.[26] The Kennedy administration was incensed by Diefenbaker's waffling on the issue and by his provocative public claim that the December 1962 Nassau agreements invited a fundamental reconsideration of NATO nuclear weapons policy. Kennedy and his advisers had a number of viable retaliatory options within reach (e.g., capital export restrictions, import restrictions on lumber or oil), but chose not pursue any of them, mostly – the circumstantial evidence suggests – because of the weight of the established diplomatic culture, and the norm against coercive linkage in particular.

Grudge linkages, on the other hand, *did* come into play, and had important effects on the process and outcomes of several concurrent disputes. Lower-level officials continued to manage the day-to-day business of the bilateral relationship as best they could, but the rapidly accelerating escalation of personal tensions between Diefenbaker and Kennedy had a chilling effect on talks to resolve ongoing negotiations on co-management of balance-of-payments problems, the Seafarer's International Union strike, and trade restrictions on oil, lumber, wheat, and lead and zinc.[27] Kennedy essentially '[gave] up on' Diefenbaker, and refused to pay much attention to his requests for renewed talks on these issues.[28] When Canadian officials asked their American counterparts for assistance with the Seafarer's Union, for example, they received half-hearted expressions of support. But the White House was not in the mood to go to bat for Canada against the powerful and well-connected union, and it made absolutely no effort to intervene on Canada's behalf.[29]

Grudge linkages are probably important in every international relationship, but they seem to be especially important in the Canada–U.S. context, for at least two reasons. First, because the relationship with Canada is so important and so complex, yet receives so little sustained and critical attention in Washington, it is that much more likely to be governed by broad impressions of the way the overall relationship is going. Second, as Safarian noted, the virtual foreclosure of 'hard' retaliation options pushes U.S. foreign policy-makers – by default – towards grudges.

Linkage Politics, Then and Now

As mentioned in the introduction to this volume, a number of things have changed since the *IFPC?* roundtable was published in 1968, and these developments have had important effects on the way that bilateral conflicts are managed. First, the shrinking of Canada's alliance contributions during the Cold War, and then the end of the Cold War itself, took away one of the primary bases for American self-restraint vis-à-vis Canada.[30]

Second, the deepening of economic interdependence between the two countries fostered the proliferation of interest groups in the United States with a stake in the health of the bilateral relationship, and with an interest in blocking particular linkages, just as Keohane and Nye had predicted. At the same time, however, increased interdependence – in the context of the United States' becoming more deeply embedded in the world economy, and therefore more vulnerable to its pressures – also catalysed the emergence of a variety of groups with an interest in 'getting tough with Canada,' and a greater responsiveness to these pressures from Congress and relevant bureaucratic agencies.

Third, the fragmentation of foreign policy decision-making in the United States in the 1970s effectively displaced the transgovernmental network that had carried and enacted the postwar diplomatic culture, and the shared norm against coercive linkage. The result was that engagement with the United States became much more complicated and unpredictable, with many more hands on the steering wheel, and far fewer of them with any real knowledge of or interest in the smooth running of the larger bilateral relationship.

And finally, the bilateral relationship became enmeshed in a web of formal institutional structures – including, but not limited to, the CUSFTA and NAFTA. There were some prominent integrative regimes in place as early as the 1960s, such as the Defence Production Sharing Agreement and the Auto Pact, but these were exceptions to the broader tendency to bilateral informalism.[31] One consequence of this shift from informal problem-solving to formal adjudication was that it contributed to the displacement of the transgovernmental network that had managed the relationship according to the old postwar diplomatic culture. More important, it set powerful limits on the range of policy instruments that each country could pursue (i.e., Canadian moves that might provoke retaliation *and* American moves through which retaliation might be pursued). The free trade agreements, in particular, set limits on the kinds of policy changes that were considered acceptable, and provided mechanisms for each country to pressure the other to follow the rules. These new institutional layers – reinforced and extended at the global level by the consolidation of the World Trade Organization – represent not only a set of constraints on state autonomy in general, but also an additional barrier to certain kinds of issue-linkages.

Beginning in the 1970s, then, interest group pressures to 'do something' about troublesome Canadian policies, and calls for retaliatory linkages, became much more common in Washington and had much more traction on executive decisions. Congress even began to experiment with its own capacity to make retaliatory linkages, as in the 1978–80 border broadcasting dispute, when members tried to force Canada to withdraw new tax laws that hurt U.S.-based television broadcasters, by taking away the Canadian exemption from U.S. taxes on professional conventions held abroad.[32] We saw this kind of thing again during the 1987 free trade negotiations, when the Senate Finance Committee tried to hold the president's 'fast-track' authority as a hostage in the softwood lumber dispute, and there have been many smaller-scale echoes of it by such notorious congressional issue-linkers as Montana's Senator Max Baucus.

However, this new inclination to 'get tough' with Canada did not lead to a sudden outbreak of direct retaliation, because the same fragmentation of power that undercut the transgovernmental network also created new obstacles to the making of issue linkages. Institutional changes in the United States made it easier for aggrieved domestic interests to push their government for retaliatory linkages, but they also made it easier for groups that might be hurt by those linkages to anticipate and oppose them.

It is important to recognize that the new mechanics of issue-linkage within the more fragmented American political system apply not only to direct retaliation, but also to grudge linkages. In that sense, these long-term historical developments have reinforced the general tendency for the foreclosure of 'hard' linkage options to push U.S. policymakers towards 'soft' linkages. But they have also complicated the way that grudge linkages work.

These continuities and changes are illustrated in recent diplomatic tensions over Iraq and BMD. Canadian participation/support was certainly not indispensable to the United States in either case, but the two back-to-back refusals – and the provocative way in which they were delivered – stirred up a great deal of frustration in Washington, and seem to have provoked a broader reappraisal of Canada's value and reliability as an ally and supporter.[33] Eruptions of this frustration in the press fuelled speculation about retaliatory linkages, particularly with respect to tightened border security protocols. The issue of border security reform was well within the White House's reach after 9/11, and the executive branch had a fair amount of latitude in setting the terms of U.S. policy on this issue, but this was not – and still is not – an especially promising basis for retaliation. There is no question that severely tightened border security measures would hit the Canadian economy hard. But they would also have readily identifiable, substantial, and concentrated effects on politically powerful interests in the United States, particularly multinational companies whose transnationalized production networks might be massively disrupted.[34]

There were, however, a variety of ways in which the political executive could make grudge linkages, by withholding attention and support in other concurrent disputes, and there is a fair amount of circumstantial evidence suggesting that it did so through 2004 and 2005. There were, during this period, a number of U.S. policy changes pending or recently undertaken that clearly hurt Canadian interests, and stirred up intense political pressure on Ottawa to deflect or overturn them. The most prominent of these were the long-running protectionist campaigns against Canadian lumber and beef, and North Dakota's Devil's Lake water diversion project. Each of these three issues, like many diplomatic frictions over the last thirty years, involved an indirect challenge to long-standing bilateral understandings or agreements, which had been initiated and driven forward by local interests in the United States, and enabled by congressional parochialism and opportunism. They were, in other words, textbook examples of Plumtre's 'erosive rats ... nibbling away' at the bilateral order.

George W. Bush's White House did not do anything to make these problems worse for Canada, but neither did it do anything to make them better. In American eyes, both Chrétien and Martin had been all too happy to put domestic politicking ahead of the bilateral partnership; why should the United States do things any differently? The administration's resentful disinterest in Canada's problems had a paralysing effect on the day-to-day governing of these issues and on bureaucratic efforts to reinvigorate stalled negotiations.[35] After the Liberals were replaced by Harper's Conservatives in January 2006, official talks on beef and lumber resumed in earnest, and formulas were quickly found for temporary 'resolutions' of the conflicts. Neither of these political settlements was as good as the new Harper government might have hoped for, but they seemed at the time to be much better than living with the economically draining and politically combustible status quo.

Retaliation and Independence, Revisited

The preceding discussion suggests two main conclusions about how coercive linkages work in the Canada–U.S. relationship, and how they might be important in thinking about the nature and limits of Canada's foreign policy 'independence.' First, the management of conflicts of interest works differently in the Canada–U.S. context than in other international relationships. Retaliation, as defined here, is a normal and pervasive feature of world politics. There are of course a number of strategic and political challenges involved in pursuing retaliation (or the threat of retaliation) effectively, but these are often overcome where the stakes are high and viable linkage scenarios are available. In the Canada–U.S. relationship, these practical obstacles are much more numerous and weighty, and they have historically been supplemented by deeply rooted norms against coercive issue-linkages, so the bar for resort to retaliation is set very high. Though we have seen some bilateral conflicts over the last sixty years that have tested this threshold, we apparently have not seen any that have clearly crossed it.

Because retaliatory linkages have essentially been 'off the table' in Canada–U.S. relations, American frustration has been channelled instead towards what I have called 'grudge' linkages. These grudge linkages set up a subtle and complex diplomatic dynamics, in which signals of resolve are often cryptic, Canadian politicians and officials have strong incentives to try to build up and maintain their stock of 'diplomatic capital' in Washington, and Canadian vulnerability often depends on ephemeral configurations of executive control in the United States.

Second, the basis for American self-restraint has evolved over time, based on long-run historical changes to the institutional structure of U.S. foreign policy-making. In the 1950s and 1960s, the executive branch in the United States was in a position to engineer direct retaliatory linkages in especially high-stakes disputes, and to make grudge linkages pretty much at will. The main obstacle to coercive linkage during this period was the policy-makers themselves, or rather their commitment to a shared diplomatic culture, which ruled out coercive linkages as fundamentally inappropriate in the Canada–U.S. context. After the early 1970s, with the increased sense of vulnerability among domestic interests in the United States, and the fragmentation of control over foreign policy-making, the old normative barriers to coercive linkage began to crumble, and the United States was increasingly inclined to consider both direct retaliatory linkages and less-direct grudge linkages. However, this same fragmentation of political power also created new obstacles to the pursuit of effective issue-linkages, by enabling relevant bureaucratic and societal groups to fight against disruptions that might sacrifice their interests for the sake of others. The result has been a much more contentious and often confusing pattern of bilateral diplomacy, where anxiety about possible retaliation is pervasive and intense, and government officials on both sides are often frustrated by their inability to influence one another's policy choices or satisfy demanding constituents at home.

Canadian thinking about how best to manage the relationship with the United States has also evolved over time. In the early Cold War decades, Canadian officials and diplomats were relatively confident about the bases and extent of American self-restraint, and therefore tended not to spend a lot of time worrying about the threat of retaliation. At the same time, they recognized how frequently favourable settlements in the past had depended on timely and energetic interventions by sympathetic and far-sighted members of the executive branch, and so also recognized the potential risks involved in failing to cultivate and maintain goodwill in the White House and the State Department. They didn't lose a lot of sleep worrying about grudge linkages, but they did work hard to maintain the spirit of 'partnership' and were often prepared to sacrifice potential gains in particular disputes when they believed that doing so would keep the larger relationship running smoothly.

In retrospect, it seems clear that Canada had little to worry about in terms of grudge linkages during this period, at least relative to the way things have been since the early 1970s. As the impacts that political and economic developments outside the United States could have on various domestic interests intensified, and control over foreign policy-making became more fragmented, the U.S. government became less generous and forbearing, more and more likely to argue in public about how best to 'get tough' with foreign trouble-makers, and increasingly inclined to consider coercive linkages. In this new political environment, U.S. officials often have irresistible incentives to talk tough, and may find it politically risky to be seen to create or maintain favourable deals for Canada, or even to come to the bargaining table with them, while recent Canadian policies are churning up resentment among domestic constituents. Canadian priorities and strategies have also become increasingly 'politicized,' and Canadian political leaders have been much more inclined to stir up speculation about retaliation while in opposition, and to make a show of pushing at the limits of U.S. restraint while they are in office.

The new U.S. foreign policy dog certainly has more bark, but it doesn't necessarily have more bite. The fragmentation of power within the United States, and the ever-tightening straitjacket of global market pressures and international institutional commitments, seem to have made it much harder for American policy-makers to translate their new inclination to make coercive linkages into diplomatic practice. But these new obstacles to linkage are less thorough and pervasive than the old ones. Whether or not the United States is willing and able to make grudge linkages in any given case varies over time, and from one issue area to another, depending on complex, shifting domestic political alignments within the country.[36]

This obviously doesn't make it any easier for Canadian officials, or the general public, to think strategically about how best to engage with the United States. In recent years we have seen both a smug complacency that seems to assume nothing important has changed since the 1960s and a near-panic that seems to believe that Canada has entrapped itself in a subordinate relationship cemented by perpetual bullying and intimidation. Neither is correct, and both are potentially dangerous as guides to diplomatic strategy. In fact, the bases for grudge linkages – like the process and outcomes of foreign policy-making in the United States more generally – has become increasingly complex over time, and so therefore have the sources and limits of Canada's foreign policy autonomy.

NOTES

1 Kim Richard Nossal, 'The Imperial Congress: The Separation of Powers and Canadian-American Relations,' *International Journal* 64 (Autumn 1989): 863–83.
2 Michael Mastanduno, 'The United States Political System and International

Leadership: A "Decidedly Inferior" Form of Government?' in *American Foreign Policy: Theoretical Essays*, ed. G. John Ikenberry, 4th ed. (New York: Addison-Wesley, 2002).

3 Robert O. Keohane and Joseph S. Nye, Jr, *Power and Interdependence: World Politics in Transition* (Boston: Little Brown & Co., 1977), esp. chap. 7.

4 Allan E. Gotlieb, 'Canada-US Relations: The Rules of the Game,' *SAIS Review* 2 (Summer 1982): 183.

5 A.F.W. Plumptre, A.E. Safarian, Abraham Rotstein, and Pauline Jewett, 'Retaliation: The Price of Independence?' in *An Independent Foreign Policy for Canada?* ed. Stephen Clarkson (Toronto: McClelland & Stewart, 1968).

6 Asked about the meaning and importance of these eruptions in the press, Allan Gotlieb dismissed them as 'the usual background noise.' Interview, Toronto, 23 May 2001.

7 K. Nash, *Kennedy and Diefenbaker: Fear and Loathing across the Undefended Border* (Toronto: McClelland & Stewart, 1990), 18–19.

8 E. Dosman, *The National Interest: The Politics of Northern Development, 1968–75* (Toronto: McClelland & Stewart, 1975), 58.

9 S. Clarkson, *Canada and the Reagan Challenge* (Toronto: Lorimer, 1982), 32.

10 These three episodes, and the assessment of them that follows, are covered at some length in Brian Bow, *The Politics of Linkage: Power, Interdependence, and Ideas in Canada-US Relations* (Vancouver: UBC Press, forthcoming).

11 J.J. Greene, '"Canada Can't Moan over Oil Cuts" – Greene,' *Ottawa Citizen*, 11 March 1970, 1, 21.

12 Plumptre, in *An Independent Foreign Policy for Canada?* 44.

13 Jewett, ibid., 52. See also the discussion of 'non-decisions' in K.J. Holsti, 'Canada and the United States,' in *Conflict in World Politics*, ed. Steven Spiegel and Kenneth Waltz (Cambridge, MA: Winthrop, 1971), 376–7.

14 See also Stephen Azzi, 'Magazines and the Canadian Dream: The Struggle to Protect Canadian Periodicals, 1956–65,' *International Journal* 54, no. 2 (Summer 1999): 502–33.

15 For an excellent review of bilateral crises in this period, see Greg Donaghy, *Tolerant Allies: Canada and the United States, 1963–68* (Montreal and Kingston: McGill-Queen's University Press, 2003).

16 Gotlieb, 'The Rules of the Game,' 183.

17 See, for example, Clarkson's account of the Reagan administration's exploration of potential linkages during the dispute over Trudeau's National Energy Program. *Canada and the Reagan Challenge*, chaps. 2–3.

18 Samuel J. Huntington, 'American Ideals vs. American Institutions,' *Political Science Quarterly* 97 (Spring 1982): 1–37.

19 Holsti, 'Canada and the United States,' 373.

20 Safarian, in *An Independent Foreign Policy for Canada?* 49.

21 Plumptre, ibid., 45, emphasis in original. The metaphor is slightly flawed because it frames the larger relationship as a zero-sum contest, but there is a lot of value in the underlying emphasis on the way particular moves are not immediate responses to the other side's last move, but rather are arrived at as the culmination of a long series of prior moves, and are based primarily on expectations about likely future choices.

22 Barry Cooper and Mercedes Stephenson, 'Ballistic Missile Defence and the Future of Canada–US Cooperation,' *Fraser Forum*, March 2005: 9–11.

23 Plumptre, in *An Independent Foreign Policy for Canada?* 47.

24 The phrase is borrowed from an interview with a former Canadian official, Ottawa, November 2006.

25 Interview with senior State Department official, Washington, August 2005.

26 This account of the dispute is based on my dissertation research. See also H. Basil Robinson, *Diefenbaker's World: A Populist in Foreign Affairs* (Toronto: University of Toronto Press, 1988), esp. chaps. 20, 23, and 27–9.

27 See Laurence J. Legere to McGeorge Bundy, no date, 'Subject: Follow-up with Canadians on Hyannis Port,' White House Staff Files, Myer Feldman, John F. Kennedy Library.

28 Robert F. Kennedy, quoted in Nash, *Kennedy and Diefenbaker*, 11.

29 Charlotte S.M. Girard, *Canada in World Affairs*, vol. 13, *1963–65* (Toronto: CIIA, 1980), 72–8.

30 Denis Stairs, 'Myths, Morals and Reality in Canadian Foreign Policy,' *International Journal* 57 (Spring 2003): 239–56.

31 K.J. Holsti and Thomas Allen Levy, 'Bilateral Institutions and Transgovernmental Relations between Canada and the United States,' *International Organization* 28 (Autumn 1974): 875–901.

32 Donald K. Alper and Robert L. Monahan, 'Bill C-58 and the American Congress: The Politics of Retaliation,' *Canadian Public Policy* 4 (Spring 1978): 184–92.

33 For example, Dwight Mason, 'Canada and the Future of Continental Defense: A View from Washington,' *CSIS Policy Papers on the Americas* 14 (September 2003).

34 Peter Andreas, 'A Tale of Two Borders: The US-Mexico and US-Canada Lines after 9/11,' in *The Re-Bordering of North America*, ed. Peter Andreas and Thomas J. Biersteker, 1–23. New York: Routledge, 2003.

35 Interview with senior State Department official, Washington, August 2005.

36 Brian Bow, 'Out of Ideas? Models and Strategies for Canada–US Relations,' *International Journal* 62 (Winter 2006–7): 123–44.

4 The Return of the Quiet Canadian: Canada's Approach to Regional Integration after 9/11

STEPHANIE R. GOLOB[1]

The Security and Prosperity Partnership of North America (SPP) is perhaps the most ambitious and noteworthy institutional innovation in the realm of North American regional integration since the North American Free Trade Agreement (NAFTA) side accords. As such, it was announced with much fanfare by the three national leaders at their summit meeting in Waco, Texas, in March 2005.[2] However, in contrast to its trinational mandate for security cooperation and regulatory harmonization and its prodigious sprawl across multiple agencies and key policy agendas of the three member states, the SPP has been, in practice and in public, a quiet affair. It represents a triumph of technical expertise over politicking, and of bureaucratic rationality over the highly emotional and irreconcilable conflicts that have plagued NAFTA and North American integration since the polemical Canadian 'free trade election' of 1988 and the battle to pass NAFTA in the U.S. House of Representatives in 1993. By all appearances, the three NAFTA partners have moved ahead by moving offstage, lowering the rhetoric, and handing off the technical details of smoothing the flow of commerce across secured borders to the professionals.

In other words, the SPP today bears all the hallmarks of 'quiet diplomacy,' that much-maligned traditional approach to foreign policy criticized by several of the contributors to *An Independent Foreign Policy for Canada?* as overly subservient and secretive. Viewed in this way, the SPP affirms the underlying assumption of the quiet diplomacy approach – that geopolitical realities and economic asymmetries are more than bothersome constraints on Canadian foreign policy; they form an inescapable web, trapping Canada in its U.S.-centric confines. As a result, the best Canada can hope for is to leverage its influence and access in

Washington, the only place where it counts, and reject as irresponsible the kind of symbolic posturing aimed at proving Canada's ability to stand up to its powerful neighbour. Independence, it seems, could never possibly begin at home.

In keeping with the provocative spirit of the original *IFPC?* volume, however, I will argue in this chapter that this perception of 'hands-tied' determinism regarding Canada's post-9/11 policy towards North American integration does not adequately appreciate the extent to which quiet diplomacy can be read as a Canadian choice, not simply an American imposition. Over the past six years, and over two governments of different ideological bents, quiet diplomacy has been embraced in the North American context with renewed vigour and with strategic purpose, in the process advancing both Canada's privileged position vis-à-vis Mexico, and the privileged position of Canadian government officials in their closed-circuit dealings with their American counterparts. In their promotion of Canadian exceptionalism via quiet diplomacy, these governments have staked out an arguably advantageous, 'insider' position for Canada; however, I will contend that their strategy has threatened to deepen two pernicious divides in the region: a *development divide* that maintains Mexico as an 'Other,' rather than a full partner and potential ally for Canada in the trilateral relationship; and a *democratic divide* that unnecessarily distances non-business 'stakeholders' in North America from the construction of new regional rules, on the pretence that such technical matters require insulation from public view and legislative politicization.

Following a brief review of Canada's role in infusing quiet diplomacy into the North American project both before and after 9/11, I will turn my attention to the SPP, arguing that its surface trilateral innovations only serve to deepen the grooves of traditional 'quiet' Canada–U.S. bilateral relations that favour American priorities for 'security' and 'prosperity' and muffle what could be a productive public debate in Canada about why belonging to and in 'North America' is in the broader national interest. In the concluding section, I will reflect on how SPP could figure in a more creative and pluralistic – and less quiet – Canadian approach to continental integration.

Plus ça change ... : Quiet Diplomacy in North America before and after 9/11

Over the course of the twentieth century, as the United States grew in power and influence, and as north-south economic ties tightened the bonds between the neighbouring countries, Canada–U.S. relations have paradoxically taken a distinctly undercover profile. Because they matter relatively less south of the 49th parallel, relations with Canada have barely registered on the U.S. political radar screen, with vast public ignorance of Canada's role as a top trading partner and source of imported oil. Meanwhile, because bilateral relations mattered so much more for Canada, and because key economic disputes could end up in the highly parochial hands of the protectionist U.S. Congress, generations of Canadian diplomats in Washington have honed their skills in back-channel influence and confidence-building within the U.S. executive branch. Moreover, because fears for Canadian sovereignty have represented an untouchable 'third rail' in Canadian politics, deep cooperation has been driven further underground, as politicians in all political parties remain sensitive to criticisms of 'selling out' to the imperialists to the south.[3] This overall pattern of 'silent integration' persisted in the postwar era, as the two countries cooperated extensively in defence (in particular through the North American Air Defense system, or NORAD) and even formalized their growing economic interdependence, first through a bilateral Free Trade Agreement (1988) and then the trilateral NAFTA accord (1994). Public expressions of Canadian 'independence' in postwar North American affairs have therefore tended to be isolated, attributable to singular figures such as Pierre Elliott Trudeau, or to calculated attempts to burnish leaders' nationalist credentials, such as Brian Mulroney's decision not to participate in the Strategic Defense Initiative.

It therefore comes as little surprise that 'North America' as a region, and Canada's policy towards its operation and governance, have conformed to these historic patterns of bilateral relations. Cleaving to the notion of the 'special relationship,' Canada entered NAFTA mainly to lock in what had been negotiated bilaterally in the FTA, and the resulting agreement is exceptionally lean in terms of trilateral institutional apparatus. Instead, given the well-oiled quiet diplomacy channels in Washington and the mutual need to shield the project from angry voters, Canadian officials joined their American and Mexican counterparts and kept the volume down on 'North America' after NAFTA. This consensual choice left the field open in the 1990s for economic integration to proceed according to NAFTA's neoliberal rules favouring transnational business, which had already begun to continentalize production, investment, and distribution. This 'privatized' pattern of regional integration eschewed any vision from political leaders. Instead, it leaves the day-to-day management of the regional economy to 'the professionals,' centred in the U.S. Department of Commerce, which was responsible for the coordination of the sectorally based and inter-agency NAFTA working groups, themselves built upon the foundation of well-developed Canada–U.S. transgovernmental relationships.

North America also lacks a formal, institutionalized commitment to 'levelling up' its poorer partner. This is in contrast with the European Union's use of regional development funds, also known as cohesion funds, designed to fund infrastructure improvement, industrial subsidies, and other programs to bridge disparities across its member states.[4] In addition to keeping the issue of political cohesion off the table, rejecting Europe's model reflects and reinforces the Canadian (and American) preference for a two-speed, double-bilateral approach to NAFTA. To be fair, the great asymmetries that characterize the region make such a configuration logical and, in the short term, even beneficial to all parties. However, over time the lack of attention to issues of equalization – that is, recognition by the more advanced partners that, without proactive measures on their part, the weaker partner will always be behind – privileges Canada at the expense of Mexico within the North American regional club. Similarly, the NAFTA side accords for labour and the environment, which enjoy at least a modicum of institutional presence via distinct secretariats, do little to equalize the three countries in terms of regionally enforced norms. These accords have primarily targeted Mexico and its failures to enforce its own law, without considering the resources (both monetary and technical/political) that are necessary for Mexico to make the kinds of 'rule of law' domestic reforms favoured by both business and human rights groups. The prohibition against pooling sovereignty – which Mexico ironically shares – makes Canada and the United States reluctant to view equalization as a legitimate part of the trilateral agenda.

'Privatized' integration has also meant minimal channels for citizen input or oversight, which again underscores how quiet diplomacy dominates the form and practice of the region's governance structures (or lack thereof). The NAFTA negotiations gave privileged access to big business, which worked closely with their national teams of trade negotiators to fashion favourable outcomes for their sectors. Not surprisingly, after the agreement was in place, its operation was overseen mainly by these same trade bureaucrats, whose phone numbers remained on the proverbial Rolodexes of the big continental corporations and their government relations staffs. Citizens, by contrast, were defined by the architects of the agreement as consumers, and as such were viewed as the main beneficiaries of regional free trade. However, as the controversy surrounding NAFTA's U.S. Congressional approval and more than a decade of national and transnational anti-NAFTA contentious politics in all three countries has shown, opposition to free trade in general and to NAFTA in particular puts the lie to this 'citizen=consumer' equation. At the same time, other than the citizen petition mechanisms within the side agreements, which lack legal teeth, there are no trilateral or trinational North American institutions designed to take into consideration the responses and demands of ordinary people.[5] Again, in keeping with the NAFTA model, those citizens are directed to their *national* representative institutions, which are outsiders to the bureaucratic insider game. Moreover, Chapter 11 dispute settlement elevates private companies to the role of plaintiffs on a par with national governments, whereas findings in the labour and environmental side agreements shield private businesses from legal responsibility.

A window of opportunity to shift these dynamics opened after 11 September 2001, when Canadians rallied to the side of their neighbours and talk of a 'North American Security Perimeter' raised the possibility of viewing both Canada and Mexico as 'inside' a regional frontier that the three countries could defend together. However, rather than rethinking anything, Canada's post-9/11 North American policy has reaffirmed a commitment to quiet diplomacy and double-bilateralism. In the immediate aftermath of the attacks, Canadian government statements announced that 'economic security' defined the national interest, making market access via the border the *sine qua non* of national survival. As bureaucracies closed ranks and President Bush's hand-picked chief of Homeland Security, Tom Ridge, began to work with Deputy Prime Minister John Manley, there was impressive activity throughout the autumn of 2001 to negotiate a Smart Border Accord and to implement the accord's main provisions to expedite legitimate commerce while deterring illegal flows.[6] Partly this was done to reinforce the perception that Canada could be trusted, in contrast with Mexico, which saw its bilateral relations with Washington deteriorate after 9/11, with the collapse of U.S. support for a draft immigration accord and the openly anti-American statements of some Mexican politicians. While Manley's very public campaign to brand Canada as 'the Good Neighbour' may seem anything but quiet, it shared quiet diplomacy's assumption that Canada must embrace its 'special relationship' with the

United States, while the Smart Border initiatives accelerated cooperative efforts already under way within American and Canadian border
management agencies. This very combination of photo ops on the outside and inter-wonk relations on the inside is the hallmark of quiet
diplomacy.

This pattern of two-speed North America, privileging quiet diplomacy within the U.S.-Canada dyad, appeared to meet its first serious
challenge in March 2005 with the launch of the Security and Prosperity
Partnership at a summit of North American leaders held in Waco,
Texas.[7] Indeed, at first glance, this trilateral summit suggested a shift
towards a new orientation for governance in the region, and the SPP is,
in many ways, a notable innovation. However, as I will argue in the following section, at base the SPP merely reinforces traditional patterns of
quiet diplomacy and double bilateralism, with consequences for the
domestic and international repercussions of Canada's North American
policy.

Speak Softly, Period: Canada and the SPP

Given the virtually institution-free nature of North American integration under NAFTA, it is easy to be impressed – or alarmed – by the scope
and apparatus of the SPP. The initiative is notable first for breaking the
decade-long official silence on the extent of deep, structural integration,
which has created 'North American' issues that transcend national
boundaries and require trinational cooperation. Each of its two separate
but related policy agendas – Security and Prosperity - is 'led' by the corresponding ministers/secretaries whose substantive mandates cover
the areas in question, and who are required to report back at set inter-
vals to the three leaders on the work of their agencies.[8] The ministers, in
turn, look to the heads of specialized offices within their organizations
to contribute studies and proposals for particular areas of regulation
that could benefit from various degrees of harmonization – or agreement on common principles and practices if not common language –
towards the declared consensus aim of advancing legal commerce while
minimizing threatening flows across borders. Aiding this proposal-
generating effort are upwards of twenty SPP trinational working
groups, which bring together the staffs of these specialized agencies.[9]
Not surprisingly, some very traditional areas related to post-9/11 security concerns and to NAFTA-led integration dominate the two agendas.
For example, the Security agenda is dominated by border management,

while initiatives to improve 'competitiveness' through streamlining rules of origin and reducing costs to business and consumers via the 'rationalization' of national regulations fill out the Prosperity side. At the same time, other innovative areas for intergovernmental cooperation are also included, such as public health responses to the avian flu threat, joint monitoring of the continental food supply, and (somewhat more controversial) information sharing for law enforcement.

Despite some of the more overwrought accusations of its critics on the right, however, the SPP is hardly the first step on the road to European-style regional integration, or to a 'North American Union' and the end of U.S. sovereignty. Replete with neoliberal references to improving 'competitiveness' and 'quality of life' through more efficient market operation, the SPP project is still very much a creature of the narrow, politically risk-averse vision that has thus far characterized the 'privatized' North American integration model.[10] First, the SPP working groups aim mostly at what can be called 'low-hanging fruit' – that is, the types of regulations or projects that are either so highly technical (for example, the size and shape of baby food jars) or in which the consensus to act is so urgent (improving border infrastructure and roads leading to border crossings) that they are unlikely to meet legal or political roadblocks to their solution by technocratic means. Second, there has been no effort whatsoever to give the SPP a 'secretariat,' or any kind of permanent institutional presence.[11] In sharp contrast to the process that created the behemoth Department of Homeland Security in the United States, or the massive bureaucracy in Brussels for that matter, the SPP design is one of maximum flexibility and minimum centralization. The working groups are, themselves, based on intergovernmental groups already established as part of NAFTA to maximize interchange of information and ideas among bureaucratic experts with a minimum of political interference.[12] Finally, there is little political will at the top in any of the three NAFTA member states to go beyond what the SPP is – a reorganization and reinvigoration of bureaucratic resources that already existed but are now being put to work to solve discreet, concrete problems whose only overarching goal is the vague notion of improving 'security' and 'prosperity' in the region. Similarly, though deadlines and periodic summit meetings do give the impression of top-level executive will,[13] timetables thus far have only required incremental 'progress' and not a coordinated outcome, such as a new 'NAFTA-plus' agreement.

Instead of representing the next step towards a European-style super-state, the 'North America' reflected in the SPP's minimalist and technocratic structure is in many ways equal to, or less than, the sum of its parts. Most notably, behind all the trilateral rhetoric, the SPP is driven first and foremost by the post-9/11 agenda of the U.S. government, and Canada's enthusiasm for the SPP can thus be read as a risk-averse choice to continue playing 'Good Neighbour' while benefiting behind the scenes from the SPP's basis in quiet diplomacy. In the aftermath of 9/11, proposals coming out of both the Canadian parliament[14] and the Canadian private sector[15] sensed a flagging interest in the United States in regional integration, and suggested that a bigger initiative would be needed to prevent the United States from turning inward. These ideas made their way into the NAFTA bureaucracy in Washington and motivated Bush administration officials to consider a new trilateral initiative.[16] Though the SPP as it emerged from the National Security Council in 2005 lacks the 'big idea' that many Canadians hoped for, it did rely upon the seamless inter-operability of Canadian and U.S. government experts and the synergy of professional ideologies that forms the basis of quiet diplomacy. Rather than reinvent the wheel, the SPP keeps everyone doing what they were already doing, and keeps the same people talking together and maintaining the continuity of relationships as well as approaches. Moreover, one SPP innovation is explicitly to allow any two countries to advance bilaterally on issues of mutual interest without the participation or consent of the third party, reinforcing the double-bilateralism norm for North American integration. It is no coincidence that there is no single Mexico-Canada initiative within the SPP.[17]

Moreover, it is almost uncanny how the 'closed-circuit' nature of the SPP parallels and in some ways reflects the same 'closed circuit' behaviour of External Affairs specialists so energetically excoriated in 1968 by Stephen Clarkson, Franklyn Griffiths,[18] and other *IFPC?* authors critical of quiet diplomacy. Indeed, three key types of insularity that characterize the SPP leave it open to related critiques. First, and most obvious, is the insulation of bureaucrats that allows them to feel that they know best and that the public need not be privy to specialized topics that are beyond their comprehension. In this looking-glass world, policy is made ostensibly to benefit the public, and yet public scrutiny is viewed as an obstacle to 'getting the job done.' Second, and related to this, is the insulation of the SPP agenda from legislative scrutiny and oversight. Indeed, a somewhat breathless report in the *Ottawa Citizen* last February announced that the SPP was 'bypassing legislators and the public to open borders,' further arguing that the SPP agendas were specifically designed to select regulations that required either no congressional or parliamentary approval, or could be legally defended through pre-existing law.[19] While the article exaggerates the conspiratorial nature of the SPP, it captures the 'perception is reality' nature of politics: the quiet, technocratic modus operandi of the SPP is easily interpreted by NAFTA's critics as a purposeful end run around public accountability to protect corporate interests.

Indeed, the SPP does allow for the input of groups outside of the government, but these 'stakeholders' are exclusively representatives of big business. This leads to the third type of insulation undermining the political legitimacy of the SPP: the restriction of access to the policy process to corporate insiders. The North American Competitiveness Council (NACC), officially launched at the second anniversary summit at Cancún in June 2006, brings together representative delegations of the region's major business organizations and serves as a conduit for private-sector views on what kinds of regulations should be harmonized under the SPP. Each NAFTA country has its own delegation. In Canada, for example, the effort is housed at the Council of Canadian Chief Executives, while in the United States the Council of the Americas and the U.S. Chamber of Commerce serve as quasi-co-secretariats, and Mexico's Instituto Mexicano de Competitividad heads up that country's delegation.[20] Thus far, the NACC has offered a way for 'stakeholders' to work with members of the expert community, first via the consensus recommendations submitted ahead of the February 2007 summit in Kananaskis, Alberta,[21] and later in projected consultations as the proposals go forward to individual working groups. Thus, the SPP envisions creating small, integrated quasi-teams of government and private-sector actors forging policy ideas and tailoring regulatory and policy reform to suit 'stakeholder' needs.

As the ultimate 'insider' operation, then, the SPP advances Canadian efforts to be viewed as an insider by the Bush administration, which has a reputation for distrusting critics and valuing loyalty. This choice, however, may yet prove costly at home, where the consensus on 'competitiveness' as the primary 'North American' value is hardly complete and where there is a healthy scepticism regarding the public-interest vocation of multinational corporations. Clearly absent from the SPP 'stakeholder' mechanism are any groups or viewpoints that would question or contradict the neoliberal orientation towards regional integration. It is hardly surprising, then, to see Canadian citizens' groups such as Common Frontiers and the Council of Canadians,[22] and more traditional left interest groups such as the Canadian Labour Congress,[23] publishing and advocating against the SPP. In addition, Canada's left-of-centre New Democratic Party (NDP) has also taken a proactive stand against the SPP,[24] setting up a 'Stop the SPP' working group,[25] sponsoring motions, and submitting citizen petitions to the Standing Committee on International Trade that call for greater legislative oversight and public communication regarding the SPP, culminating in four days of televised hearings in the spring of 2007.[26] Meanwhile, NDP leader Jack Layton went on Lou Dobbs's program on CNN in early March 2008 to announce that the party's international trade critic, Peter Julian, had plans to take the NDP's 'Stop the SPP' working group trilateral.[27] Although the NDP is a small party, even by Canadian standards, it is a national party drawing upon a long history advancing 'defence of sovereignty' positions, and it has mobilized its parliamentary resources to bring the SPP out of the shadows.[28] Add to this its alliance with the labour movement and contentious political groups skilled in new media and transnational activity, and the NDP looks less like a voice in the wilderness and more like a small but considerable thorn in the side of the Canadian government's SPP agenda.[29] And, as seen vividly in the protests of Mexican farmers and the resurgence of anti-NAFTA voter rage in Ohio and Texas, voices calling for the renegotiation or repeal of the agreement are not as absent as they appear within the SPP mechanism. The more subtle and profound message sent by these dissenting voices is that the North American integration project is opposed by those who were ostensibly meant to benefit – consumers – because they continue to define themselves first as citizens.

While the quiet diplomacy model embodied in SPP is widening this 'democratic divide,' the SPP's double-bilateral approach is similarly widening the 'development divide' that separates the two wealthy North American nations from their poorer southern neighbour. We may never see a EU-style program of public investment in Mexico, owing to the U.S.-driven neoliberal model that has shaped NAFTA and the SPP. However, I would argue, in agreement with a 2005 trinational study group sponsored by the C.D. Howe Institute,[30] that neither Mexico's continued poverty, nor its marginalization within the double bilateral framework, is in Canada's interests. This is not to imply that a two-speed North America is inherently bad, nor that it is more in Canada's interest to negotiate trilaterally as a rule. There is a general agreement that the two bilateral agendas are sufficiently asymmetrical that such a two-track approach is often most pragmatic, particularly in the security realm. However, I would suggest that this overemphasis on the short term and the pragmatic has made it more difficult to see what is long term and potentially visionary about even the narrow and privatized NAFTA-based North American integration project: that cooperation towards *Mexico's* security and prosperity could conceivably achieve the same kind soft-power-generating 'doing well by doing good' that the United States and Canada enjoyed in the dawn of Bretton Woods and the venerated postwar moment. At that time greater prosperity and security for Europe were achieved through institutions of what G. John Ikenberry has called the 'liberal democratic order' and through the 'postwar bargain' of the welfare state.[31] While the chances are slim that the neoliberal model of NAFTA would allow for such deviation towards state intervention, one wonders how many more Canadian products would be consumed, how many more Canadian consulting companies would be employed to advise in the restructuring public and private institutions, and how many more Canadian teachers and students would be participating in efforts to (re)vitalize Mexico's lagging primary and secondary education, if Mexico were viewed more emphatically and concretely as a true partner, just as postwar Europe was.

That said, there are some more short-term and pragmatic reasons why Canada should devote more sustained attention to its other NAFTA partner. In strategic terms alone, empowering Mexico within trilateral NAFTA mechanisms can have concrete advantages when the two weaker partners negotiate with their mutual superpower neighbour. Mexico and Canada are also middle powers who could cooperate in a number of ways within the UN system and the WTO, as well as the OAS. Prime Minister Harper's July 2007 trip to Latin America coincided with Mexican President Felipe Calderón's reorientation of his country's foreign policy back towards Latin America; one wonders if this common interest might further forge solidarity out of the shadow of the current, or any future, U.S. administration.

Finally, recent polls have shown that Canadians want their country's foreign policy to become more active and to assume more global responsibility. One such survey, 'Canada's World Poll,' sponsored by the Simmons Foundation among others and released in January 2008, concluded that 'Canadians feel strongly connected to the world outside their borders,' and that they supported a world role for Canada, with more responsibility and activism in solving global problems such as hunger, human rights abuses, and global warming.[32] Another poll, discussed by EKOS president Frank Graves at its release in February 2008, shows Canadians with a 'vision hunger' for a 'bold new vision for the country' in both domestic and foreign policy.[33] The EKOS poll also found that Canadians showed 'a new focus on transparency, inclusiveness, and results' in government, and were looking for 'legitimacy' and 'relevance.'[34] By following a closed-door approach to SPP that also puts Mexico's unique and pressing development agenda on the back burner, the Canadian government is arguably missing an opportunity to place SPP and North American integration into a broader and more politically winning foreign policy frame. Canada's role in North America could hypothetically be enhanced by cultivating the Canada–Mexico relationship as a contribution towards development in Mexico – of democracy, free markets, health and education, and environmental protection – and as an expression of a new commitment to global responsibility on the part of Canada.[35]

Towards a Not-So-Quiet Canadian Voice in North America

In this essay I have made the case that quiet diplomacy is alive and well, and deeply rooted in Canada's North American policy. While this may be chalked up to the exigencies of political and economic asymmetries, a more accurate picture reveals that Canadian governments have purposefully chosen the quiet diplomacy path. The benefits of following this path – ease of dealing with the prickly U.S. political system, insulation from bothersome public interference with experts' problem-solving activities, privileging of Canada (over Mexico) and Canada–U.S. bilateral issues within the North American agenda, and the maintenance of all-important market access for Canadian goods at a time of heightened U.S. distrust of outsiders – have been legion. Still, my analysis points to the possibility that what Canada gives up by going underground and forging its North American policy in the back room is the ability to legitimate its position both at home and abroad. In the name of pragmatism and *realpolitik*, quiet diplomacy in the post-9/11 North American context has arguably contributed to today's sense of 'vision hunger' abroad in the land, which echoes the yearning for Canadian moral authority so eloquently if quixotically described and celebrated by the contributors to the original *IFPC?* volume. This is not simply because Canada has chosen a policy of 'close alliance' with the

United States; it is because the price of this close alliance is distancing Canada from values that could, if expressed within the 'North American' context, lead the region towards a more equitable and just future for all of its members. For example, Canada's commitment to universal health care, its long tradition of multilateralism, and its vibrant, transnationally oriented NGO sector all point to ways that the *plural* voices of Canadians could be drawn upon to enrich the discussion of what it means to live together in a highly integrated regional economic system. Breaking free of the 'Quiet Canadian' deference in the North American context may not amount to a truly 'independent' foreign policy, but it could border on liberating.

NOTES

1 The research in this article forms part of a larger trinational study of the origins and development of the Security and Prosperity Partnership of North America and its working groups. The author gratefully acknowledges the generous support of the Canadian Studies Faculty Research Grant Program, 2005–6, administered through the Canadian embassy in Washington, DC. The author also gratefully acknowledges the intellectual contribution to this work of Stephen Blank, and the generosity of the officials in the U.S. Commerce and State departments who agreed to be interviewed by Dr Blank and the author in January 2007. Many thanks also to Brian Bow and Patrick Lennox for the invitation to contribute to this exciting project, and for their insightful and constructive comments on an earlier draft. Any errors are my own.

2 The key documents for the 2005 Waco summit regarding the Security and Prosperity Partnership can be found on the SPP website: see '2005 Launch of SPP,' http://www.spp.gov/2005_launch.asp, and the 'Report to Leaders (June 27, 2005),' at http://www.spp.gov/report_to_leaders/index.asp ?dName=report_ to_leaders.

3 Indeed, this concern about nationalist critcisms was the reason given, posthoc, by Prime Minister Mackenzie King for walking away from secret negotiations for a bilateral free trade agreement with the United States in the late 1940s. See Robert Cuff and J.L. Granatstein, 'The Rise and Fall of Canadian-American Free Trade, 1947–8,' *Canadian Historical Review* 58 (December 1977): 459–82; and Michael Hart, 'Almost but Not Quite: The 1947–48 Bilateral Canada-US Negotiations,' *American Review of Canadian Studies* 19 (Spring 1989): 25–58.

4 For an analysis of the European Development Funds (EDFs) with an eye

to how such policy could be designed in the North American triad, see Nina Peacock, 'New Lessons from the Old World: Side-Payments and Regional Development Funds,' *Norteamérica* 1, no. 2 (July-December 2006): 99–125.

5 See Jeffrey Ayres and Laura Macdonald, 'Deep Integration and Shallow Governance: The Limits of Civil Society Engagement across North America,' *Policy and Society* 25, no. 3 (2006): 23–42.

6 The Smart Border Declaration of 12 December 2001 was accompanied by a 30–point Action Plan. For the full text, see the posting on the Border Cooperation section of the Canada-U.S. Relations site of Foreign Affairs and International Trade Canada (DFAIT-MAECI), 'Key Border Documents, and What's New,' at http://geo.international.gc.ca/can-am/main/border/key_border-en.asp.

7 See note 2 above.

8 The most recent of which was held 21–22 April 2008 in New Orleans.

9 On the Prosperity side, for example, there are working groups in the following areas: Manufactured Goods and Sectoral and Regional Competitiveness; Movement of Goods; Energy; Environment; E-Commerce and Information Communications Technologies; Financial Services; Business Facilitation; Food and Agriculture; Transportation; and Health. See 'SPP Prosperity Working Groups,' at http://www.spp.gov/prosperity_working/index.asp?dName=prosperity_working.

10 The following section draws upon confidential interviews, Departments of Commerce and State, Washington, DC, 17 January 2007.

11 Reflecting the U.S.-centric nature of the SPP, the de facto coordinator of the Prosperity Agenda appears to be the Commerce department's Office of NAFTA and Interamerican Affairs, which is in the Market Access and Compliance directorate of the International Trade Administration. See Work Reference (Organizational) Chart, International Trade Administration, at http://www.ita.doc.gov/ooms/MACCHART.pdf.

12 Joseph McKinney, 'NAFTA-Related Institutions in the Context of Theory,' in *Created from NAFTA: The Structure, Function and Significance of the Treaty's Related Institutions* (Armonk, NY: M.E. Sharpe, 2000), 14, quoted in Stephen Clarkson, Sarah Davidson Ladly, and Carleton Thorne, 'De-Institutionalizing North America: NAFTA's Committees and Working Groups,' Third EnviReform Conference (Toronto, 8 November 2002), 3; at http://www.envireform.utoronto.ca/conference/nov2002/clarkson-paper2.pdf.

13 Jason Ackelson and Justin Kastner refer to executive summits and their subsequent calls for reporting back by specified dates as 'action enforcing events,' but remain unclear as to who, or what offices formulate these goals.

See Ackleson and Kastner, 'The Security and Prosperity Partnership of North America,' *American Review of Canadian Studies* 36, no. 2 (Summer 2006): 221.

14 See House of Commons Standing Committee on Foreign Affairs and International Trade, *Partners in North America: Advancing Canada's Relations with the United States and Mexico*, tabled 12 December 2002, at http://cmte.parl .gc.ca/Content/HOC/committee/372/fait/report s/rp1032319/faitrp03/ faitrp03–e.pdf.

15 A major spokesman for this 'Big Idea' point of view was Thomas D'Aquino, president of the Council of Canadian Chief Executives. See Thomas D'Aquino, 'Security and Prosperity: The Dynamics of a New Canada–United States Partnership in North America,' presentation to the Annual General Meeting of the Canadian Council of Chief Executives, Toronto, 14 January 2003. See also Wendy Dobson, 'Shaping the Future of the North American Space,' *Commentary* [C.D.Howe Institute], *The Border Papers*, no. 162 (April 2002).

16 Confidential interviews, Washington, DC, 17 January 2007.

17 See Danielle Goldfarb, 'The Canada-Mexico Conundrum: Finding Common Ground,' *The Border Papers*, C.D. Howe Institute, no. 91 (July 2005), 8.

18 Franklyn Griffiths, 'Opening up the Policy Process,' in *An Independent Foreign Policy for Canada*, ed. Stephen Clarkson (Toronto: McClelland & Stewart, 1968), 110–18.

19 Kelly Patterson, 'Integrating North America "By Stealth,"' *Ottawa Citizen*, 7 February 2007 (received via e-mail from a colleague).

20 Confidential interview, Washington, DC, 17 January 2007. On the U.S. side the private sector was already organizing itself to be a player in the SPP; meeting in Louisville, Kentucky, in January 2006, delegates to a meeting sponsored by UPS and the Council of the Americas began strategizing about the priorities the U.S. business community would communicate to the governments. This meeting is featured prominently on the Council of the Americas website; see http://www.councilofhteamericas.org.

21 North American Competitiveness Council, 'Enhancing Competitiveness in Canada, Mexico, and the United States: Private Sector Priorities for the Security and Prosperity Partnership of North America – Initial Recommendations of the NACC,' February 2007; available at http://www.as-coa .org/files/PDF/grp_10_4.pdf.

22 For materials generated ahead of the Montebello SPP summit in August 2007, see Council of Canadians et al., 'Behind Closed Doors: What They Are Not Telling Us about the SPP,' at http://www.canadians.org/integratethis/ backgrounders/guide/index.html. It should be noted, too, that this and

similar sites offer forms to send via e-mail to entire lists of friends, through portals such as Facebook. American anti-SPP sites tend to be sponsored by conservative, anti-immigrant groups who similarly provide means for electronically contacting representatives or broadcasting documents to groups. See, for example, 'Stop the SPP,' at http://stopspp.com/stopspp/?p=43.

23 For a representative sample of the CLC/CTC's advocacy against the SPP, see 'Deep Integration in North America: Security and Prosperity for Whom?' 22 March 2007, at http://canadianlabour.ca/index.php/Deep _Integration/Deep_Integration_in.

24 'Continental Integration' is one of ten main party issues highlighted on the NDP website. See 'Blowing the Whistle on SPP: Deep Concern over Deep Integration,' at http://www.ndp.ca/continentalintegration.

25 See, 'NDP Launches Stop SPP Working Group,' press release, 29 October 2007, at http://www.ndp.ca/page/5823.

26 The hearings, held 26 April and 1, 3, and 10 May 2007, were announced by NDP International Trade Critic Peter Julian. See 'Throwing Cold Water on Deep Integration,' article published 28 April 2007, at http://www.ndp.ca/ page/5270.

27 The NDP website redirects viewers to the following site on YouTube: Jack Layton on Lou Dobbs, 6 March 2008, http://www.youtube.com/ watch?v=N_MR7tL7tWs.

28 For a spirited critique of the power of bureaucrats and the need for Canada's political parties to establish think tanks to regain control of the policy process, see Irvin Studin, 'Revisiting the Democratic Deficit: The Case for Political Party Think Tanks,' *Policy Options*, February 2007, available at http://www.irpp.org/po/.

29 Recent polling data from Nanos, for example, show Canadians and Americans alike *favouring* free trade by comfortable margins. For Canadians, 27.2 per cent called free trade with the United States 'extremely important' for future prosperity, with a total of 83.2 per cent voting 6 or higher on a 10–point scale. However, as Daniel Drezner points out in his analysis of the politics of outsourcing, it is virtually an 'iron law of politics' that interests hurt by open trade are concentrated and more organized (labour, especially), and those benefiting from open trade more diffuse and less organized (consumers). Thus, the diffuse polling data may tell us less, politically, about the relative strength or weakness of opposition to trade than other key variables, such as the electoral calendar, geographic distribution, economic growth, and unemployment figures. For the polling data, see Nik Nanos, 'SES-*Policy Options* exclusive poll: Canadians, Americans Agree Both Better Off with Free Trade,' in web edition of Special Issue, 'Free Trade at 20,' *Policy Options*,

October 2007, at http://www.irpp.org/po/. For a summary of the 'iron
political rules' of trade politics, see Daniel W. Drezner, 'The Outsourcing
Bogeyman,' *Foreign Affairs* 83 (May/June 2004): 22–34.

30 For the consensus document, see Goldfarb, 'Canada-Mexico Conundrum'
    (2005).

31 G. John Ikenberry, 'The Myth of Post–Cold War Chaos,' *Foreign Affairs* 75,
    no. 3 (May/June 1996): 79–91.

32 'Canada's World Poll,' January 2008, at http://www.igloo.org/community
    .igloo?r0=community&r0_script= /scripts/folder/view.script&r0
    _pathinfo=%2F%7B0f2c2935–322d-40c1–b053–6c1c022faa81%7D%2
    Flearnmor%2Fquizzesa%2Fpollresu&r 0_output=xml, 4–5.

33 See Frank Graves, 'Canadian Values: Understanding Our Values in a Global
    Context,' presentation to the 'Connecting with Canadians' Canadian Policy
    Research Networks Leadership Summit, 18 February 2008, 6; at http://
    www.cprn.org/documents/49412_EN.pdf.

34 Ibid., 11.

35 One optimistic sign is the little-known Canada-Mexico Partnership (CMP),
    established in 2004, which boasts SPP-style working groups in areas such
    as trade, investment, science and technology, labour mobility, and human
    capital (which includes education). See http://www.canadainternational
    .gc.ca/mexico-mexique/cmp-pcm.aspx?lang=en.

PART THREE

Finding Security in the Continental System

The traditional concept of sovereign security seems to be unravelling under the stresses of globalization, global climate change, and the transnational terrorist threat. Indeed, critical international relations scholars, NGOs, and Canada's own Department of Foreign Affairs and International Trade have been pushing for a broadening of the traditional notion of security to include important 'human security' concerns. There has been some evolution in the way that security is understood in the context of the bilateral defence relationship with the United States – particularly after the terrorist attacks of 9/11, which dramatically highlighted the new importance of non-state actors, unconventional weapons, and the national security aspect of issues like immigration and policing. But the pivotal issue in Canada–U.S. defence relations today remains essentially the same as it was forty years ago: Canada wants to keep defence costs and constraints under control, yet it must guard against becoming too reliant on the United States for its security, or losing influence over the joint defence of the continent. In an era in which Canadian and American security perceptions and priorities are often out of sync (both at home and abroad), and the United States has made it clear that it is ready to do whatever it thinks necessary to protect itself, Canada is confronted with the possibility that it might be shut out of the decision-making in a crisis, or even that the United States might be prepared to intervene in Canadian domestic affairs in order to further its own security.

Keeping up appearances, then, is the name of the security and defence game in North America. This is true as much for Canada as it is now for the United States, as Christopher Sands, one of our American contributors, maintains chapter 5. Independence in terms of security and defence policy for both Canada and the United States is illusory according to Sands. Nevertheless, the illusion is one that both states are willing to cooperate to maintain. Ironically, Sands argues, this might make things easier for all involved.

Not so easy for all involved are re-emerging contentions over the issue of Canada's Arctic sovereignty. Interestingly, it was just one year after the publication of the original *IFPC?* volume that the voyages of the SS *Manhattan* through the Northwest Passage first brought this ongoing controversy to a boil. In chapter 6, Rob Huebert argues that this is the one issue that pertains to Canada-U.S. defence and security where Canadian politicians have not been afraid to break with quiet diplomacy and publicly air their views. Unfortunately, this loud talk has not been backed up with any serious commitment to invest the resources required to exercise effective, independent jurisdiction over the region, and thereby support Canada's legal and political claims.

5 An Independent Security Policy for Canada in the Age of Sacred Terror?

CHRISTOPHER SANDS

In 1968, when the University League for Social Reform gathered lead-ing Canadian thinkers together to ponder the possibility of an indepen-dent foreign policy for Canada, the context included Vietnam, where the United States was escalating its engagement in what Washington viewed as a key battleground in the Cold War. In 2008, as this question is raised again, the context includes Iraq, where the United States recently escalated its engagement (in the form of a counter-offensive popularly called 'the surge') in what Washington views as a key battle-ground in the war against al Qaeda.

Although Canada's freedom to take an independent position would arguably be limited in the case of retaliation of some kind by the United States, the contributors to the 1968 volume concluded that there was not much evidence that Washington 'retaliated' against Canada for not providing troops for the fighting in Vietnam.[1]

The focus on retaliation in the 1968 discussion reveals that indepen-dence was being defined in the sense of freedom of action – the ability of Canada to reject a U.S. position, and even U.S. pressure, successfully. Given the past American reluctance to engage in tit-for-tat retaliation, this sort of an independent security policy seems manifestly attainable for Canada. Alternatively, independence can be defined as freedom from dependence – the ability of Canada to take action to secure its ter-ritory and protect its citizens, and perhaps even to promote Canadian values abroad through international operations without permission or assistance from the United States. Low spending on security, a ten-dency to cede certain security responsibilities to the United States (as in the case of missile defences), and the transnational nature of the terror-ist threat make an independent Canadian security policy less possible today than in 1968.

In 2008 the defence of Canada and Canadians must include two critical national security domains: traditional military security – what is normally meant by defence policy – and domestic security policies that are central to the protection of citizens from terrorist attacks. The challenge for governments in Ottawa associated with achieving either freedom of action or freedom from dependence differs substantively in each national security domain.

Military Security

Canadian policy independence in the area of traditional military security is achieved at a price. No Canadian government has ever directly opposed a U.S.-led war to the point of siding with American enemies openly or covertly, which might prove too costly. However, governments have traditionally demonstrated policy independence from the United States, not just by opting out of major conflicts, but also in rejecting U.S. appeals to fund and sustain Canadian military procurement and capabilities at a higher level. Progressive critics of Canadian defence policy see these two policies as consistent with desired Canadian policy independence: Canada avoids foreign conflicts as its capacity to participate in them is diminished. Advocates of a stronger Canadian military point out that in a crisis the price that Canada pays for this independence is that it must rely more on allies, principally the United States.

The tension between the pursuit of security policy independence as defined by freedom of action and security policy independence as defined by freedom from over-reliance on the United States is difficult for Canadian policy-makers to reconcile. In the area of military security, governments in Ottawa have tended since 1945 to opt for the appearance of freedom of action in the short term while downplaying reliance on the United States on a routine basis. This politically appealing solution nonetheless can be risky in the event that an international security crisis emerges and the actual dependence of Canada peeks through the veil of perceived independence of action. Successive governments in Ottawa have succeeded in escaping the political price of independent stances on military security thanks to a public inattentive to military security issues, self-interested U.S. discretion, and a relative lack of local security crises.

This strategy has been undermined in recent years thanks to the gap between U.S. and Canadian defence spending. Even after the end of the

Cold War, U.S. defence spending continued to outpace that of other countries, much of it devoted to research and development. As a result, the United States has regularly added new military capabilities and, in most such cases, given Canada the option to participate in the development of new systems, purchase them for its own defence, or partner in the use of such systems through alliances. For Ottawa this presents a challenge for an independent security policy: if Ottawa responds favorably to U.S. overtures, it may appear to lose some freedom of action owing to implicit conditionality. Yet when Canada chooses to reject all U.S. offers to participate in the development or deployment of new defence systems, its future freedom of action, should it want to participate in the allied response to a crisis overseas, may be limited. This was the case during the NATO war in Serbia, Operation Allied Force, when Canadian planes lacked sufficient 'smart' munitions. The Canadian Forces dropped 10 per cent of the munitions used in the 78-day bombing campaign, but could not do more for lack of equipment.

A different type of challenge to Canadian security policy independence occurs when Canada opts not to participate, but the United States proceeds and subsequently provides protection to Canada anyway. Whether Ottawa intends it or not, in such cases Canada appears to U.S. policy-makers to be 'free riding' on U.S. military security spending.

The most important recent example of the free-rider dilemma has emerged over missile defences. In response to U.S. invitations of partnership in developing missile defences, Canadian governments from Brian Mulroney's to Stephen Harper's have declined to participate. In the twenty-plus years since Ronald Reagan announced the Strategic Defense Initiative, much has changed. The threat from missile attacks has grown as the technology necessary to produce ballistic missiles has become cheaper and more widespread, and the proliferation of chemical, radiological, biological, and even nuclear materials that might be placed in a missile warhead has increased. Four successive American presidents, from Reagan to George W. Bush, have supported the development of missile defences, and U.S. expenditures on related research and development have led to a variety of defensive systems from the Patriot II missile system deployed to protect troops in the 1991 Gulf War to the ship-based defences of the Aegis-class cruiser. In 2002 the United States invoked its right to withdraw from the Anti-Ballistic Missile Treaty it signed with the Soviet Union in 1972, removing the sole obstacle in international law to the further development of missile defences. The United States, Russia, and China have successfully tested missile-launched anti-satellite weapons, and missile technologies obtained by North Korea, Iraq, and Iran have been used to threaten neighbouring states.

Canadian politicians from Mulroney to Harper have chosen not to get involved in U.S. missile defences in part to demonstrate independence from Washington. As the U.S. deploys missile defence systems to protect North America and missile technology becomes cheaper and easier to obtain, the odds of an attack that might force the United States to protect Canada from a missile attack, however low, will rise. Yet as missile technology proliferates among enemies of the west, it becomes less and less likely that an attack would consist of a single missile; with still limited missile defences, the odds will grow that U.S. commanders will one day have to choose between protection of a Canadian city or saving missile defences to protect U.S. targets from subsequent attack. Many in Washington wish Canadian leaders would engage voters on the risks and value of such defences.[2]

Where Canada chooses not to 'free ride' on the military contributions of others, it can make a significant contribution to its own national security and that of its allies. The current example of this is Afghanistan. Canada contributed 750 soldiers to the campaign against the Taliban and al Qaeda in Afghanistan in 2002, where they served under U.S. command and joined in Operation Anaconda. As of the end of 2007, Canada had deployed 16,000 personnel and 20 warships to Afghanistan and the Persian Gulf since 2001. Canadian ship-borne helicopters, patrol, and transport aircraft had flown more than 5000 sorties and more than 22,500 hours of mission flights. At present Canada has troops in Afghanistan and leads the NATO mission. The Canadian Forces have suffered numerous casualties. This is a major contribution, and contrasts favourably with the contributions of other NATO countries (other than the United States, which shoulders the largest burden in Afghanistan and elsewhere).

As with the quest for policy independence, the preference of Canadian governments for high-profile expeditionary missions outside North America rather than increasing capabilities in North America itself is tied to its quest for perceptible independence. Deployments of Canadian Forces outside North America are expensive and dangerous, yet seem to feed the Canadian desire for a presence internationally to compensate for relative geographic isolation. Contributions to continental defence are always overshadowed by those of the United States, and the absence of regular threats to Canadian territory makes the operations of the Canadian Forces in Canada inherently low-profile.

Formal alliance membership was an important manifestation of Canada's commitment to international security throughout the Cold War; alliances also allowed governments in Ottawa to portray Canada as a member of a mutual aid pact, rather than as a security dependent. Standing alliances also served U.S. strategy in extracting commitments from other countries for collective defence. In an alliance such as the North Atlantic Treaty Organization (NATO), individual countries could specialize in certain areas so that, collectively, the countries would be able to offer a wide array of offensive and defensive strengths. The American nuclear arsenal would be pledged to defend allied countries as a deterrent against invasion or sudden attack, allowing U.S. allies to reduce overall defence expenditures.

No country exploited the United States more consistently than Canada within Cold War alliances. Successive Canadian governments saw the political symbolism of alliance membership as the main benefit and continued to allow Canadian military spending to decline in real terms while capabilities degraded. Without an expulsion clause in NATO, there was little that the United States or its allies could do to reverse the Canadian decline. It was up to the United States to make up the difference where Canada fell short, and although U.S. governments upbraided Canadian governments during this period, this only compounded the problem: Canadian politicians could reap the domestic political benefits of alliance membership 'on the cheap,' and also gain politically by being seen to resist U.S. pressure.

In 2008 the Canadian positions on participation in missile defence in North America and in the NATO mission in Afghanistan are having very different effects on Canada's two principal alliances with the United States, NATO and the North American Aerospace Defense Command (NORAD).

NORAD was established in 1957 to detect and counter attacks by Soviet bombers and, soon after, intercontinental ballistic missiles (ICBMs), and, later, cruise missiles. When bombers were the main threat, there was no question that U.S. and Canadian fighter jets would scramble in response to a violation of North American airspace and, if necessary, shoot down hostile aircraft to prevent an attack on American or Canadian cities. When missiles became the main threat, Canada remained committed to early detection and warning, but there was no means of responding to such an attack.

This conventional wisdom was challenged in 1987 as the United States began researching new technology to permit missiles to be shot down, and offered Canada the opportunity to participate in the development of deployable systems. Canada refused, showing its capacity for adopting an independent military security policy. The United States did not retaliate, and in fact continued to ask Canada to participate (thus giving Canada regular opportunities to refuse, and to renew the perception of policy independence).

As the first U.S. missile defence systems began to be successfully deployed, the United States hoped to have NORAD take responsibility for systems that would protect North America. However, Canada refused to participate in missile defence, maintaining its independence but weakening the rationale for NORAD, and the United States began shifting defence assets and responsibilities away from the joint command structure. Unlike air defences in a bygone era, current missile defence systems have been designed so that Canadian territory is not required for either sensors or interceptors. Canada's vast geography does not guarantee Canada a place in U.S. plans, or a veto over them.

In contrast, Canada's participation in NATO has been significantly increased through the NATO mission in Afghanistan. The value of NATO after the end of the Cold War was questioned in many capitals, including Washington. In Afghanistan NATO has undertaken its largest 'out of area' mission to date, and has performed well. Certain countries have offered token commitments or placed conditions on their commitments that keep their troops away from combat, but the Canadian Forces have taken on very dangerous assignments in rough country, and have suffered significant losses. Canada's independent security policy is strengthening NATO at a time when this alliance badly needs its members to be willing to undertake major burdens if it is to remain relevant.

In the area of military security policy, Canada has significant freedom of action and a high degree of dependence on the United States and other countries. Formal alliances have made the protection of others appear to be another Canadian choice, since Canada is never forced to reciprocate; Canadian governments are in a position to claim that they can maintain low defence expenditures and exempt Canada from missions with full freedom of action and at no risk to its alliance memberships. The United States and other Canadian allies have been complicit by not retaliating (except through periodic chastisement) against Canada for exploiting independence for domestic political gain; at the same time, the United States and other allies have taken Canadian policy into account in adjusting their own security policies (as in the case of missile defences).

Why have Canada's allies not complained more vociferously at the blatant injustice of this arrangement? Sadly, it was the United States that complained the loudest and most consistently during the Cold War with little effect. It gave and loaned equipment to Canada on generous terms (for example, building the Distant Early Warning, or DEW, Line stations in the Canadian arctic for free, and giving them to Canada to operate and maintain). Washington offered Canada a unique defence partnership, the NORAD agreement for the defence of continental air space. None of this was accepted without gratitude, but neither did such gestures reverse the slow decline of Canadian defence investments.

Over time, the expectations of Canada held by U.S. military planners and presidents fell precipitously, although they continued to hope that Canada might join in continental missile defences as late as 2004, when President George W. Bush made the public case for Canada to get involved in his visits to Ottawa and Halifax. Although the Cold War was won, the state of Canadian defence expenditure for its duration marked one of the greatest U.S. diplomatic failures of the period. Other NATO allies, as well as the United Nations (which relied on Canadian contributions for peacekeeping) chided and nudged Ottawa to do better, but if the United States as the leader of the western alliance and Canada's senior ally was unsuccessful despite its repeated exhortations, inducements, and pressures, it is not a surprise that others gave up on Canada more quickly.

Domestic Security

Domestic security, now referred to in the United States as homeland security, has become more important in 2008 than it was in 1968, when few would have included it in a discussion of Canadian defence. Yet the threat of terrorist attacks on North American soil has to be defended against through the use of intelligence, border inspection, and law-enforcement activity within each country under threat. Two features of domestic security are important when fighting terrorism. First, although foreign countries can help Canada, there is no substitute for Canadian efforts in monitoring threats and responding to risks within Canada. Second, as the al Qaeda attacks in 2001 demonstrate, terrorist groups are capable of planning attacks in one country and executing them in another. This means that the intelligence information that the Canadian government may require to prevent an attack on Canadian citizens could come from outside Canada; and that the protection of

American citizens and other non-Canadians from such attacks requires cooperation from Canada.

This simple fact reduces the capacity for, and the desirability of, an independent domestic security policy for Canada. Naturally, constitutional and other legal protections for civil liberties bind most Western countries to insist on sovereign control of activity within their territory. Yet the logic of cooperation is so powerful, following the nature of the threat from terrorism, that indulging independence for its own sake would be politically dangerous for any government.

Canadian policies since 11 September 2001 have reflected a full recognition of the need for cooperation in ensuring domestic security. The U.S.–Canada Integrated Border Enforcement Teams (IBETs) established at the suggestion of the Cross-Border Crime Forum in 1997 have been expanded across the country. The IBETs serve as joint task forces drawing law enforcement and intelligence agencies from across the federal governments and from state, provincial, and local governments as well. By 2003, thirteen IBETs had been established to cover the entire length of the border between Canada and the lower forty-eight states, and operate in both countries. Each IBET is named for the region it covers: Pacific, Okanagan, Rocky Mountain, Prairie, Red River, Superior, Detroit/Windsor, Niagara, Thousand Islands, St Lawrence Valley Central, Valleyfield, Champlain, Eastern, and Atlantic.[3]

Both the U.S. and Canadian governments work together on the border through the Free and Secure Trade program, building on the Customs-Trade Partnership Against Terrorism (C-TPAT) to obtain private-sector cooperation in reducing the risk of tampering with legitimate commerce. The two countries' customs authorities collaborate in the Container Security Initiative, with U.S. Customs inspectors working in the ports of Halifax, Montreal, and Vancouver and Canada Customs officers working in New York–New Jersey and Seattle-Tacoma. Teams in the Canadian Department of Finance and the U.S. Department of Treasury have worked closely to stop terrorist financing from moving through North American financial institutions, a difficult forensic task, and have shut down charitable organizations whose fund-raising had benefited terrorist groups.

Cooperation with Canada in the context of the U.S.-Canada Smart Border Action Plan has been necessary, but not sufficient to correct security weaknesses apparent since 9/11. Following the strong and specific recommendation of the bipartisan National Commission on Terrorist Attacks Upon the United States (informally known as the 9/11 Commission), Congress passed legislation to require that U.S. citizens present valid passports when returning from all foreign countries including Canada (where previously other identity documents were accepted by U.S. immigration officials). In 2005 Congress passed new federal mandates on states to improve the security of driver licences. These measures generated resistance from the Canadian government, which saw them as potentially inconvenient for Canadians and for Americans who crossed the border regularly. The U.S. Congress appropriated funds for the U.S. Departments of State and Homeland Security for a 'Western Hemisphere Travel Initiative.' which was to develop secure identity documents as alternatives to passports, and to increase the capacity for passport issuance in an effort to mitigate the effects of the passport requirement. The Martin and Harper governments lobbied for delays in implementation of the new rule and other changes, generating bewilderment and frustration on the part of Bush administration officials and showing that the two governments did not completely see eye-to-eye on border policy.

Since the perception of freedom of action is paramount for Canada, the mutuality of interdependence among countries in protecting their domestic populations against terrorist attacks is important. Whereas for military security, it requires effort to preserve the perception that Canada is not inappropriately dependent on others, for domestic security the United States itself has been forced to acknowledge interdependence. As a result, actual policy independence is illusory for all states. The goal for Canadian governments in domestic security, as in military security, is simply to avoid appearing to need too much help with basic security tasks.[4] The goal for governments in the United States is to show that they are doing everything necessary to protect their citizens. Listening to Canadian concerns in a spirit of neighbourliness is good politics for American officials, but they cannot accept a reduction in security levels to placate Canada.

Notwithstanding friction over domestic and border security, both countries have little option other than increasing their close cooperation in response to the increased risk of future terrorism in North America. Bilateral two-way trade is valued at more than $1.7 billion (in Canadian dollars) every day, a total of $626 billion in 2006.[5] September 11 security responses at the U.S.-Canada border resulted in a brief but expensive increase in commercial inspection and clearance times for trucks entering the United States from Canada; delays went from the normal one to two minutes to ten to fifteen hours.[6] Both governments have become keenly aware of the economic costs of a future disruption.

Nonetheless, the Chrétien government rejected U.S. proposals to develop a common security perimeter by upgrading the security screening of individuals and goods entering North America from the outside. The border with Canada was therefore an important line of defence where the U.S. government could act to protect its citizens. The effects of this action on cross-border commercial traffic were of secondary concern. Arguably, with a significant U.S. investment in infrastructure and personnel at the border, it is now too late to shift back to a perimeter approach entirely, despite recent suggestions from the Harper government that it would reconsider its position on perimeter screening.

The United States and the Quest for Security Policy Independence

In 1968 and in 2008 the perceived risk to Canadian security policy independence came from the United States. This brief review of Canada's policy independence in the areas of military security (mixed, but cosmetically good) and domestic security (less independence, but sovereignty secure) has shown that Canada remains capable of sustaining independent national-security policy positions and avoiding U.S. retaliation in both areas. Thus, the final questions to be addressed in this chapter on Canadian security policy independence are, what U.S. policy-makers think about Canada's exercise of autonomy, and whether the threat of terrorism altered the calculus in Washington such that there may be an effort to limit Canada's freedom of action in the near future.

U.S. strategies for military and domestic security have taken different approaches. For military security planning, the U.S. policy emphasizes the 'unipolar moment' and freedom of action against attempts by rival states and even allies to check the exercise of American power.[7] Ad hoc coalitions have been favoured over alliances, at least initially, for military action during the Bush administration; in its aftermath, burden sharing by other countries and even the United Nations is welcomed for stabilization and reconstruction work. For domestic security, U.S. planners have viewed foreign governments as either partners or as enablers of terrorist groups; most countries, such as Canada, fall into the former category, and their ability to provide intelligence and cooperation is highly valued.[8]

In 2008 the world has entered into what Benjamin and Simon have called the 'Age of Sacred Terror'[9] and Podhoretz has termed 'World

War IV.'[10] The skill with which terrorists have exploited the openness of Western societies in order to kill civilians creates a different kind of threat. Asymmetric warfare against terrorist cells requires close co-operation in intelligence-gathering, counter-insurgency tactics, law enforcement, and counter-terrorist operations. The increased sense of vulnerability in the United States to terrorist attacks led Bush administration policy-makers to take steps to develop an independent security policy of its own after 11 September 2001, which in the American context meant reducing dependence on others except where necessary.

In North America, the Bush administration established a new command structure for U.S. military operations, similar to those in place for other regions of the world. The U.S. Northern Command (NORTH-COM) now plans and coordinates U.S. defence in North America in the same way that Southern Command (SOUTHCOM) organizes U.S. military activity in Latin America and the Caribbean. It is not a treaty or alliance, but a division of the American military.

In 2005 Canada established a new Canada Command to organize and plan military activities within Canadian territory. U.S. NORTHCOM and Canada Command work together closely, but unlike with NORAD, there is no joint command structure uniting the two militaries.[11] Measured in terms of freedom of action, Canada is thus more independent in its military security policy in the North American theatre than it has been at any time since 1957. So, too, is the United States.

However, U.S. NORTHCOM protects the continent from missile attacks, defends American and Canadian satellites, and engages the U.S. Navy off the Atlantic, Pacific, and Arctic coasts of North America, all without a Canadian voice in command decisions (although in some limited cases consultations may be triggered under old NORAD protocols). In effect, but without attracting attention from most Canadians, Canada has become more dependent on U.S. protection because governments in Ottawa have freely chosen not to protect, or to participate in the protection of, Canadians from missile threats and to 'free ride' on American technology and expenditure. Yet with the capacity to distinguish between attacks on U.S. and Canadian targets and strong public pressure on the U.S. military to protect Americans first in the event of missile attacks, Canada may be getting exactly what it is paying for in terms of missile defence protection: nothing.

In 1968 this sort of Canadian behaviour would have prompted steady pressure from the United States for Ottawa to reconsider its position. In February 2000, U.S. Deputy Secretary of Defense John J.

Hamre remarked that the United States might be the only country in history that wanted a stronger military power on its borders.[12] This comment reflected the thinking of most American policy-makers during the Cold War, but also a sense that Canadian attitudes towards burden-sharing and U.S. security concerns after the Cold War were making continued close cooperation impossible.[13]

In 2008 the outlook for some U.S. defence planners is different. To combat groupthink, Pentagon strategists form teams of analysts identified by colours (e.g., red, yellow, blue) to consider potential threats from different angles. The teams compete, challenging one another's arguments and recommendations. The result is not a consensus, but leads to a final decision taken by the President, Secretary of Defense, or other senior civilian leaders.

To borrow from the colourful U.S. defence planning approach, immediately after the 11 September attacks it was possible to discern two rival camps among U.S. policy-makers regarding Canada: a 'red team' that sought to prepare to meet 100 per cent of any risk with U.S. resources and to welcome Canada's contributions as supplemental afterward; and a 'blue team' that argued for incentives to coax larger contributions from Canada than the red approach was expected to produce.[14]

On military security, the parallelism of U.S. NORTHCOM and Canada Command suggests that the red team approach has won out. At least for the Bush administration, the red team approach meant reducing apparent dependence on Canada for North American defence. One military analyst wrote that the United States today might even prefer a weaker Canada:

> For the United States, Canada epitomizes friendliness – not because Canadians themselves are friendly (although they are) but because Ottawa poses no hint of a threat and entertains no illusions about who wields the upper hand when it comes to Canadian-American relations. The United States will never feel fully secure until the world consists of nations like Canada, both genuinely free and reliably acquiescent.[15]

This comment demonstrates the advantage of a red team approach to the military relationship: the less dependent the United States is on Canada for what it considers essential, the less pressure it will place on Canada to share military burdens; and the less the U.S. pressures Canada, the easier it is for Ottawa to claim freedom of action in setting its own goals, and even joining coalitions and accepting alliance missions such as that in Afghanistan. There is also less temptation now for Ottawa to rebuke the United States publicly to show independence. It has been observed that this may be a healthier foundation for the bilateral relationship on military security than the dynamic leftover from the Cold War.[16]

There is still concern about the military security relationship between Canada and the United States with regard to expeditionary missions outside North America. The concern is whether Canadian governments will develop an approach to military security based on national interest that would see missions such as that in Afghanistan as essential to Canadian security.[17] This approach to independence, reducing by even just a little the degree of Canadian dependence on others for international peace and security, would be welcomed by Canada's allies. Meanwhile, a former Canadian defence minister recently argued that Canada should incorporate plans for increasing military capabilities into a new grand strategy for Canadian foreign policy outside North America[18] because the United States can no longer be relied upon to establish a grand strategy framework that Canadian foreign policy could supplement. Given the debate in the United States about the Bush administration's robust new grand strategy for fighting global terrorism,[19] the argument that the United States does not currently have a grand strategy seems to be ill founded and strangely uninformed, but it hardly matters to Washington. The U.S. red team strategy ensures that if Canada does not change its policy, for whatever reason, U.S. security will not suffer.

On domestic security, the approach of the United States has followed the blue team model, with incentives for Canadian contributions above the bare minimum. A dramatic red team approach to domestic security, such as a U.S. invasion of Canada similar to Israeli incursions into Lebanon, is not a practical or necessary option. The United States can and will continue to take actions that Canadian governments disagree with, such as mandating the use of passports by its citizens travelling abroad. But this is an exercise of its domestic sovereignty, and should not be read as an example of the red team approach, since no Canadian contribution to implementing this policy is necessary.

The most concrete example of blue team security strategy has been the Security and Prosperity Partnership (SPP), launched in Waco, Texas, in March 2005. Through the SPP, Canada and Mexico get annual leaders' summits with the United States, engagement from U.S. cabinet-level officials in a trilateral, interagency negotiating process that, while not institutionalized (and thus, a 'coalition of the willing') is open-ended.[20] The logic of the blue approach is more compelling in domestic security, where interdependence is strongest. Just as Canada reduced the appearance of dependence through alliances designed to portray members as helping one another, the United States is settling for the perception of independence in the form of freedom of choice.

The goal of independence in national security policy in an interdependent world characterized by globalization and transnational terrorist networks is attainable only in perception and dreams. The high degree of integration between the United States and Canada that existed in 1968, and which is even deeper today, makes it pointless to debate whether the United States can act without reliance on allies, including Canada, for material or moral support. In contrast to perceived freedom of action, actual freedom from dependence in a world that is increasingly interdependent is a holy grail, not a realistic option for Canada, or even the United States. It is thanks to North American integration that this is just as true for the United States in 2008 as it was for Canada in 1968.

Ironically, now that both sides are pretending to have independent security policies, it may make U.S.-Canada security cooperation easier. Complicity in keeping up appearances may be a strange basis for a security alliance, but it is not uncommon among friends.

NOTES

1 Pauline Jewett, A.F.W. Plumptre, Abraham Rothstein, and A.E. Safarian, 'Retaliation: The Price of Independence?' in *An Independent Foreign Policy for Canada?* ed. Stephen Clarkson (Toronto: McClelland & Stewart, 1968), 43–56.

2 Dwight N. Mason, 'Canada Alert: Canada and the U.S. Missile Defense System,' *CSIS Hemisphere Focus*, 9 January 2004.

3 United States, 'Integrated Border Enforcement Teams Now Cover Canada-U.S. Border from Coast To Coast,' press release, 19 November 2003 (Washington: U.S. Department of Justice).

4 Patrick Lennox, '"Defence against Help": Canada and Transnational Security after 9/11,' in *Revolution or Evolution? Emerging Threats to Security in the 21st Century*, ed. Riley Hennessey and Alexandre S. Wilner (Halifax: Centre for Foreign Policy Studies, Dalhousie University, 2005); see also his 'From Golden Straightjacket to Kevlar Vest: Canada's Transformation to a Security State,' *Canadian Journal of Political Science* 40, no. 4 (December 2007): 1017–38.

5 Canada, 'Table 13: Goods by Georgraphic Area, Annual' in *Canada's Balance of International Payments: System of National Accounts Second Quarter 2007*, Statistics Canada catalog no. 67-001. http://www.statcan.ca/english/ freepub/67-001-XIE/2007002/t017_en.htm (accessed 10 September 2007).

6 Peter Andreas, 'A Tale of Two Borders: The U.S.-Canada and U.S.-Mexico Lines after 9/11,' in *The Rebordering of North America*, ed. Peter Andreas and Thomas J. Biersteker (New York: Routledge, 2003), 1–23.

7 United States, *The National Security Strategy of the United States of America*. (Washington: The White House, 2006).

8 United States, *The National Strategy for Homeland Security* (Washington: Office of Homeland Security, 2002).

9 Daniel Benjamin and Steven Simon, *The Age of Sacred Terror: Radical Islam's War against America* (New York: Randon House, 2002)

10 Norman Podhoretz, *World War IV: The Long Struggle against Islamofascism.* New York: Doubleday, 2007.

11 Devin Fisher, 'Canada's New Chief of Defence Staff Visits NORAD, USNORTHCOM,' *USNORTHCOM News*, 25 April 2005.

12 John J. Hamre, 'Address to the Calgary Chamber of Commerce,' as delvered by the Deputy Secretary of Defense (Washington), available at http://www.defenselink.mil/speeches/speech.aspx?speechid=531 (accessed 3 March 2008).

13 Joseph T. Jockel and Joel J. Sokolsky, 'The End of the Canada–U.S. Defense Relationship,' CSIS Policy Papers on the Americas, 1996.

14 Christopher Sands, 'Canadian National Security after 9/11: What Does the United States Expect?' *Canadian American Strategic Review* (Simon Fraser University) 1 (August 2002).

15 Andrew J. Bacevich, 'No Disrespect to Canada ...,' *The National Interest* no. 90 (July/August 2007): 12–13.

16 Kim Richard Nossal, 'Defense Policy and the Atmospherics of Canada-U.S. Relations: The Case of the Harper Conservatives,' *American Review of Canadian Studies* 37, no. 1 (Spring 2007): 23–34.

17 J.L. Granatstein, *Whose War Is It? How Canada Can Survive in the Post 9/11 World*, (Toronto: HarperCollins Publishers Ltd, 2007).

18 David Pratt, 'Is There a Grand Strategy in Canadian Foreign Policy?' *Policy Options*, September 2007: 6–11.

19 John Lewis Gaddis, *Surprise, Security, and the American Experience* (Cambridge, MA: Harvard University Press, 2004.)

20 Greg Anderson and Christopher Sands, 'Negotiating North America: The Security and Prosperity Partnership,' *Hudson Institute White Paper*, Fall 2007.

6 Walking and Talking Independence in the Canadian North

ROB HUEBERT

This chapter examines the relationship between Canada and the United States in the Arctic. In thinking about Canadian independence and dependence in the Arctic one immediately faces the problem of attempting to determine what independence means, what independent action looks like, and whether or not independent action is possible, or even desirable.

In the original *IFPC?* volume, Stephen Clarkson defined an independent Canadian foreign policy as one that is made by Canadians for Canadian interests. In the introduction he asked what caused the lack of a Canadian independent foreign policy: was it that the United States did not allow Canada to act independently, or was it because domestically Canada lacked the strength to pursue an effective, independent foreign policy? Ultimately, Clarkson came to the conclusion that Canadian dependence is best represented by 'quiet diplomacy.' He made it clear that Canadian policy-makers and diplomats have found it easier to deal with Canadian foreign policy issues with the United States through a 'back-door' approach instead of spending the necessary resources to think through the problems for themselves. While 'quiet diplomacy' of this nature tended to ensure that Canadian issues were heard by the Americans, it also meant that Canadian foreign policy would be meek. Clarkson accordingly advocated a Canadian foreign policy that was not based on 'quiet diplomacy' and was more assertive in challenging the United States.

Of all the issues in Canada–U.S. relations, Arctic sovereignty is the one on which Canadian leaders have been most assertive with their U.S. counterparts. Indeed, it would appear that Arctic sovereignty is the one issue in Canada–U.S. relations over which successive governments in Ottawa have not shied away from talking an 'independent' line. Walking an independent line, however, is a much different matter, as this chapter will explore.

Land Disputes

In the period between 1945 and the middle of the 1960s, Canada and the United States prepared their joint defences against a possible attack by the USSR.[1] Canada faced the challenge that while it agreed with the United States about the Soviet threat, officials in Ottawa tended to downplay its severity.[2] Nevertheless, there was mutual agreement in both Ottawa and Washington that precautions had to be taken against a Soviet attack from the north. The Americans began to build airstrips and other associated infrastructure in the Canadian north. When the Soviet Union acquired nuclear weapons and developed long-range bombers and then intercontinental missiles, both Canada and the United States recognized the need for developing a defensive shield across the Canadian north that included fighter aircraft bases and electronic warning systems.[3]

The challenge for Canada in this period was that while it accepted that the USSR was a threat to Western security, it was concerned over the increase in American activity in its own backyard. Yet, on its own, Canada could not provide the necessary resources to defend the continent against the threat from above. Canadian concerns were periodically heightened when various American officials would muse about the possibility of 'taking control' of Canadian territory to allow them to better prepare the defences against the Soviet threat.[4] Both Canada and the United States agreed to the construction of a line of radar sites that spanned from the westernmost tip of Alaska, across all of northern Canada to Greenland, which became known as the Distant Early Warning (DEW) Line. The issues that developed between Canada and the United States were ultimately resolved. The United States paid for and built most of the DEW Line, then passed to Canada control over the components located in its national territory.

There is some controversy in the growing literature on early Cold War defence cooperation in the north, but it is clear that Canadian sovereignty concerns about the land it claimed in the Arctic were respected by the Americans.[5] While there may have been some Americans who thought about annexing some of the Canadian north that was uninhabited and seemingly ignored by the Canadian government, it was clear that the main American concern was to develop a shared system that defended against a possible Soviet air attack and warned of a possible missile strike. If the systems developed responded to these requirements, the Americans were satisfied.

In many ways the Canadian government's approach during this period can be seen as quite shrewd. It was able to ensure that its security against the Soviet threat was protected, but it also was able to ensure that its own sovereignty was not challenged by the United States. Furthermore, once the Americans had built and paid for the bulk of the system, and then transferred it to Canada, Ottawa had an improved ability to assert control over the region. Thus, it acquired new instruments to know what was happening in its north and was therefore better prepared to protect Canadian sovereignty. And it had gotten someone else to foot the bill!

Whether luck or skill allowed Canadian officials to gain so much for Canadian sovereignty and security while doing so little themselves is an open question. It is hard to suggest that this was the result of careful policy development. The assessment of most of those who have examined this era is that the driving force for Canadian officials was to limit American control as cheaply as possible.[6]

A paradox thus arises. Canadian 'independence' on this issue existed as long as it ultimately went along with the American will. If Canada had 'independently' opted for a 'neutral' position and refused U.S. requests, then it is reasonable to expect the Americans would have taken a more assertive position about what they wanted done in the region. But what would that have been? Would the United States have treated Canada as the USSR treated Finland, allowing it independence over its domestic policies, but maintaining a veto over its foreign and defence policies? Or would it simply have annexed the Arctic territory it deemed necessary for its security, as Canada, the United Kingdom, and the United States did to Iceland during the Second World War?

The real issue comes back ultimately to Canadian core interests. It was never in Canada's interests to refuse American requests to build a defensive system against the USSR for the mere sake of being able to say no to Washington. The USSR posed a real and direct threat against all Western states, Canada included.[7] Canada needed to be able to defend against and deter the USSR. Thus, it was acting cooperatively, but not necessarily dependently, by allowing the United States to build the bulk of the northern defences.

Maritime Disputes

All the contemporary disputes between Canada and the United States concern Arctic maritime zones. The most widely known dispute is over the status of the Northwest Passage.[8] The United States has maintained since 1969 that the passage is an international strait, while Canada's position is that the passage is part of Canada's historic internal waters. The predominant implication of this legal distinction centres on the control of international shipping. If the Americans are correct, Canada cannot stop international maritime traffic from transiting the passage. If the Canadian position is correct, then Canada has the right to grant or deny permission to whomever it wishes. However, despite the limited scope of the issue (i.e., it only affects international shipping), this dispute has achieved an emotional status within Canada, and is known popularly as the 'Arctic sovereignty dispute.'

This dispute began in 1969 following the discovery of oil along the north slope of Alaska. Once this discovery was found to be substantial, the Americans needed to determine the best means of bringing the oil to market. The two main options considered were to build a pipeline north to south across Alaska or to ship the oil out by tanker in the summer months. To test the feasibility of shipping the oil by tanker through the Northwest Passage, the American company Humble Oil (later to become Exxon) chartered a supertanker that it modified for use in ice-covered waters. The U.S. Coast Guard provided an ice-breaker to escort this vessel through the Northwest Passage from the east coast to the north coast of Alaska.

The Canadian response was to grant its 'permission' to the Americans and to send a Canadian ice-breaker to assist in the voyage.[9] The Americans stated that they did not need to ask for Canadian permission: they had the right to transit the passage. However, they were happy to receive the assistance of the extra ice-breaker. The voyage proved to be much more difficult than expected. Without the assistance of the Canadian ice-breaker and information on ice conditions provided by the Canadian Ice Service there is serious doubt that the transit would have been successful. The next year the Americans made the return voyage, travelling west to east. Once again it was very difficult. The net effect of the challenges of making the voyage convinced the Americans that the construction of the pipeline was the preferable means of transporting the Alaskan oil.

However, the ramifications of the American refusal to concede Canadian control of the passage resulted in widespread public concern. In the summer of 1969 the voyage became front-page news in Canada. It became clear to the recently elected Trudeau government that it needed to take action. There were those in the Cabinet who believed that the best course of action would be to declare Canadian sovereign control over the passage.[10] However, this course of action was deemed too provocative. Trudeau himself believed that international law did not support such action. Instead, the government opted for a more innovative but less challenging route. They declared that the harsh climatic conditions and sensitive ecology of the Arctic required special protection. To do so, the Canadian government enacted the Arctic Waters Pollution Prevention Act (AWPPA). The focus of the act was to give Canada the power to unilaterally require all foreign vessels (and domestic ones) to follow Canadian marine environmental regulations. It was hoped that this action would be seen as less provocative than if the government had simply declared its right to control all aspects of shipping in its northern waters. Thus, the Canadian government was attempting to assert functional sovereignty.

At the same time, the Trudeau government also mounted a campaign to seek international support for its actions.[11] Canada called for a meeting of Arctic nations, but Soviet suspicions and American coolness prevented such a meeting from occurring. However, the Canadian government was successful in incorporating the international need for better northern maritime environmental protection into the ongoing negotiations for the Law of the Sea that were conducted throughout the 1970s. Ultimately, when negotiations were completed in 1982, Canada's efforts were rewarded with the inclusion of article 234 into the final draft of the United Nations Convention of the Law of the Sea (UNCLOS). Known either as the Canadian article or the Ice-Covered Waters article, article 234 gave states with maritime regions that were ice-covered for most of the year the right to unilaterally create stronger environmental regulations for activity in such waters. However, any such rules needed to be applied in a non-discriminatory fashion and could not favour domestic shippers. Canadian officials believed that the inclusion of this clause gave them international recognition of their control over the Northwest Passage through the AWPPA.

However, while the act appears to require all international and domestic vessels to comply, the reality is quite different. In order to ensure compliance with the act the Government of Canada created a reporting system titled the Vessel Traffic Reporting Arctic Canada Traffic Zone (NORDREG). Vessels entering Canadian Arctic waters are expected to report to a Canadian Coast Guard Marine and Communications Traffic Service centre. At this point the ship's captain is supposed to provide information to let Canadian officials know if it meets the requirements of the AWPPA. If the ship's captain complies, the vessel will be allowed to sail into Canadian Arctic waters. If s/he does not, the vessel is presumably denied entry, thus demonstrating Canadian control of the waters. The problem with this system is that NORDREG is voluntary. Ships are only encouraged, not required to report. What makes this situation even more problematic is the lack of surveillance capabilities. Canada does not have the ability to know if a ship is entering its waters without reporting unless it is lucky and one of its few air or sea assets stumbles across the foreign vessel. However, this may be soon changing. In August 2008 Prime Minister Harper announced his government's intention to make the reporting system mandatory for all vessels entering Canadian Arctic waters.

While the Trudeau government acted in an innovative manner by creating the AWPPA and then pursuing international acceptance of it though the UNCLOS, it never bothered to develop the tools necessary to ensure that Canadian officials knew what was going on in its waters. Thus, the government pretended that it was requiring international shipping to submit to Canadian jurisdiction, but was never willing to spend the money necessary to ensure that this was happening.

The American government protested the AWPPA through a démarche, but did nothing else.[12] It is unlikely that the existence of a much stronger Canadian response would have created a stronger American position. It is difficult to think of what the Americans could have done, beyond issuing a diplomatic protest, had Canada made the NORDREG system mandatory and provided the means for its enforcement. Even more to the point, it is also likely that, had Canada invested in equipment at the time to improve its surveillance and enforcement capability, the Americans would have viewed such action in a positive light. While Canada would have done so under the requirements of improving its sovereignty, the Americans would have viewed it as important for the defence against the USSR. This suggests that Canada was free to defend the Canadian Arctic much more robustly than it chose to.

The next chapter in this dispute began in the winter of 1984. The Americans have requirements for their coast guard ice-breaking fleet to provide services in the eastern and the western Arctic. At this time the western Arctic was serviced by the USCGC *Polar Sea*, which was home-ported in Seattle. Specifically, it was required to service various research projects in the waters north of Alaska. The main requirement in the eastern Arctic was the annual resupply to the military base in Thule, Greenland, which was normally done by the USCGC *Northwind*. This vessel was older, and when it went in for normal servicing in the fall of 1984, significant mechanical problems were found. The decision was made not to spend the resources to fix the problems and the vessel was retired. This left the Americans with the problem of meeting both of their commitments with only one vessel. Canada was approached with a request to provide the resupply to the Thule base. Its Auxiliary Oil and Replenishment (AOR) supply vessels had a limited ice-strengthened capability and one of them could have made the voyage. But all had been committed and the Canadian government declined to use them.[13]

Senior American coast guard officials then met with their Canadian counterparts to see if an alternative arrangement could be made. While there was time for the *Polar Sea* to travel from Seattle through the Panama Canal and then proceed to Thule, there was not enough time for it to return the same way to make its commitments in Alaska. The Americans were aware of the political sensitivities of sailing through the Northwest Passage and asked the Canadians if they could still do this. They offered to issue a statement in which both sides would agree that the voyage was only for operational needs and would in no way prejudice either side's position. An agreement was reached by late winter and the voyage seemed set to go. However, when both the Canadian media and senior officials from External Affairs learned of the forthcoming voyage, a political storm ensued. The media presented the voyage as an effort by the Americans to undermine Canadian sovereignty, while External Affairs dissociated itself from the earlier agreement and demanded that the United States ask permission. The Americans did not do so, but Canada still 'granted' permission and once again sent one of its ice-breakers to sail with the *Polar Sea*.[14]

This incident illustrates the political and sensitive nature of the issue. Senior members of the Canadian government should have understood what the Americans needed to do when the initial request to resupply Thule was made.[15] But the fact that no one had appreciated the likely impact of not being able to handle the request shows that there was no capacity (or desire) to understand actions taken in the north. Thus, the Canadian government was independent enough to be able to say no to the American request for a resupply to Thule, but did not seem to understand the full consequences of such actions.

Ultimately the voyage went ahead. But it created a large media and public outcry, which in turn led Mulroney's Conservative government to want to 'do something.' That something was a six-part policy platform announced in September 1985. Of these promises, the government moved quickly to implement three that did not require new resources: (1) declaring straight baselines to enclose the Arctic; (2) ensuring passage of the Canada's Law Offshore Application Act; and (3) removing Canada's reservation to the International Court of Justice on its claim to the Northwest Passage.[16] Of the three actions requiring new resources, only one was actually completed. The promised Polar 8 ice-breaker was cancelled within four years. The pledge to extend and enhance the military's capacity for air and sea sovereignty patrols amounted to virtually nothing. While there was a marginal increase in air overflights, there was no meaningful increase in capability, except for the purchase of three additional stripped-down Aurora long-range patrol aircraft, called Arctus. The government considered buying nuclear-powered submarines, but these were deemed to be too expensive and also abandoned.

The last of the six promises was the commitment to negotiate a deal with the Americans over the use of the Northwest Passage. Considerable political and diplomatic effort went into the negotiations. After two years, direct discussions between Prime Minister Brian Mulroney and President Ronald Reagan led to the Arctic Waters Cooperation Agreement of 1988. The agreement starts by stating that it does not prejudice the position of either state on the status of the passage. It then states that the United States will ask the consent of Canada when it wants to send its ice-breakers through it. Canada in turn is expected to give that consent. Although a limited agreement, it did ensure that there would be no repeat of the 1985 crisis over the sailing of a small fleet (two vessels at the time).

The issue then receded from public attention until the beginning of the 2000s. At this time there was a growing awareness that climate change was transforming the Arctic. Specifically, as global temperatures increased, the ice cover of the Arctic was melting. As the ice melted, the possibility of using the Northwest Passage as a navigable route for surface vessels was seen as an increasing possibility. In the minds of the Canadian public and media there was a renewed sense of the need to take action.

Paul Martin's Liberal government engaged in studies to determine the seriousness of this challenge. In its foreign and defence policy papers – Canada's International Policy Statement – there was a recognition that Canada faced a future where there would be increased international use of its Arctic waters. Under Martin, the Canadian government did restart visits by Canadian naval vessels to the north as well as reinitiating northern defence exercises. It also seemed to make a decision that its new replenishment vessels would be given some abilities to operate in limited ice conditions.

During the 2005–6 federal election, the Conservative Party under Stephen Harper made the protection of Canadian Arctic sovereignty an election issue.[17] Following their electoral success, the Conservative government began to develop plans to improve Canada's limited ability to enforce its will in the Arctic. These have included the promise to build six to eight Arctic Coastal Patrol vessels and nine large icebreakers, building a resupply port in Nanisivik and an Arctic training base at Resolute Bay, and the commitment to make NORDREG mandatory.

If the Canadian government follows through on these initiatives, they will represent an important improvement of Canada's ability to monitor and enforce its jurisdiction in the Northwest Passage. What is most striking about this flurry of new activities has been the almost complete silence from the United States, which has not questioned, condemned, or supported any of these Canadian initiatives. Periodically the serving American ambassador will be asked his opinion on the status of the disagreement over the passage, and the standard response is that the United States continues to disagree with Canada. But the Americans have not mounted a campaign to undermine the Canadian efforts, nor have they offered any public statements attempting to build support for their position. Rather, the United States is remarkably silent on the entire issue, which suggests that Canada has the latitude to be much more assertive than it has been. Thus, one cannot help but conclude that Canada has always had the ability to both walk and talk 'independently' from the United States on this issue of Arctic sovereignty.

Emergent Shelf Disputes

While the Northwest Passage issue tends to dominate the Arctic sovereignty discussion in Canada, another related issue has begun to attract the interest of the Canadian government and the general public. In the summer of 2007 the Russian government sent a mini-submersible to the North Pole and planted a flag on the sea bottom. At the same time, extensive media attention was given to Russian efforts to map the seabed of the Arctic and, in particular, an underwater feature known as the Lomonosov Ridge.[18]

The Russian activities have been inspired by the new rights given to coastal states by the UNCLOS. Negotiated between 1973 and 1982, UNCLOS is a comprehensive international treaty that codified existing international maritime law and created new means of controlling and regulating the oceans and their resources. One new concept created by the convention was that of the continental shelf. At its simplest level, this is the extension of the land area of the continent that happens to be under water. If the continental shelf of a coastal state extends beyond the 200-nautical-mile Exclusive Economic Zone (EEZ) (also created by UNCLOS), the coastal states are allowed by the new treaty to claim – up to a distance of 350 nautical miles – the right to the resources on the seabed and subsoil. This means that any oil and gas in this area are controlled by the coastal state. Under the terms of article 76 (which creates this zone), the coastal state must first scientifically determine that it has a continental shelf that goes beyond its EEZ. Then it must submit its claim within ten years of ratifying the convention.[19] This means that any oil and gas in this area are controlled by the coastal state. The Russian government ratified UNCLOS in 1997 and was therefore required to submit its claim by 2007. Moscow submitted a formal claim in December of 2001, but the Commission on the Limits of the Continental Shelf (CLCS) determined that it would need additional scientific information in support of the submission. The Russians engaged in further research and there are reports that they submitted new information in 2008, but there is still much uncertainty surrounding the status of the Russian claim.

There are four circumpolar nations – Russia, Canada, the United States, and Denmark (for Greenland) – that can make a continental shelf claim under UNCLOS. Norway can also claim some of the Arctic Ocean, but its ability to go to the pole is blocked by the geographic position of Russia. Of the remaining states, Canada ratified UNCLOS in 2003 and Denmark in 2004. The United States has not yet ratified it. In theory, all the bordering states must make their claim and submit it to the CLCS, which then reviews the claims on the basis of their hydrographic findings. The CLCS in effect checks the science of the submitting state. It is then up to the states themselves to resolve any overlaps that may exist with their neighbours' claims.

The American refusal to ratify UNCLOS is the result of inertia within the U.S. domestic political system. In 1982 the newly elected Reagan government took issue with part 11 of the convention. This section attempted to establish a resource-sharing mechanism for deep seabed mining. The idea was to create a principle of 'the Common Heritage of Mankind,' which would allow the developing world to share in the exploitation of minerals that were expected to be mined beyond national jurisdiction in the high seas. The new administration viewed this as an unfair economic practice, which would hurt U.S. industries wishing to exploit these resources. Under pressure from the United States (which had quiet support from the newly elected Mulroney government), the international community agreed to renegotiate part 11 of the convention. By the middle 1990s agreement was reached that effectively nullified the efforts to provide for a shared development of these resources. The irony is that no company has pursued the development of these minerals since the costs are still too high. But even more troubling is the fact that despite getting its way on this issue, the United States still has not ratified the treaty. Both the Bill Clinton and George W. Bush administrations have talked about the need to accede to the treaty, but neither has been able to gain the Senate support necessary to accomplish the task. It is not entirely clear why some Republican senators are still opposed, but it would appear that they continue to labour under the impression that the United States did not succeed in removing the application of the Common Heritage principle for deep seabed mining.[20]

The four states will soon face the problem of resolving possible overlaps of their individual claims. UNCLOS only came into effect in 1994, and since that time its dispute settlement provisions are largely untested. Thus it is not known how the four will settle their differences. Furthermore, the fact that the United States has not ratified UNCLOS has created a great deal of uncertainty around the entire process. It is not clear how the three parties to the treaty need to proceed once they have completed the studies of their regions; nor is it clear what potential American disagreement with the three states' remaining claims will mean. Canada does not yet know what its own or the American claim will be, if they will overlap, and what could be done to resolve the resulting policy frictions.

The problem for Canada is clear. Despite being a major contributor to the creation of UNCLOS in the period 1973 to 1982, and therefore being fully aware of the need to determine the limits of its continental shelf, it was not until the Chrétien government's second last budget in 2004 that funds were allocated to accomplish the task. Furthermore, Canada is the only nation among the four that does not have access to a nuclear-powered submarine to assist in this task. (The Danes have entered into an agreement with the United Kingdom to use one of their submarines to assist in their efforts).

Ultimately, the problem facing Canada can again be traced to its refusal to act independently in the Arctic. The Americans have not been able to proceed on developing their claim because of their internal politics surrounding UNCLOS. Canadian leaders have been well aware of what was required of them since 1982. Although Canada did not ratify UNCLOS until 2003, eventual ratification was known to be a certainty well before this date. Yet Canada did not allocate the needed resources to begin its determination of its claim until 2004. Thus, it now finds itself significantly behind an increasingly aggressive Russia. In theory, Russia has to wait to resolve any disagreement with its neighbours before it can begin the economic development of its shelf. But because Canada has been so slow in determining its position, it is not even known if the Russian claim does cross over into Canada's, let alone whether Russia will wait.

The third area of dispute between Canada and the United States is with respect to continental shelf issues. During the UNCLOS negotiations, it became clear that the treaty was going to create a new maritime zone of control for coastal states now known as the Exclusive Economic Zone. The EEZ gave coastal states the rights over the living and non-living resources found in their offshore region to a distance of 200 nautical miles from their coastline. As the negotiations developed, nations including Canada and the United States rushed to extend their jurisdiction even before the treaty was completed. This created a disagreement in the Beaufort Sea.[21] Canada and the United States selected different (but equally acceptable in international terms) means for determining their maritime boundary. The Canadian government chose to extend the land boundary between the Yukon and Alaska. The Americans decided to create their version of the boundary by drawing a line ninety-degrees perpendicular to the coast line. Not surprisingly, each technique favours the country that put it forward. The net effect, however, is to create a disputed area that resembles a triangle. Contained within this triangle may be significant oil and gas resources, a potentiality that raises the stakes of the dispute and accordingly makes it more difficult to resolve.

Since the late 1970s Canada and the United States have both made competing claims to be able to regulate the area, with each side's claims meeting with diplomatic protest from the other side. But the collapse of oil and gas development in the Arctic at the end of the 1970s has meant that both states could afford to ignore the problem because no oil company was willing to develop the area. The recent rise of oil and gas prices, however, in combination with the expectation of more accessible sites as the ice of the Northwest Passage recedes under the pressure of global climate change, has created a new round of anticipation that resource development in the area could occur. Thus, since 2002, the U.S. Department of the Interior has been offering lease rights in the zone. Currently no oil company has opted to bid on one of the sites. But it is only a matter of time until this happens. At that point, Canada will be faced with a major political and diplomatic challenge.

Given the political sensitivities that erupted over Denmark's claim to the economically unimportant and physically small Hans Island, it is easy to speculate that American oil and gas development in Arctic territory claimed by Canada will cause a major public outcry. This will indeed be the test of Canadian independence. The government will face tremendous pressure to defend Canadian interests. But the Americans have shown that they will always mount a strong defence of their energy security. Of course, if Ottawa was willing to take the initiative, it could attempt to develop a joint management scheme with the Americans to develop the resources in the disputed zone. This could mitigate the worst elements of a dispute by sharing the resources. However there is no sign that anyone is thinking that far ahead. Nor is there a guarantee that such a move would not be seen as a sell-out by the Canadian public. The paradox of such a move would be that while taking the action would be an act of independence, and the result of the action would be an act of interdependence, there is a danger that it would be seen as an act of dependence!

One last word needs to be said about a final complicating factor for the development of the Canadian position. Since Canada has a federal system that is reliant on its bureaucracy, there have been and continue to be different positions on what Canada should do to protect its Arctic sovereignty. The Department of National Defence is now slated to become the department with the largest numbers of physical assets to protect Canadian sovereignty. It also is the only government department that makes a sustained effort to teach its mid-level personnel to think about the issue as a matter of routine training. As such there are many in the forces who tend to favour an assertive Canadian position on the issues. However, there are also some who believe that the Arctic is not the region where DND should be spending its limited resources. At the same time, the Department of Foreign Affairs seems to believe that each of the main Arctic issues should be treated as unique. Therefore, the department tends to believe that the issues are not serious and can ultimately be resolved by patience and diplomacy. The dire financial circumstances in which the coast guard continues to find itself mean that it seldom has the ability to examine the issue carefully. Instead, it is forced to simply put all its efforts into maintaining its operations in the north. Finally, the territories have also begun to develop positions on the issue.[22] Thus, it is easy to find serious differences over the issue.

Still, when the federal government does take the time to plan and act, these bureaucratic differences disappear. When the government decided to act on the issue of Hans Island, the various bureaucracies came together to arrange for the landing of Canadian troops and the defence minister on the island. Departments can and often do disagree when there is a lack of direction from above, but when political leadership is demonstrated, these differences disappear.

Conclusion

Arctic sovereignty is often popularly portrayed as one of the areas where a bullying United States forces its will upon a subordinate Canada. While it is clear that there are significant differences between the formal positions of the two countries on this issue, a close examination paints a different picture. The picture that emerges is, rather, one in which successive Canadian governments are determined to avoid the suggestion that they are being weak relative to the United States. Talking the tough talk of independence, Canadian governments have been equally determined not to back up this talk with the resources needed to defend the north. It does not seem to matter if the issue concerns the building of the DEW Line or the status of the Northwest Passage; Canadian governments have been unwilling to walk the walk of independence by building the necessary capacity to provide adequate surveillance and enforcement to let the world know that they are truly serious about controlling Canada's Arctic region.

It would appear that there would have been few consequences from the United States if Canada had simply gotten on with the job of ensuring that it could observe and act in the Arctic. Even if the United States had continued to protest, had Canada built up its capabilities and then enforced the requirement that all foreign ships follow AWPPA, Canada would have at least de facto control of the passage. The United States, owing to the need to defend the principle of rights of passage internationally, would not have dropped its protests. But following the events of 9/11, Washington could have easily been convinced that a strong Canadian presence in the north would be a wise security measure.

Likewise, there has been no real effort on the part of the United States to influence Canada's position on the continental shelf. The last ten years would have been the ideal time for Canada to have developed the hydrographic capabilities to make and defend its position. Yet, once again, there has been little evidence that it was willing to do so.

Climate change will soon be bringing the world to the Arctic. Only now is Canada willing to spend the money to acquire the capabilities that it has needed for so long.

Thus, this chapter reasserts Stephen Clarkson's conclusion in 1968 that Canada's 'dependence' on the United States is self-inflicted. Had Canada carefully determined what its Arctic interests were and then allocated the necessary resources to promote and protect them, it would not be reduced to simply responding to the United States whenever it acts in the north. Instead, there could have been a United States that would have come to depend on a Canada. Perhaps it is not too late.

NOTES

1 One of the best examinations of this era is provided by Shelagh Grant, *Sovereignty or Security: Government Policy in the Canadian North 1936–1950* (Vancouver: UBC Press, 1988).
2 R.J. Sutherland, 'The Strategic Significance of the Canadian Arctic,' in *The Arctic Frontier*, ed. R. St. J. Macdonald (Toronto: University of Toronto Press, 1966), 264.
3 K. Eyre, 'Forty Years of Defence Activity in the Canadian North, 1947–87,' *Arctic* 40, no. 4 (1987): 292–9.
4 United States, Army Air Force Headquarters, Atlantic Division, Air Transport Command, *Problems of Canada – United States Cooperation in the Arctic*, 29 October 1946 [NARA RG 319, Records of the Army Staff, Publication files, 1946–51, box 2785].
5 While the best-known study of these issues was completed by Shelagh Grant, *Sovereignty or Security*, some newer scholars are starting to add new twists to her specific findings. See Whitney Lackenbauer and Matthew Far-

ish, 'The Cold War on Canadian Soil: Militarizing a Northern Environment,' *Environmental History* 12, no. 3 (October 2007) and Adam Lajeunesse, 'The Distant Early Warning Line and the Canadian Battle for Public Perception,' *Canadian Military Journal* 8, no. 2 (Summer 2007); available at http://www.journal.forces.gc.ca/engraph/Vol8/no2/09-lajeunesse_e.asp.

6 Lajeunesse, 'The Distant Early Warning Line.'

7 Ron Purver, 'The Arctic in Canadian Security Policy, 1945 to the Present,' in *Canada's International Security Policy*, ed. David Hewitt and David Leyton-Brown (Scarborough: Prentice Hall, 1995), 85–7.

8 Donat Pharand, *Canada's Arctic Waters in International Law* (Cambridge: Cambridge University Press, 1988).

9 Edgar Dosman, 'The Northern Sovereignty Crisis 1968–70,' in *The Arctic in Question*, ed. Edgar Dosman (Toronto: Oxford University Press, 1976).

10 Ivan Head and Pierre Trudeau, *The Canadian Way: Shaping Canada's Foreign Policy, 1968–1984* (Toronto: McClelland & Stewart Inc., 1995), 37–48.

11 Don McRae, 'The Negotiation of Article 234,' in *Politics of the Northwest Passage*, ed. Franklyn Griffiths (Kingston and Montreal: McGill-Queen's University Press, 1987), 98–114.

12 John Kirton and Don Munton, 'The Manhattan Voyages and Their Aftermath,' in *Politics of the Northwest Passage*, 93.

13 'Polar Vision or Tunnel Vision: The Making of Canadian Arctic Waters Policy,' *Marine Policy* 19, no. 4 (July 1995): 343–63.

14 Ted McDorman, 'In the Wake of the *Polar Sea*: Canadian Jurisdiction and the Northwest Passage,' *Marine Policy* 10 (1986): 243–6.

15 Rob Huebert, 'Steel, Ice and Decision-Making: The Voyage of the *Polar Sea* and Its Aftermath: The Making of Canadian Northern Foreign Policy,' unpublished MA thesis (Dalhousie University, 1993), 208–17.

16 McDorman, 'In the Wake of the *Polar Sea*.'

17 'Harper Pledges Larger Arctic Presence,' 22 December 2005, at http://www.ctv.ca/servlet/ArticleNews/story/CTVNews/20051222/harper_north051222/20051222?s_name=election2006&no_ads=.

18 BBC News, 'Russia Plants Flag at Northpole,' 2 August 2007, at http://news.bbc.co.uk/1/hi/world/europe/6927395.stm.

19 United Nations, Ocean and Law of the Sea, Commission on the Limits of the Continental Shelf (CLCS), 'The definition of the continental shelf and criteria for the establishment of its outer limits' (2007), at http://www.un.org/Depts/los/clcs_new/continental_shelf_descr iption.htm.

20 Kevin Mooney, 'Law of Sea Treaty Hurts U.S. Security, Sovereignty Activists Say,' *CNSNews.com*, 4 October 2007, at http://www.cnsnews.com/ViewNation.asp?Page=/Nation/archive/2 00710/NAT20071004d.html.

21 Chris Kirkey, 'Delineating Maritime Boundaries: The 1977–78 Canada-U.S. Beaufort Sea Continental Shelf Delimitation Boundary Negotiations,' *Canadian Review of American Studies* 95, no. 2 (Spring 1995).
22 Governments of Yukon, Northwest Territories, and Nunavut, *Developing a New Framework for Sovereignty and Security in the North: A Discussion Paper* (April 2005).

PART FOUR

Economic Policy-Making in a Complex Environment

The two chapters in this part of the volume help us to appreciate the sheer complexity of the context for policy-making in Canada today – particularly with respect to economic relations with the United States – and some of the varied, cross-cutting implications for Canada's independence. We often think of Canada–U.S. economic relations in terms of Robert Putnam's 'two-level game' model of international bargaining, where two diplomats face off against one another, struggling to find a favourable but mutually acceptable settlement, and thereby satisfy their own domestic constituents. In practice, of course, there are more than two levels, and the game itself is much more complicated. National policy-makers have to contend with a vast array of mobilized interest groups, plus sub-national governments, trans-national firms and organizations, and an ever-expanding latticework of sub-national, national, and international legal and institutional structures. But Putnam's central insight still seems to hold true: rather than a true chess match, diplomacy today often takes the form of a very difficult balancing act, where each side is mostly concerned with finding a policy equilibrium – almost any equilibrium – that might satisfy all of the various sub-national and trans-national interests and institutions with a stake in the outcome.

In chapter 7, Geoffrey Hale argues that 'independence' is a red herring, and that the only sensible standard for evaluating Canadian policies is 'whether particular policy frameworks provide Canadian governments with sufficient discretion to adopt policies that directly address or accommodate both distinctive domestic conditions and shared policy challenges.' He looks carefully at three different kind of 'inter-mestic' issues, where ostensibly 'domestic' policies have profound effects on other societies, and thus create frictions and demand for some kind of coordination: macro-economic, sectoral/micro-economic, and border management/security. Canadian policy-makers, he concludes, have been constrained by a variety of forces – including American policy choices, past Canadian choices, international agreements, and domestic political conflicts – just as other governments all over the world have been. But Canada still has a lot of discretion in the kind of policy objectives and instruments it chooses, and – contrary to Clarkson's 'independentist' interpretation – is therefore able to make autonomous, effective policies.

In chapter 8, Christopher Kukucha switches the focus from the independence of the Canadian federal government to the independence of the provincial governments, with a specific focus on trade policy. He finds that provincial governments are certainly not in a position to direct national trade policies, but they have been able to collect their own information, do their own analysis and construct their own policy agenda, and even exercise substantial influence over policy outcomes. Through general arguments and specific examples, he is able to shed new light not only on provincial autonomy, but on that of the federal government as well, and on the nature of an emerging structure of multilayered, transnational governance that encompasses both.

7 Maintaining Policy Discretion: Cross-Border Policy-Making and North American Integration

GEOFFREY HALE

Stephen Clarkson's prescriptions for an 'independent foreign policy' for Canada are firmly rooted in the assumptions and normative commitments of 1960s English Canadian economic nationalism – whatever the subsequent adjustments of his analysis in response to changes in global and North American political and economic conditions.[1] He views an independent foreign policy, at least in part, as a means of providing a national project capable of overcoming domestic political divisions by enhancing policy distinctions from the United States in pursuit of a more independent role in the world.

Achieving greater economic independence from the United States is intended both to foster nation-building and reduce Canadian dependence on U.S. markets and investment. As such, Clarkson's prescriptions apply to governmental capacities to exercise autonomy or discretion in policy fields traditionally viewed as 'domestic' – not just to the design of the political and security dimensions of foreign policy. Indeed, he sometimes equates failure to appreciate the supposed American threat or to support active measures to limit it with 'subservience' to the United States.[2]

However, a growing cross-section of academics and policy commentators decline to be pigeon-holed in such rigid categories, taking more nuanced views of Canada's national interests and the capacity of Canadian governments to pursue them in the contemporary context of interdependence – whether within North America or in a broader context.[3] These outlooks typically reflect three major developments in Canadian political economy during the past forty years:

- the progressive decentralization of the Canadian federation, partly

offset by the restoration of the federal government's fiscal capacity in the late 1990s and early twenty-first century;
- the continuing fragmentation of Canada's identity and culture in response to the continuing realities of Quebec nationalism, multiculturalism and the disappearance of 'English Canada,' urban-rural divisions, aboriginal nationalism, and the growing distinctiveness of Canada's regional economies – resulting in the world's first 'postmodern' society;[4]
- Canada's progressive, but variegated, integration within North America, reflected in the fact that most Canadian provinces now export as much or more of their production to other countries, primarily the United States, as to other provinces.

This chapter addresses the degree to which Canadian governments have sustained a capacity for relative autonomy in policy fields traditionally considered to be primarily domestic, but which are subject to significant degrees of interdependence with other countries: macro-economic policies, micro-economic and sectoral policies governing energy policies, capital markets and securities regulation, border management and related security issues. It emphasizes the practical challenges facing governments of many smaller countries: the need to accommodate economic, societal, and policy trends involving their own citizens arising from their growing interaction and interdependence with counterparts in other countries, while maintaining the political and policy discretion necessary to serve the distinctive, often diverse, needs and preferences of Canadians.

Conceptualizing the National Interest: 'Low' Politics and the Context for Policy 'Discretion'

For the past forty years, Clarkson's narrative of Canadian political economy has emphasized a broader nation-building project in response to what he views as the threat of an allegedly expansionist United States to Canada's political, economic, and cultural identity. Clarkson fears for the sustainability of what he describes as its 'state system' between the 'extremes of externally-determined dysfunctionality' derived from the interaction of globalization and the policies of international institutions, and 'self-imposed truncation' allegedly derived from a pervasive neoconservative agenda and 'the country's loss of sovereignty to transnational corporations.'[5]

However, others have framed concepts of the national interest that neither deny the reality of the American elephant nor adopt Clarkson's often binary view of Canadian interests as sharply differentiated from those of its larger neighbour. These observers tend to approach policy autonomy or 'independence' as relative concepts reflecting different aspects of state capacity. This very broad concept includes the capacity to address *domestic* (or *'intermestic'*) *political issues*: those combining domestic and international dimensions, reflecting various patterns of interdependence. Public expectations of governments also require policies capable of combining *relative policy effectiveness* – the capacity to achieve defined policy goals over a reasonable period – with *political legitimacy* – the acceptance of particular policies by a broad public or key stakeholders – in light of realistically available alternatives.

The concept of relative autonomy also addresses the capacity of governments to deal with political and economic interdependence in ways that serve their broader political and policy goals. Equally vital is the capacity to manage external political challenges in ways that allow Canadian governments sufficient discretion to accommodate or manage the expectations and demands of societal interests.

Political legitimacy under such circumstances is often the by-product of 'low politics': the interaction and competition of governmental and societal interests with different and often partial views of the public good or national interest. Canada's open political and economic systems still allow governments to take prescriptive actions in particular policy fields – for example, in organizing major social systems such as those governing education and health care, or designating 'strategic sectors' – including banking, telecommunications, and cultural industries.

However, state capacity in Canada is affected by two major factors that can both reinforce one another and work at cross-purposes: its growing internal diversity, whether characterized in regional, cultural, or urban-rural terms, and the growing stake that many Canadians have in open economic and social systems characterized by considerable degrees of interdependence and autonomy from day-to-day government control. These realities are embedded within the systems of Canadian federalism and the different ways in which Canadians relate to their own country. They also challenge the unitary vision of Canada that, while not inherent to Clarkson's outlook, given his openness to Quebec's aspirations, tends to view other regional interests as peripheral or opposed to broader 'national' (read: Toronto- or Ontario-centric) priorities.

Successive Canadian governments have deliberately sought to encourage greater engagement and interdependence with the North American and global economies so that these assumptions are deeply embedded within the expectations of most citizens and businesses. Consequently, it is unrealistic (and possibly fatuous) to conceptualize policy autonomy or 'independence' in terms of immunity from foreign influences, whether political, economic, or even societal.

The appropriate test for the legitimacy and effectiveness of government policies is not whether they are radically different from broader trends in the United States or other advanced industrial countries in an increasingly interdependent world. Rather, it is whether particular policy frameworks provide Canadian governments with sufficient discretion to adopt policies that directly address or accommodate both distinctive domestic conditions and shared policy challenges. A related test is whether governments can manage (and, in some cases, resist) international pressures where these are seen by senior policy-makers to be detrimental to Canadian interests – whether those of Canadian citizens or of the Canadian state. Rather than being static constructs, both policy settings and policy capacity need to be dynamic in order to evolve with changing domestic and external circumstances.

CUSFTA and NAFTA may serve to some extent as a supra-constitution, as contended by Clarkson. However, these treaties coexist with formal political constitutions and enduring cultural differences between and within Canada, the United States, and Mexico in ways that constrain processes of integration as much as they enable them. As such, the interaction of globalization and North American integration with various forms of particularism more closely resembles the concept of 'fragmegration' outlined by political scientist James Rosenau: 'the pervasive interaction between fragmenting and integrating dynamics at every level of community.'[6] These realities may be seen in the three broad policy fields surveyed in this chapter: Canada's macro-economic policies, key sectoral and micro-economic policies, and border management and related security policies.

Macro-Economic Policies: Seeking Policy Autonomy amid Global Competition

Clarkson's normative standard for state autonomy is the interventionist Keynesian state capable of providing both economic growth and full employment for its citizens by its management of both macro-economic and micro-economic policy functions. Clarkson's approach may be contrasted with the so-called 'right' Keynesianism of the federal finance department during the postwar era,[7] which stressed macro-economic management over prescriptive micro-economic policies, except for a limited number of strategic sectors.[8] Arguably, the federal government's medium-term fiscal and monetary policies since the early 1990s are an adaptation of earlier liberal Keynesian models to the realities of a regionally diverse, trade-dependent economy open to large-scale capital flows. However, they are anathema to the relatively centralized state-centred model of economic development that is Clarkson's normative ideal.

Post-FTA monetary and fiscal policies may be said to have gone through three broad phases: the initial 'trial-and-error' efforts to reduce deficits, curb inflation, and adapt to globalization and free trade (1985–94), the consolidation of these policies during the Chrétien government's first two terms (1994–2000), and Ottawa's efforts to retain control of its policy priorities with the institutionalization of federal surpluses since 2000.

Monetary Policies

The federal government's substantial delegation of authority over monetary policy to the Bank of Canada raises significant issues of what is meant by 'policy autonomy' – particularly in the absence of effective coordination between monetary and fiscal policies. For example, central banks may pursue similar goals, with varying degrees of independence, using different mixes of policy tools.[9] They are also influenced by one another's shared outlooks and understandings of monetary policies – as well as by the need to cooperate in dealing with periodic international disruptions.

The relative autonomy of Bank of Canada policies in an international context has gone through several cycles over the decades. During the 1960s, Canada successfully defended its exemption from U.S. restrictions on foreign capital flows in order to preserve its access to American capital markets – in part, by accepting some constraints on its monetary policy choices.

However, Clarkson notes that the Bank adopted monetarist anti-inflation policies during the 1970s before the U.S. Federal Reserve did. Decisions to float the Canadian dollar, and later to focus on inflation-reduction targets led to growing distinctions between Canadian and

U.S. monetary policies – albeit within the consensus of the central banking 'club.' Governor John Crow's decision to establish a target of price stability – a policy more restrictive than that of the Federal Reserve – is generally conceded to have increased the severity of the 1990–1 recession and prolonged the subsequent economic recovery.[10]

Improved policy coordination with the Department of Finance after 1993, based on an agreed inflation target range of 1 to 3 per cent and more restrictive fiscal policies, helped to reduce inflation and interest rates to their lowest levels in more than thirty years by the late 1990s. These trends reinforced economic growth and spurred major changes in Canada's financial markets. As a result, Canadian governments enjoyed increased policy capacity and greater autonomy at the end of the 1990s than at any time since the phasing out of exchange controls in the early 1950s.

This autonomy was tested after 2001 when several prominent economists challenged the Bank of Canada's floating-exchange-rate policy, which had allowed the Canada-U.S. exchange rate to fall to a low of 61.8 cents in January 2002 from 89 cents in 1989, and called Ottawa to move towards some form of common currency arrangement with the United States to impose the kinds of external policy disciplines associated with the European Union's introduction of the Euro.[11]

Subsequent debates noted the implications of a common currency for Canadian sovereignty. However, most analyses held that exchange rate fluctuations clearly reflected global shifts in prices and Canada's relative dependence on commodity exports. They also helped Canada's regionally diverse economy to adjust to changing economic conditions without massive increases in unemployment.[12] However, while the subsequent commodity-driven rebound of Canada-U.S. exchange rate since 2002 has vindicated the positions of the Bank and its supporters, . the subsequent overvaluation of the Canadian dollar has triggered calls from some provinces and business groups for intervention of other kinds.

The Bank of Canada cooperated with other central banks, including the Federal Reserve, to contain an international financial panic in 2007 resulting from problems in the U.S. sub-prime mortgage market and related financial innovations. However, different circumstances in Canadian markets resulted in a different mix of policy responses – including support for a deal brokered by Quebec's *Caisse de Dépôt* to stabilize the $35 billion Canadian market in 'asset-backed commercial paper.'[13]

Fiscal and Tax Policies

Applying concepts such as 'independence' and 'national interest' to varied fiscal policies and the national tax system is a complex task – particularly in the space available for this chapter. However, the federal government (and most provinces) have developed greater capacity to manage international policy pressures related to their fiscal and tax policies since the mid-1980s – if perhaps less than at the beginning of this decade.

In some cases, Ottawa's management of intermestic pressures has differentiated Canada from policy trends in the United States and other industrial countries. In others, U.S. (and other foreign) policy decisions have facilitated the pursuit of Ottawa's preferred goals. At the same time, Canadian governments' pursuit of greater economic integration within North America has often encouraged domestic interests to press for greater degrees of policy parallelism with the United States. However, successive governments have also demonstrated the capacity to subordinate business pressures for more extensive tax policy changes to their own fiscal, tax-policy, and partisan political objectives.

The prevalence during the 1990s of neo-liberal policy styles, rather than (with limited exceptions) a neo-conservatism inspired by the efforts of British and American politicians to 'shrink the state,' suggests that the evolution of both federal and provincial government policies were shaped at least as much, if not more, by domestic circumstances than by external ones. In this context, Clarkson's social democratic commitments often make it difficult for him to engage the analytical contexts of policy-makers to whom he is fundamentally opposed.

The federal government's October 1994 'Framework for Economic Policy'[14] provided the clearest, most explicit agenda for economic change tabled by the federal government since the Second World War. The Chrétien Liberals' decision to shift from the fiscal gradualism of their 1993 Red Book to a more thorough-going assault on the federal deficit certainly reflected external influences such as the Mexico peso crisis of 1994–5 and suggestions by the U.S. business media that the Canadian dollar could be relegated to the status of a 'Hudson Bay peso.' However, it also reflected their determination to control the terms of restructuring Canada's public sector rather than seeing them dictated by others. The fact that comparable measures were pursued, if often in different ways, by Canadian governments of very different political stripes, suggests that domestic political institutions determined the timing and methods by which they would mediate these pressures.[15]

Arguably, these measures have helped to enhance Ottawa's fiscal autonomy in the medium term, enabling it to finance a significant increase in federal transfers to support post-secondary education and research after 1998, and to use the federal spending power to increase the conditionality of health care transfers to the provinces after 2000. Rather than 'dismantling the state,' these measures are more suggestive of the reallocation of functions described as 'shape shifting' by Clarkson and Lewis in their 1999 analysis of the evolving federal state.[16]

Between 1998 and 2002, Ottawa's commitment to 'fiscal balance' between new spending initiatives and tax- and debt-reduction measures – the so-called '50–50' approach – enabled it to maximize its discretion in the targeting and timing of spending increases and tax cuts. A key thrust of federal policies was to increase the sustainability of public services in the face of an aging society by allocating substantial amounts for debt reduction, and by refinancing the Canada Pension Plan with sizeable tax *increases* that largely offset its personal tax reductions during this period.[17] However, longer-term initiatives intended to promote an 'innovation agenda' that aimed at fostering greater microeconomic competitiveness ran aground – one of several casualties of Liberal leadership politics and growing restiveness over chronic federal surpluses.

Although successive governments have gradually reduced effective corporate tax rates, broadly paralleling the measures taken by some European and Asian countries, both federal and provincial corporate tax reductions have been secondary to other fiscal priorities and short-term political considerations. At least, that was the case until Opposition leader Stéphane Dion's endorsement of larger corporate tax cuts in late 2007 in lieu of the Harper government's promised GST cuts provided the latter with a political opening to commit to both sets of measures in its October 2007 Economic Statement.[18] Marginal effective tax rates (METRs) for Canadian corporations – a measurement of the cumulative tax rate on each additional dollar of income after accounting for assorted deductions, credits, and other allowances – dropped about 17 per cent, on average, between 1997 and 2006. Even so, sharply rising corporate profits during the same period enabled governments to substantially increase their revenues from this source. Nevertheless, Ottawa's fiscal priorities – personal tax cuts in 2001–3 and substantial spending increases since then – have relegated corporate tax reductions to a decidedly secondary priority.[19]

Federal capacity to exercise policy autonomy, whether from political or policy motives, can also be seen in the Harper government's 2006 cut in GST rates against the strongly held opinions of most business and tax economists. Despite Finance Minister Jim Flaherty's commitment to reducing CIT rates to the lowest among G-7 industrial nations by 2012, almost three-quarters of the multi-year tax reductions introduced in his October 2007 economic statement came from cuts to sales and income taxes paid by individuals.[20]

More controversial, if congenial to policy elites, was its Halloween 2006 decision to scrap tax preferences for income trusts, ostensibly on the grounds of limiting corporate tax avoidance (despite posing as champions of small investors on the issue during the previous election campaign). However, it remains to be seen if its subsequent efforts to curb international tax arbitrage will survive widespread criticisms from both corporate elites and many tax experts.[21]

In summary, the federal government, in particular, has substantially increased its capacity to define and implement its fiscal policies independently of external pressures since the early 1990s. In doing so, it has succeeded in promoting sustained economic growth, greater fiscal discretion, and the long-term sustainability of major social programs. These successes have largely insulated Canadian governments from the pressures of business and other groups to imitate foreign-inspired policy models – whether originating in the United States or Western Europe.[22] Although business interests and priorities still play a major role in shaping federal fiscal and tax policies, as they did even during the most interventionist of the Trudeau years, Canadian governments continue to demonstrate a substantial capacity to manage the pressures of globalization, rather than being controlled by them.

Micro-Economic Policies: Sectoral and Regional Decentralization,
Cross-Border Coalition Building, and Managing External Pressures

Clarkson's central critique of Canada's institutionalization of 'free trade' under CUSFTA, NAFTA, and the Uruguay Round was that such neo-liberal policies largely deprived the federal government of the policy tools necessary to develop a national industrial strategy capable of insulating Canada's economy from the effects of economic globalization.

The broad outlines of Canada's neo-liberal micro-economic policies since 1985 are well known. Trade agreements reduced barriers to the movement of goods, services, and capital, reinforcing existing trends towards economic restructuring – particularly of Canada's branch-plant manufacturing sector. Ottawa and some provinces moved away from the use of Crown corporations as policy instruments, shifting towards commercial mandates and, in some cases, outright privatization, and separating regulatory from commercial functions.

Ottawa has also responded to international regulatory trends transforming global capital markets. It allowed the partial restructuring of Canada's financial sector – enabling major chartered banks to expand their activities. It also reduced (and ultimately eliminated) foreign ownership limits on pension funds and RRSPs, allowing Canadians to diversify their investments and forcing Canada's financial sector to compete with foreign-backed firms and syndicates for the right to manage and invest these savings.[23] These policies have reinforced the shift of English-speaking countries from managerial capitalism to shareholder capitalism, making corporate executives more vulnerable to shareholder demands and potential takeovers, and substantially changing incentive structures for businesses, politicians, regulators, and citizens.

Canadian governments have also tacitly encouraged the development of Canadian multinationals and cross-border alliances, with the practical effect of blurring the distinctions between domestic and foreign ownership. Large Canadian firms are organized increasingly to supply North American rather than mainly domestic markets, often as part of international supply chains. These policies provided an important safety valve for most provincial economies as governments reduced deficits during the 1990s. They also made it more difficult for protectionist U.S. interests to target Canadian firms without adversely affecting American interests too. At the same time, the balancing of regional interests in north–south (and other international) trade became increasingly important for federal trade policies.[24]

Regional and sectoral variations in micro-economic policies have four major implications for the calculation of Canada's national interests, and the development of 'national' (and not just 'federal') policies in its interactions with the United States and other countries. First, the evolution of Canadian federalism increasingly suggests that 'national' policies require the participation and mutual accommodation of *both* federal and provincial orders of government. (See Kukucha, this volume.) Second, patterns of North American integration will take significantly different forms in sectors characterized by significant levels of provincial regulatory controls, federal regulatory controls, or limited federal *or* provincial economic regulation.[25] Third, the need to secure provincial approval for international or cross-border economic policies often parallels the need of U.S. presidents to accommodate congressional policy preferences when negotiating cross-border policies. This observation applies particularly to sectors subject to significant levels of provincial regulatory control and in sectors located primarily in a single province or region of Canada. These realities have significant implications for the regulatory strategies of Canadian governments, as well as for patterns of policy coordination across North America – particularly in the development of energy policies and the regulation of capital markets.

Energy Policies

Few policy debates of the Trudeau era triggered the passions released by the collision of domestic and international interests over energy policies – particularly those related to the ownership and development of Canada's oil and gas resources and the economic rents from them. Nationalist historiography, including Clarkson's discussions of these issues,[26] has focused on repeated clashes between the Trudeau government, international oil companies, and successive U.S. administrations culminating in the battle over the National Energy Program (NEP).

However, Trudeau's state-centred nationalism also ran afoul of strong domestic interests – not least, oil- and gas-producing provinces and large segments of Canadian business. Far more than external political pressure, memories of the NEP and Trudeau's neo-colonial and statist approach to energy policies prompted these groups to entrench the more market-oriented policies of the Mulroney government in CUSFTA.

Canadian and U.S. energy policies have evolved broadly in parallel since the mid-1980s, but with three major exceptions. First, policies in both countries are heavily segmented by the differing regulatory and market conditions of major energy sources – oil, natural gas, electricity, and nuclear power – and inter-jurisdictional transmission systems that, in turn, reflect *very* different degrees of integration with international markets.[27] Second, provincial ownership and jurisdiction over resource development have significantly limited the extent to which the federal government can control, as opposed to influence, domestic policy developments. Third, the prevalence of regionally based businesses, including Crown corporations, as leading or dominant firms reinforces this decentralization of power. As a result, federal policies have accommodated significant provincial and market-driven discretion and diversity in both domestic and cross-border energy relations, while carefully controlling formal relations with other governments.

The Canadian and U.S.-based energy sectors have become increasingly interdependent, with growing interpenetration of large and medium-sized firms in both countries and the emergence of several major Canadian firms capable of both competing and partnering with American-based (and other foreign) counterparts on relatively equal terms.[28] The persistence of Canadian energy surpluses is central to this process, complementing growing U.S. dependence on energy imports. Other important factors include the effects of significant technological changes on the development (and economic viability) of new energy sources; changing economic concepts of natural monopoly, especially in electricity generation and distribution; and growing U.S. concerns over energy security in the aftermath of 9/11.

The Bush administration's National Energy Policy of 2001 has had far less effect on Canadian policies than anticipated or feared in some quarters – largely because of U.S. domestic debates resulting in prolonged congressional gridlock.[29] Indeed, Canadian diplomats worked closely with some U.S. interests to block legislative provisions allowing energy exploration in the Arctic National Wildlife Reserve (ANWR). However, most cross-border issues arising from the long, drawn-out congressional debate were resolved through quiet diplomacy and technical log-rolling.[30]

Traditional domestic debates over royalty levels, the location of processing and upgrading facilities, equity ownership of new energy developments (mainly in Newfoundland), and the implications of resource depletion on sustainability have been largely limited to the producing provinces. However, even in areas of notionally federal jurisdiction such as the proposed Mackenzie pipeline, the devolution of regulatory powers to territorial and First Nations governments – even if mediated by the National Energy Board – has resulted in a lengthy process of competition and brokerage among regional, aboriginal, and assorted private-sector interests. Ottawa strongly resisted pressures from the Exxon-led consortium for major subsidies or to take an equity stake in the project, along with demands from competing pipeline interests to accelerate development of a competing link to a planned Alaska natural gas pipeline. These factors may have contributed to Exxon-Mobil's 2007 announcement of plans to pass the leadership of the Mackenzie project to Canadian-based Trans-Canada Corp., although there appears to be little difference between the rent-seeking proclivities of either firm.[31]

Taken together, these factors suggest that domestic considerations – especially the desire of energy-exporting provinces and Canadian energy producers to exploit the insatiable U.S. market – have both complemented external pressures on energy policies and shaped federal responses to them. Provincial governments retain greater policy capacity and discretion in managing energy issues than does Ottawa. Although U.S. federal electricity regulations require reciprocal market access for utilities connecting to the U.S. grid, 'reliability' regulations implemented following a 2003 blackout that affected large sections of both countries were developed with strong federal support – and with the active involvement and cooperation of utilities in both countries.

Strong political opposition to the Kyoto Accord in the United States may have created significant barriers to Canadian measures to implement it in ways calculated to limit transitional costs. However, growing environmental policy engagement by U.S. state governments has created a platform for cross-border cooperation with like-minded Canadian provinces. Energy policies are contested to some extent in both countries as part of the broader interplay of competing interests and priorities among different societal groups – if arguably less so than in the 1970s and 1980s. However, the decentralization of policy processes in both countries has tended to diffuse the polarization of debate and to limit the capacity of politicians to engage in zero-sum political conflicts capable of wrecking the fragile fabric of Canadian nationhood. As a result, North American integration has strengthened the capacity of *provincial* governments – if not that of the federal government – to exercise policy discretion in the management of their energy policies.

Foreign Investment, Capital Markets, and Securities Policies

The federal government's 1985 conversion of the Foreign Investment Review Agency to Investment Canada signalled a major change in official views of the national interest from restricting to encouraging foreign investment in Canada. These changes were reinforced by Quebec's 1986 decisions to remove restrictions on both foreign and Canadian chartered bank participation in the province's securities markets, followed soon afterward by Ontario. Subsequent federal policy shifts allowed large-scale chartered bank entry and ultimately dominance of Canada's securities industry from 1988 to 1992. CUSFTA, NAFTA, and the Uruguay Round cemented these policy commitments into place, based mainly on principles of non-discrimination (with some sectoral exceptions) and national treatment.

Canadian corporations greatly increased their investments abroad during the 1990s, as well as taking advantage of the rationalization of Canadian branch plants by foreign multinationals. Since 1997, the total value of Canadian foreign investment abroad has exceeded that of foreign direct investment in Canada. Private and institutional investors also greatly increased their foreign holdings during the same period – accommodated by the progressive relaxation of federal restrictions on investments abroad. However, Canada's opening to capital markets and the growing two-way flows of both direct and portfolio investment have created much greater levels of interdependence that, in turn, have created several major challenges for Canadian governments.

Are Canada's national interests in traditionally protected sectors served better by domestic oligopolies focused primarily on competition for domestic markets or in opening domestic markets to greater foreign competition while encouraging the consolidation and external expansion of dominant Canadian firms? Does the current, relatively open market for corporate control provide a net benefit to Canadian corporations, investors, and workers, and if not, does Ottawa possess the capacity to take effective regulatory action without undermining its core economic objectives? Does Canada's decentralized system of securities regulation provide an effective balance among the interests of major national stakeholders, domestic and regional interests, and ordinary investors? And if not, does the federal government possess the capacity to do a more effective job in balancing these interests?

The federal government loosened entry requirements for the telecommunications, banking, and rail and air transportation sectors during the 1990s. However, substantial restrictions remain, and these sectors remain dominated by domestically focused oligopolies. Efforts by two pairs of major banks to merge in 1998 prompted a political firestorm that led Ottawa to reject the mergers – effectively stalling the trend towards financial sector consolidation and market opening. Ottawa has also restricted most 'cross-pillar' mergers of banks and other large integrated financial services firms, although allowing three major semi-integrated insurance firms to rise above the crowd. Overall, historic political arguments for giving priority to domestic competition and the protection of domestic markets in these sectors have prevailed in the absence of strong external pressures or an independent political constituency for market opening.

The debate over foreign investment and foreign takeovers is far more complex. Despite two record-setting waves of foreign takeovers in 1998–2000 and 2004–7, the number and value of foreign takeovers by Canadian firms had been even higher over both business cycles – at least until June 2007.[32] Although foreign control of Canadian manufacturing assets has grown, overall levels of foreign control – whether as a share of Canadian business assets or of Canada's largest 800 corporations – has remained fairly stable.[33]

The recent takeover boom reflected the openness of Canadian (and other international) markets for corporate control – and the shift from direct restrictions on foreign investment to an emphasis on competition policy to limit undue corporate concentration. It also reflects the steady decline of deference to corporate executives by institutional investors and much of the investing public. Such attitudes are often sceptical of the notion of fostering 'national champions' – and of the political cronyism and elite entitlements to public support often associated with this concept. Legislative barriers to foreign takeovers or controlling ownership blocs – including those of privatized Crown corporations such as Air Canada, Canadian National, and Petro-Canada are residual effects of such policies. Other major factors include the growing activism of several major public sector pension and investment funds following federal and provincial government decisions to mandate independent governance structures and investment strategies designed to maximize long-term returns to stakeholders.[34]

These developments have highlighted the gulf between the interventionist reflexes of much of the Canadian public (including many corporate executives faced with unsolicited takeover bids) and government policy-makers deeply sceptical of the capacity of politicized investment policies to serve a broader national interest – as opposed to those of powerful, well-connected elites.

Similar factors have influenced provincial responses to proposals for the creation of a national securities regulator. Although inter-governmental cooperation through the Canadian Securities Administrators was greatly extended during the 1990s, competing interests and philosophical differences of provincial regulators have blocked Ontario's efforts to create a single securities regulator,[35] despite bank-controlled securities dealers' domination of Canadian markets and the consolidation of Canada's major stock exchanges between 1998 and 2002. It has also limited the extension of federal authority in this sector except at the margins.

The regionalized structure of securities regulation reflects the three-tier character of Canada's securities market for publicly traded companies. Most of Canada's largest 200 multinationals are listed on foreign markets – mainly in New York. A bigger group of larger publicly-traded corporations is open to more centralized approaches to regulation. However, a sizeable majority of small-and medium-sized firms, based largely in Western Canada, appears sceptical of the capacity of Ontario-based institutions to understand or serve their interests.[36]

Regulatory changes introduced in 2004 and 2005 brought Canadian corporate governance and financial disclosure standards closer to U.S. Sarbanes-Oxley standards, although some remaining differences reflect variations in market structures and regulatory philosophies between the two countries.[37]

A federal government proposal for negotiation of a bilateral agreement on 'free trade' in securities with the United States, tabled in its 2007 budget, reflects the decision of G-7 finance ministers to move towards 'mutual recognition' systems that reduce barriers to cross-border purchases of securities by foreign nationals – while looking to British rather than U.S. regulatory models for their inspiration.[38] More controversial are budget proposals to revise Canada's tax treaty with the United States to eliminate withholding taxes on interest paid to arm's-length non-residents and remove the deductibility of interest on money borrowed to finance the foreign affiliates of Canadian-based multinationals.[39]

On balance, rapid shifts in global capital markets and the distinctive evolution of American and European (especially British) regulatory regimes have forced Canadian governments into largely reactive responses. Federal tax policies have accommodated (if not necessarily encouraged) the growth of large Canadian multinationals, usually outside traditionally protected sectors, and major Canadian pools of investment capital that have become increasingly autonomous players in both domestic and foreign capital markets.

Clarkson would respond in dismay to these trends and see the relatively arm's-length response to them of Canadian governments as antithetical to his well-developed world view. However, they are consistent with Ottawa's broader strategic approach to economic policies and to its efforts to maintain some level of discretion in balancing competing domestic and international interests.

Border Management and Related Security Issues

Few issues speak to concerns over national independence and policy autonomy more intrinsically than the management of national borders and related issues of national security. CUSFTA and NAFTA contributed to the blurring of borders in several ways – not least by making trade facilitation and economic integration a key objective of Canadian (and to a lesser extent U.S.) policies. The events of 9/11 triggered a paradigm shift, especially in the United States, as security came to 'trump trade' as the primary focus of American policy.

Clarkson and others have noted the practical effect of these security preoccupations – emphasizing American hegemony and Canada's relatively greater dependence on U.S. markets, but also U.S. dependence on the cooperation of neighbouring states, including Canada, for the effectiveness of their security measures. He portrays 'the dominant reality of Washington as *rule maker*, strengthening the sovereignty of the United States ... [and of] the peripheries as *rule-takers* [whose] sovereignty has been reduced by accepting constraints on their policy-making powers.'[40] Harvey has described another feature of this approach as the ratchet effect, by which U.S. officials secure compliance or negotiate agreement over one set of security rules – only later to 'ratchet up' their security requirements in response to ongoing games of 'cat and mouse' with organized criminals and evolving terrorist networks. Canadian officials have adapted to these pressures with what Anderson and Sands have described as 'minimal, satisficing' responses to proposals that could unduly limit their operational discretion or run the risks of politically embarrassing legal or civil liberties challenges within Canada.[41]

These issues affect a wide range of security-related matters. Both governments and business interests emphasize the need to 'balance' and 'integrate' trade facilitation and security, although these terms often mean different things to different interests and government agencies on each side of the border. At a micro-policy level, officials continue to discuss the requirements and standards for identity documents, overlapping visa policies applying to citizens of third countries, and information-sharing protocols between security services. These issues

provoke widespread concerns over the protection of civil liberties and
the possible misuse or theft of personal data in both countries.

These developments have provoked serious debates over the nature
of Canada's national interest and Canadian governments' capacity to
pursue security policies that are effective in containing criminal and
terrorist activities, while protecting their capacity to resist or negotiate
changes to American demands that may undermine their ability to
achieve other domestic goals.

There is little doubt that, as Clarkson has noted, initial Canadian
responses to U.S. security concerns such as the Smart Border Accord of
December 2001 reflected pressures from Canadian business groups
whose economic security was seriously disrupted by tightened U.S.
border controls after 9/11 – even if much of Ottawa's 30-point Action
Plan had already been discussed by officials in previous years.[42] Canada's national economic interest was and remains clearly linked to
secure access for its firms to U.S. markets. Since 2001, Canadian officials
have also cooperated closely with their U.S. counterparts at the World
Customs Organization and other international bodies to implement initiatives such as the Container Security Initiative and common standards for the development of electronic passports.[43] The government
reorganization that created Public Safety and Emergency Preparedness
Canada (PSEPC) and the new, more security-focused Canada Border
Services Agency (CBSA) in December 2003 reflected, at least in part, the
need for closer coordination of security initiatives following the creation of the U.S. Department of Homeland Security – albeit with important exceptions.[44]

However, both the Martin and Harper governments have worked to
maintain clear distinctions for Canadian security policies that recognize
both overlapping and diverging interests, including the constraints of
Canada's domestic legal system and other international commitments.
The Martin government's National Security Policy of April 2004 sought
to strike a careful balance between security and civil liberties aspects of
Canada's national interest – as well as the need for extensive international cooperation.[45] The deportation of Canadian dual-national Maher
Arar to his native Syria by U.S. officials, partly on the basis of information shared by the RCMP, triggered a substantial tightening of information-sharing protocols among security services, as well as significant
political fallout.[46] Extended negotiations for a joint land pre-clearance
project for cross-border shipments, a major priority of North American
business groups, fell apart in May 2007 when Canadian officials refused

to allow the extra-territorial application of U.S. laws likely to conflict with previous Charter rulings. Both the Martin and Harper governments have rejected proposals to introduce a system of national ID cards, linked to a comprehensive government database on all Canadians, despite pressures from parts of the security lobby.[47] Working closely with complementary U.S. domestic interests, Canadian officials have persistently and successfully lobbied for delays and revisions to documentation requirements for both American and Canadian citizens in crossing the border under the 'Western Hemisphere Travel Initiative' – while carefully avoiding the U.S. domestic political crossfire over immigration and security issues. Rather than endorsing business calls for a North American security perimeter, both the Martin and Harper governments have pursued carefully calibrated policies of operational cooperation and incremental change intended to facilitate 'low-risk trade and travel' while maintaining existing distinctions between U.S. security policies along the Canadian and Mexican borders.[48]

These patterns suggest the capacity to manage external and domestic policy challenges based on a coherent, consistent approach to Canada's national interests that transcends both partisanship and interest group pressures – while accommodating legitimate U.S. security interests. Canadian governments have demonstrated the capacity to negotiate changes in rule-making processes, to adapt proposed changes to serve distinctive Canadian interests, and to reject or defer measures in which losses in policy discretion are not offset by substantial benefits.

Canada's capacity to maintain this relative autonomy depends in large part on the success of security officials in deterring or diffusing potential terrorist threats to avoid the inevitable backlash that would result from another 9/11. Ottawa has demonstrated growing political skill in engaging an American political system in which cross-border issues are frequently dealt with as subsets of U.S. *domestic* politics and policies. However, that is another, equally complex subject in itself!

Conclusion

Clarkson's persistent view of the United States as an existential threat to Canadian independence, rather than a dynamic and diverse set of external realities to be managed in Canada's interests, reflects both the persistent insecurities of Canada's nationalist academic circles and a failure of imagination that often hinders their capacity to develop strategies that would enhance Canada's relative autonomy. As Clarkson himself has noted on occasion, Canada's relatively peripheral status in U.S. foreign diplomatic, economic, and security policies allows Canadian governments the luxury of concentrating their resources in managing bilateral interests and issues to a degree that is almost unimaginable in Washington.

The effectiveness of Canadian decision-makers in doing so depends partly on their capacity to define a national interest – however segmented by policy field – that can attract the support of major Canadian interests, including provincial governments. It often depends on the capacity to cultivate complementary interests in the United States, simultaneously engaging the executive branch, elements of Congress, and the multitude of interest groups which compete for their attention and support. In some cases, it also depends on the ability to identify policy approaches in other countries that complement Canada's institutional, economic, and social realities more effectively than existing American patterns or models. These dynamic processes require creativity, skill, and a capacity to relate to a variety of interests within and beyond Canada's borders. The events of recent years suggest that, whatever their limitations, both Canada's governments and its citizens may be up to the task rather more than Clarkson and many of his ideological soulmates are willing to admit.

NOTES

1 Stephen Clarkson, 'The Choices to Be Made,' in *Readings in Canadian Foreign Policy*, ed. Duane Bratt and Christopher Kukucha (Toronto: Oxford University Press, 2006) 46–61; Stephen Clarkson, *Uncle Sam and Us: Globalization, Neoconservatism, and the Canadian State* (Toronto: University of Toronto Press, 2002).
2 For example, see Stephen Clarkson et al., 'The Primitive Realities of North America's Transnational Governance,' in *Complex Sovereignty: Reconstituting Political Authority in the Twenty-First Century*, ed. Edgar Grande and Louis Pauly (Toronto: University of Toronto Press, 2005), 188.
3 For example, see William Watson, *Globalization and the Meaning of Canadian Life* (Toronto: University of Toronto Press, 1998); John F. Helliwell, 'Globalization: Myths, Facts, and Consequences,' lecture, C.D. Howe Institute, (Toronto, 2000); Reg Whitaker, 'Made in Canada: The New Public Safety Paradigm, in *How Ottawa Spends: 2005–2006 – Managing the Minority*, ed. G.

Bruce Doern (Montreal and Kingston: McGill-Queen's University Press, 2006), 77–95.

4 Richard Gwyn, *Nationalism without Walls: The Incredible Lightness of Being Canadian* (Toronto: McClelland & Stewart, 1995).

5 Clarkson, *Uncle Sam and Us*, 3–4.

6 James N. Rosenau, *Distant Proximities: Dynamics beyond Globalization* (Princeton, NJ: Princeton University Press, 2003), 11.

7 For example, see Robert M. Campbell, *Grand Illusions: The Politics of the Keynesian Experience in Canada: 1945–1975* (Peterborough, ON: Broadview Press, 1987); and W. Irwin Gillespie, *Tax, Borrow and Spend* (Toronto: Oxford University Press, 1991).

8 Clarkson (*Uncle Sam and Us*, 130) rightly notes the use of targeted tax preferences to support particular political objectives during this period. However, such measures were increasingly attacked from the left as unduly shifting discretion from governments to businesses and individual citizens.

9 John Crow, *Making Money: An Insider's Perspective on Finance, Politics and Canada's Central Bank* (Toronto: Wiley, 2002), 25–44. See also David A. Dodge, 'The Interaction between Monetary and Fiscal Policies,' *Canadian Public Policy* 28, no. 2 (June 2002): 187–201.

10 Clarkson (*Uncle Sam and Us*, 140–2). Numerous observers have argued that high-interest-rate policies perversely compounded the debt-deficit trap by increasing the costs of borrowing, as Ottawa had to borrow to cover the interest payments on existing deficits. See Lars Osberg and Pierre Fortin, eds, *Hard Money, Hard Times* (Toronto: James Lorimer, 1998).

11 A related objective was to force Canadian businesses to increase investments necessary to boost productivity, maintain their competitiveness, and raise Canadian standards of living rather than relying on the 'artificial' stimulus imposed by a cheap dollar. Thomas J. Courchene and Richard G. Harris, 'From Fixing to Monetary Union: Options for North American Currency Integration,' *Commentary* 127 (Toronto: C.D. Howe Institute, 1999); Herbert G. Grubel, *The Case for the Amero: The Economics and Politics of a North American Monetary Union* (Vancouver: Fraser Institute, 1999).

12 For example, see John McCallum, 'Engaging the Debate: Costs and Benefits of a North American Currency' (Toronto: Royal Bank Economics, April 2000); William B.P. Robson, 'No Small Change: The Awkward Economics and Politics of North American Monetary Integration,' *Commentary* 167 (Toronto: C.D. Howe Institute, July 2002).

13 For example, see David Parkinson, 'Bank of Canada Seen Setting Own Course,' *Globe and Mail*, 22 August 2007, B1; Heather Scoffield, Andrew

Willis, and Tara Perkins, 'A Deal That Was 10 Hours in the Making,' *Globe and Mail*, 17 August 2007.

14 Canada, *Agenda: Jobs and Growth – A New Framework for Economic Policy* (Ottawa: Department of Finance, October 1994).

15 Persistent deficits and the relative size of Canada's federal debt increased Ottawa's vulnerability to a run on the dollar triggered by the Mexican peso crisis, to which the Bank of Canada responded with sharp increases in interest rates. See Edward Greenspon and Anthony Wilson-Smith, *Double Vision* (Toronto: Doubleday, 1996), 235–8. For examples of varied approaches to deficit reduction, see Geoffrey Hale, *The Politics of Taxation in Canada* (Toronto: Broadview Press, 2001); and Janice McKinnon, *Minding the Public Purse* (Montreal and Kingston: McGill-Queen's University Press, 2003).

16 Stephen Clarkson and Timothy Lewis, 'The Contested State: Canada in the Post–Cold War, Post-Keynesian, Post-Fordist, Post-National era,' in *Shape Shifting: Canadian Governance toward the 21st Century – How Ottawa Spends: 1999–2000*, ed. Leslie A. Pal (Toronto: Oxford University Press, 1999), 293–340.

17 Ottawa has substantially achieved its target of achieving a debt-to-GDP ratio of 25 per cent in less than a decade, rather than the 15 years originally forecast.

18 Geoffrey Hale, 'International Capital and Domestic Politics: Stumbling towards Tax Reform?' in *How Ottawa Spends: 2008–2009*, ed. Allan M. Maslove, (Montreal: McGill-Queen's University Press, forthcoming).

19 Chen and Mintz have noted that average METRs on corporations have dropped from 44.3% in 1996 to 36.6% in 2006, with promised reductions to 33.5% by 2010. Duanjie Chen and Jack M. Mintz, 'Federal-Provincial Combined Marginal Effective Tax Rates on Capital: 1997–2006, 2010' (Toronto: C.D. Howe Institute, 2006), 20 June; Jack M. Mintz, *The 2006 Tax Competitiveness Report: Proposals for Pro-Growth Tax Reform* (Toronto: C.D. Howe Institute, 2006), 10.

20 Canada, Department of Finance, *Strong Leadership, A Better Canada: Economic Statement* (Ottawa, 30 October 2007), 72.

21 Hale, 'International Capital and Domestic Politics.'

22 Business interests actively pressured governments to follow policies that contributed to the U.S. technology boom and the rapid growth of the Irish economy during the 1990s. However, strong fiscal and economic performance gave Ottawa, in particular, considerable discretion in deciding how to pick and choose among these policies, and over what time period. The Chrétien government's five-year phase-in of assorted tax reductions and

increases in social and inter-governmental transfers after 2000 suggests considerable policy autonomy – while taking advantage of the complementary policies of the Clinton administration during the 1990s, and of George W. Bush's 'big government conservatism' of expanding social entitlements and budget deficits since 2001.

23 Encouraged to diversify their holdings geographically and by investment class, Canada's pension fund sector increased its assets by 140 per cent between 1996 and 2006, substantially faster than in most major industrial countries. Lori McLeod, 'Pension Funds on Steroids,' *Globe and Mail*, 7 July 2007, B4.

24 Between 2000 and 2005, despite a relative decline in overall dependence on U.S. markets, every single Canadian province exported a greater value of goods and services to the United States than to other provinces – some by substantial amounts. Geoffrey Hale, 'Canadian Federalism and North American Integration: Managing Multi-level Games,' paper presented to conference on 'Different Perspectives on Canadian Federalism: Retrospective and Prospective,' University of Waterloo, 27 April 2007.

25 Most sectoral policies are governed by principles of national treatment and mutual recognition – although Canada still retains significant restrictions on foreign firms operating in the banking, telecommunications, and rail and air transportation sectors.

26 For example, see Christina McCall and Stephen Clarkson, *Trudeau and Our Time*, vol. 2, *The Heroic Delusion* (Toronto: McClelland & Stewart, 1994).

27 G. Bruce Doern, and Monica Gattinger, *Power Switch: Energy Regulatory Governance in the Twenty-First Century* (Toronto: University of Toronto Press, 2003); André Plourde, 'The Changing Nature of National and Continental Energy Markets,' in *Canadian Energy Policy and the Struggle for Sustainable Development*, ed. G. Bruce Doern (Toronto: University of Toronto Press, 2005), 51–82.

28 In 2006 seven of Canada's ten largest oil and gas producers were Canadian-controlled firms, while its two largest pipeline companies had become diversified energy companies with extensive operations in the United States. 'Report on Business 1000,' *Globe and Mail*, July–August 2007, 109.

29 Bush's 'NEP' did not result in the passage of a comprehensive energy bill until mid-2005, and that only as a by-product of a series of bipartisan compromises. The challenges of petro-nationalism in Latin America, Russia, and Central Asia are far more pressing concerns for U.S. policy-makers than are energy relations with Canada, especially in the absence of serious frictions in U.S.-Canada relations.

30 Canadian diplomats have identified five Canadian priorities when engag-

ing the U.S. Energy Bill of 2005: ANWR; ensuring Canada's hydro-electric exports were not affected by internal debates over 'renewable portfolio standards' for domestic electricity generation; U.S. restrictions on the exports of uranium to Canadian manufacturers of medical isotopes; the process for cross-border coordination of electricity reliability standards; and proposed subsidies for the construction of an Alaskan natural gas pipeline. Outcomes satisfactory to Canadian officials were achieved on four of the five issues. Confidential interview, Government of Canada.

31 Shawn McCarthy, 'Trans-Canada Ups Mackenzie Role,' *Globe and Mail*, 13 December 2007, B1; Jon Harding, 'Mackenzie Partners See Ottawa Aid,' *Financial Post*, 19 December 2007, FP1.

32 Yvan Guillemette and Jack M. Mintz, 'A Capital Story: Exploding the Myths around Foreign Investment in Canada,' *Commentary* 201 (Toronto: C.D. Howe Institute, August 2004); Jeff Rubin, Peter Buchanan, and Avery Shenfeld, 'A Merger Driven Market' (Toronto: CIBC World Markets, 1 June 2007), 4–6. The multi-billion-dollar takeovers of Alcan by Rio Tinto and BCE by a consortium led by the Ontario Teachers' Pension Plan reversed this balance for the 2003–7 business cycle – due to the minority stakes of OTPP's American partners. Geoffrey Hale, 'The Dog That Hasn't Barked: The Political Economy of Contemporary Debates on Canadian Foreign Investment Policies,' *Canadian Journal of Political Science* 41, no. 3 (September 2008): 1–29.

33 Guillemette and Mintz, 'A Capital Story'; *Financial Post 500*, May 2007.

34 Seven major public sector pension and investment funds, including the Ontario Teachers' Pension Fund, the Caisse de Dépôt, and the Canada Pension Plan Investment Board, control almost half of the $1 trillion in current Canadian pension assets. These funds, often working with 'private equity' firms, have become increasingly active investors in both Canadian and foreign capital markets, as witnessed by the Ontario Teachers' Pension Fund's heavily leveraged takeover of Bell Canada Enterprises in mid-2007. This approach is a sharp departure from previous approaches – especially for Quebec's Caisse de Dépôt and Alberta's Heritage Trust Fund.

35 Both the Ontario government's 'Crawford Panel, composed of a panel of leading institutional investors and national corporate and securities executives, and a 2007 federal budget policy paper advocate a 'common securities regulator' with 'an equal voice [for] all participating jurisdictions.' Crawford Panel on a Single Canadian Securities Regulator, *Blueprint for a Canadian Securities Commission – Final report* (Toronto, 7 June 2006); at http://www.crawfordpanel.ca/Crawford_Panel_ final_paper.pdf. Most other provincial governments have preferred to retain the existing confed-

eral arrangements of the Canadian Securities Administrators, while introducing a 'passport system' based on mutual recognition of one another's standards, rather than trusting in the capacity of the proposed regulator to avoid domination by either the federal or Ontario governments. A recent Alberta Securities Commission report notes that the four largest provinces have 92% of public companies and 86% of aggregate market capital listed on Canadian exchanges – including 47% and 41% respectively for Ontario-based firms. Alberta Securities Commission, *The Alberta Capital Market: A Comparative Overview: 2007 Report* (Calgary, May 2007), 2–3.

36 Trading volumes of Canadian equities on U.S. exchanges totaled $603 billion or 41.7% of overall trading volume in 2004, the first year of the current takeover boom. Cecile Carpentier, Jean-François L'Her, and Jean-Marc Suret, 'How Healthy Is the Canadian Stock Market?' (Ste-Foy, working paper, University of Laval, 28 August 2005). In December 2005, Alberta- and BC-based firms accounted for 52% of publicly traded Canadian corporations (vs. 31% for Ontario), and 32% of aggregate market capital (vs. 42% for Ontario). Alberta Securities Commission, 'The Alberta Capital Market: A Comparative Overview' (Calgary, May 2006), 2.

37 Christopher Nicholls, 'The Characteristics of Canada's Capital Markets and the Illustrative Case of Canada's Legislative Regulatory Response to Sarbanes-Oxley,' Research Report for Task Force to Modernize Securities Legislation in Canada (Toronto: Government of Ontario, 15 June 2006), 133–8; at http://www.tfmsl.ca/docs/V4(3A)%20Nicholls.pdf.

38 In practice, it could well reduce incentives for Canadian regulators to follow U.S. regulatory shifts unsuited to the different structures of Canadian capital markets, thus increasing domestic policy discretion, while creating stronger incentives for the development of uniform securities legislation (and a single regulator) in Canada. Canada, 'Creating a Canadian Advantage in Global Capital Markets,' *Budget 2007* (Ottawa: Department of Finance, 19 March 2007), 18, 29–31; at http://www.budget.gc.ca/2007/pdf/bkcmae.pdf. These proposals were rejected by the U.S. Securities and Exchange Commission in April 2008. However, at the time of writing, there were ongoing discussions between the interprovincial Canadian Securities Administrators and the SEC.

39 Ibid., 31; Paul Vieira, 'Flaherty Flip Sparks Confusion,' *Financial Post*, 15 May 2007, FP4.

40 Clarkson et al. 'Primitive Realities,' 190.

41 Frank P. Harvey, 'Canada's Addiction to American Security: The Illusion of Choice in the War on Terrorism,' *American Review of Canadian Studies* 35, no. 1 (Summer 2005): 265–94; Greg Anderson and Christopher Sands,

Negotiating North America: The Security and Prosperity Partnership (Washington: The Hudson Institute, 2007), 4; confidential interviews, Government of Canada.

42 For example, even before 9/11, Citizenship and Immigration Canada had strongly advocated a 'Safe Third Country Agreement' to enable it to control both 'asylum shopping' and the number of economic migrants seeking refugee status in Canada. However, CIC has strongly resisted U.S. proposals to harmonize the two countries' visa waiver programs that exempt citizens of selected countries from requirements to obtain a visa before travelling to either country.

43 Geoffrey Hale, 'WHTI: Now for the Hard Part,' *Fraser Forum*, December–January 2007: 14–17.

44 For example, in contrast to the United States, most immigration functions were retained by a separate department of Citizenship and Immigration. Public Safety Canada oversees federal police and security functions, which in the United States remain under the authority of the Department of Justice, the CIA, and other agencies.

45 Whitaker, 'Made in Canada.'

46 Confidential interviews, U.S. government, Government of Canada. The Martin government's decision to create a Canadian no-fly list, subsequently implemented by the Harper government, suggests efforts to accommodate U.S. security concerns while doing so on substantially Canada's own terms.

47 Martin-era Immigration Minister Denis Coderre initially championed the idea of a national ID card before a political backlash derailed the idea. The Harper government has quietly advised officials that the issue is a non-starter. Confidential interviews, Government of Canada.

48 A key factor in this debate is the relative functionality of Canadian and American immigration policies – especially given the latter's complete breakdown in managing orderly migration flows from Mexico, Latin America, and the Caribbean. Geoffrey Hale, 'Getting Down to Business: Rebuilding Canada–US Relations,' in *How Ottawa Spends: 2007–2008*, ed. G. Bruce Doern (Montreal: McGill-Queen's University Press, 2007).

9 An Independent Foreign Policy for Canadian Provinces?: International Trade and Sub-Federal Autonomy

CHRISTOPHER J. KUKUCHA

During the past several decades Canadian provinces have demon-strated an increasing interest in international affairs. Initially, Quebec pursued nationalist goals related to language and culture. Today, how-ever, provincial governments engage a wide range of political and eco-nomic objectives external to the Canadian state. British Columbia, for example, recently signed an environmental agreement with California on climate change. Ontario has challenged New York on issues of gov-ernment procurement. Quebec now has a 'formal' role in the United Nations Educational, Scientific and Cultural Organization (UNESCO) and is seeking similar representation in other international forums. The government of Alberta has also opened an office in Washington, DC, to directly lobby the White House and members of Congress.

For the most part, there are three responses to these sub-federal initi-atives. Some, such as Paul Heinbecker, Canada's former ambassador to the United Nations, have suggested that Quebec's activity is simply 'the same old bullshit.'[1] Others, such as Andrew Coyne, have argued that the foreign presence of Canadian provinces 'blurs our international identity' and duplicates the activity of federal officials at considerable taxpayer expense.[2] The third attitude, the one shared by the majority of Canadians, is ambivalence.

This study will engage these perspectives in the context of foreign trade policy – the one issue area where every provincial government has some international presence. For the past two decades trade agree-ments, such as the North American Free Trade Agreement (NAFTA) and the World Trade Organization (WTO), have increasingly impinged on areas of provincial jurisdiction. This discussion will focus on the capacity of sub-federal institutional, sectoral and societal interests to maintain autonomy in response to these developments. Specifically, are there provisions under international law or domestic judicial decisions that guarantee the compliance of Canadian provinces with federal trade policy? Have intrusive international pressures altered federal–provincial relations or the role of non-central executive and bureaucratic actors? Are business and societal interests more relevant in this altered policy environment?

In order to answer these questions it is necessary to evaluate the impact of provincial governments on both Canadian trade policy and the evolution of international norms and standards. If significant sub-federal autonomy exists, and this is reflected in Canada's trade policy and the final legal text of international agreements, this creates potential problems for Ottawa in the pursuit of broader national objectives in this policy area. Specifically, if federal and provincial priorities diverge it can limit Ottawa's capacity to negotiate and implement foreign trade commitments. This study will suggest that provincial institutional and sectoral interests have maintained a degree of autonomy in relation to both the federal government and international trade regimes. It is important to note, however, that sub-federal pressures are not constant, and restrictions on central autonomy are limited to specific actors and policy areas.

For the most part, provincial autonomy is enhanced by a lack of binding international enforcement mechanisms focusing on sub-federal compliance. Domestic judicial rulings also fail to exclude the foreign initiatives of provinces in relevant areas of jurisdiction. These two realities have influenced the practice of Canadian federalism. In fact, intergovernmental consultative linkages now exist in the area of trade policy, although they do not guarantee full provincial participation in international negotiations. Political executives in Canadian provinces have also demonstrated increased attention to matters of trade policy, although this interest is surprisingly ad hoc and does not often result in tangible national or international outcomes. In contrast, provincial bureaucratic actors do have a considerable impact despite challenges related to limited resources and the expanding relevance of outside legal counsel. Finally, provincial sectoral interests will be shown to have directly influenced Canadian foreign trade policy and rules-based outcomes in foreign trade agreements, especially in terms of liquor, agriculture, and softwood lumber. Societal actors, however, despite their interest and mobilization on international economic issues, are primarily excluded for a wide range of reasons, including consultation fatigue and a tendency to target federal officials.

Evaluating Autonomy

In the original volume that inspired this collection, Stephen Clarkson explored Canada's capacity to pursue an independent foreign policy in the context of international and domestic considerations. External pressures were tied directly to the asymmetry of Canada's economic and political relationship with the United States. Internal limitations included Quebec's international pursuit of nationalist objectives, an inefficient and complex bureaucracy, and a lack of societal input in the foreign policy process. Finally, Clarkson pondered the 'purpose' of Canadian autonomy, if it could in fact be achieved. Specifically, what role should Canada play in multilateral institutions such as the United Nations and the North Atlantic Treaty Organization (NATO), and was there a future for the country in the specific areas of international peacekeeping and foreign development assistance? Clarkson answered the 'independence for what purpose' question with an emphatic call for a more dynamic, independent, and demanding approach to Canada's external relations.

Clarkson's decision to include a chapter on the role of the provinces in Canadian foreign policy reflected the early stages of provincial interest in Canada's international affairs. In Quebec, the aftermath of the Quiet Revolution sparked a new sense of nationalism in the province, which included an active international agenda. It was also during this period that British Columbia aggressively protected its interests during the negotiation of the Canada-U.S. Columbia River Treaty and Saskatchewan was targeted by the United States for dumping potash into the New Mexico market. Louis Sabourin's contribution, however, focused specifically on the question of special international status for Quebec. Sabourin argued that provincial initiatives in the late 1960s were directly tied to the survival of French culture. Specifically, Sabourin suggested that Quebec had limited confidence in Ottawa's ability to address these challenges. Sabourin was not calling for a rejection of federal legitimacy, especially in terms of the negotiation and implementation of international agreements, but he did emphasize the need for Quebec to assert its autonomy in this issue area.[3]

This chapter suggests that developments during the past four decades require a re-evaluation of both the 'independence' question and the role of the provinces in Canadian foreign policy. First, any contemporary discussion of autonomy must move beyond Canada's relations with the United States. State autonomy is also a complex issue that requires clear measures of analysis. Therefore, it is important to define not only autonomy, but also its relationship with sovereignty, and intrusiveness. As Kim Nossal has noted, autonomy is not 'independence,' which is the 'ability to be free from the control of others.' Sovereignty, on the other hand, focuses on the 'juridical recognition' of modern Westphalian states to control territory and exercise authority over citizens. Autonomy, however, is the 'ability' to achieve specific preferences. Although all political communities pursue these goals, none are able to consistently exercise complete autonomy. Therefore, autonomy is reduced by internal 'limitations, or by the demands, actions, and constraints of others.'[4] For the purpose of this study the autonomy of specific actors, the dependent variable, will be evaluated on a continuum ranging between *minimal*, *partial*, and *substantive*.

In terms of intrusiveness, the independent variable, it is important to evaluate the impact of international pressures on domestic policy space. Specifically, do external developments place limitations on Canada's ability to protect its self-interest? In the decades following Clarkson's volume few observers questioned the evolution of a competitive neo-liberal global economy, with increased market pressures that reduced, or minimized, state protectionism and regulatory capacity. At the same time, this chapter accepts that intrusiveness is not a zero-sum equation, where state autonomy is vulnerable in all scenarios. Therefore, when examining international pressures and the role of the provinces in Canadian foreign policy it is necessary to make clear distinctions between issues of *process* and *outcome*. In terms of *process*, there is a need to expand 'two-level' games beyond the priorities of central governments.[5] Specifically, issues of autonomy include provincial and other sub-federal interests, which also face challenges from intrusive international pressures. These developments can be evaluated by comprehensive *institutional*, *sectoral*, and *societal* categories. In the case of foreign trade policy, institutional issues include constitutional and judicial realities, the role of the executive, provincial legislatures, bureaucratic interests, and intergovernmental relations linked to international affairs. Sectoral actors consist of industry associations, corporations, individual executives, and advisory groups, as well as consultative links with provincial government departments or officials. In addition, societal interests, which are typically treated as secondary considerations, incorporate organized labour, environmental groups, First Nations, civil society, and a wide range of other non-governmental organizations.

What is missing, however, is the acknowledgment that domestic actors, even at the provincial level, can have a direct impact on international *outcomes*. The institutional policies of central and non-central governments, for example, created by executive, legislative, and bureaucratic interests, are often transferred between levels of analysis as states consult, negotiate, and implement global trade commitments. Business interests and industry associations with the capability to develop an international profile also have a presence in the global political economy that is distinct from the nation-state. In some cases, societal groups also contribute to transnational linkages that extend beyond national boundaries. Therefore, when evaluating sub-federal trade relations it is important to recognize that causal relationships are 'top-down' and 'transnational,' with an additional emphasis on 'bottom-up' linkages. Finally, it is crucial to understand that 'change' does not occur if institutional or non-state actors support policy positions already endorsed by government.[6] The key, therefore, is to look for examples where pressure from non-central governments alters Canadian policy and does not simply reflect original federal concerns.

International Initiatives and Canadian Federalism

There is some ambiguity regarding the legitimacy of provincial foreign activity in terms of international law, the Canadian constitution, and previous Supreme Court decisions.[7] This has obvious implications for Canadian federalism. Historically, Ottawa attempted to limit the provinces to a consultative role. During the Tokyo Round of the General Agreement on Tariffs and Trade (GATT), for example, the Canadian Trade and Tariffs Committee (CTTC) was established, which was responsible for gathering briefs from business, unions, consumer groups, the provinces, and other interested parties. In 1975 a more direct forum for the provinces was created with an ad hoc federal-provincial committee of deputy ministers. In 1977 a Canadian Coordinator for Trade Negotiations (CCTN) was appointed with the mandate to coordinate information from the provinces, the federal bureaucracy, industry, and other non-governmental organizations. Ultimately, these linkages evolved into provincial representation in the Trade Negotiations Office (TNO) of the Canada–United States Free Trade Agreement (FTA), and the Committee for the Free Trade Agreement (CFTA). For NAFTA, the CFTA remained in place, but Ottawa and the provinces also agreed to create the Committee for North American Free Trade Negotiations (CNAFTN).[8]

Ultimately, the CNAFTN process evolved into the CTrade committee system, which involves a series of meetings between Ottawa and the provinces four times annually. Initially, some provincial governments expressed concerns with the content and quality of information available through CTrade. More recently, however, Ottawa has prioritized provincial input owing to the complexity of issues such as services and improved access to information and the agenda-setting process.[9] At the same time, however, there is ongoing pressure from specific provinces, such as Quebec and Alberta, for a more formalized role in the policy process. Quebec, for example, has previously supported a European Union (EU) model, in which member states are direct participants in EU negotiating teams. Other provinces, however, do not endorse calls for a formalized structure. Specific concerns include the need for additional bureaucratic resources and expertise, as well as support for the current flexible consultative framework. As a result, it would appear that substantial alteration to the existing CTrade system is unlikely in the near future.[10]

Provincial Institutional Factors – The Political Executive and Bureaucracy

Surprisingly, the role of provincial political executives is somewhat marginalized in the formulation of sub-federal foreign trade policy. This suggests that when provinces do impact federal trade policy these pressures originate from areas within provincial governments other than the executive. The reason for this is the selective interest of provincial executives in this complex policy area. In fact, executive involvement is typically limited to crisis situations, such as those involving Bovine Spongiform Encephalopathy (BSE) in Alberta and Avian Flu in British Columbia. Members of the political executive also tend to be active in the late stages of international negotiations or during trade disputes, such as those over softwood lumber. Another area of executive involvement is federal and provincial trade promotion. At other times, senior cabinet members attempt to represent specific sectoral interests, such as Ralph Klein's meetings in Washington regarding a continental energy strategy and a potential oil pipeline through Canada to connect Alaska to the 'lower 48' states.

There are, however, specific examples of provincial political executives directly engaging issues of trade policy. One of the best-documented case studies is Ontario's opposition to NAFTA during the 1990s. Bob Rae's New Democratic Party (NDP) government openly opposed NAFTA with several strategies, including a critical report questioning the agreement and a constitutional legal challenge. The position of the Rae government was not based solely on ideology. Questions regarding the province's commitment to international trade first emerged when David Peterson's Liberals opposed the FTA in 1988.[11] For Peterson there were direct political costs associated with the FTA, in terms of organized labour and numerous business interests that relied on protectionist import barriers. As a result, Peterson was motivated to ensure the FTA was perceived by Ontarians as an 'imposed' agreement, reluctantly accepted by Queen's Park. Peterson's concerns were not universally shared throughout the government. In fact, the Ministry of Economic Development and Trade (MEDT) supported greater trade liberalization.[12] By January 1993, however, Rae transferred responsibility for the negotiations from MEDT to the Ministry of Intergovernmental Affairs (MIA), which better reflected Rae's caution concerning NAFTA. A series of cabinet committee hearings, which supported provincial opposition to the agreement, soon followed.

According to Donald Abelson and Michael Lusztig, although 'little documentation exists, sources within MEDT and MIA suggest that Ontario's policy shift created significant disruption of the NAFTA process.'[13] This came as a surprise to federal officials who were looking to Ontario for leadership in the later stages of NAFTA discussions. The government's position also made it difficult for provincial officials to protect Ontario's interests. As one participant recalled, 'It wasn't long before we [Ontario] lost all credibility at these meetings.'[14] Prime Minister Brian Mulroney eventually ratified the agreement by passing legislation within the House of Commons without requesting direct legitimization from provincial legislatures. In the end, Ontario also did not pursue the constitutional reference case or additional proposed legislation on water protection. Regardless, it is clear that political executives from separate Liberal and NDP governments openly opposed Ottawa on matters of international trade, which contributed to an ad hoc approach to foreign trade policy.[15] In subsequent Harris, Eves, and

McGuinty governments there was no direct involvement of the provincial political executive on issues of Canadian trade policy.[16]

In contrast, provincial bureaucracies have factored significantly into the process of Canadian trade policy development. The small number and long tenure of officials in this policy area grant provincial bureaucrats considerable influence. Federal counterparts, by contrast tend to be rotated out of positions focusing on sub-federal trade, thereby preventing the development of a comparable 'institutional memory.' The two provinces with the most developed bureaucratic commitment to international trade are Ontario and Quebec. In Ontario the responsibility for the negotiation and implementation of global trade agreements rests with the Trade and International Policy Branch of MEDT. Quebec also has its own Ministry of International Relations (MIR), although oversight of trade policy has shifted between MIR and the Ministries of Industry and of Finance. By 2003 foreign trade policy was located in the Ministry of Economic and Regional Development (MERD), which subsequently became the Ministry of Economic Development, Innovation and Export Trade. Other provinces, however, commit fewer bureaucratic resources in this issue area. In Alberta, for example, there are three to four officials responsible for trade policy within the Trade Policy Branch of the Ministry of International and Intergovernmental Relations (MIIR), whereas Manitoba has one official, who is the director of policy, planning and coordination in the Administration and Finance Division of the Department of Industry, Economic Development and Mines. Numerous line departments are also involved in the formulation of trade policy, dealing with finance, agriculture, forestry, justice, and environmental issues. As a result, some provinces, such as Alberta, New Brunswick, and Quebec, have institutionalized committees to oversee the priorities of bureaucratic interests. In other provinces, however, there are no formalized committee systems in place. Instead, policy positions are established through an ad hoc system of information sharing between relevant ministries.

Regardless, it is crucial to emphasize that only a select number of provincial officials have an impact on the formulation of foreign trade policy. Put simply, only a limited number of bureaucrats at the provincial level have the information and expertise to engage this policy area. Several provinces have also developed close working relationships and in some cases share workloads on specific files. In Ontario, for example, MEDT makes a point of copying most departmental memos to other provinces and the federal government in an effort to avoid duplication.[17] In some cases, provincial cooperation is based more on sectoral considerations and mutual interest. Alberta, for example, worked closely with British Columbia and Saskatchewan on softwood lumber. The province also shared a close working relationship with Saskatchewan on wheat and Quebec on more general questions of jurisdictional concern.[18] Quebec and Alberta also worked together in the final stages of the Uruguay Round negotiations in Geneva. At the same time, however, it is important to not over emphasize this cooperation. In the words of one provincial bureaucrat, 'provinces have competing interests, and it does not always make sense to share information.'[19] Another issue challenging the impact of provincial bureaucracies is reduced budgets and staffing. The on-going legalization of trade policy, and the increasingly prominent role of outside legal counsel, create additional financial limitations on provincial bureaucracies, in addition to raising normative issues of legitimacy.[20]

Sectoral and Societal Considerations

Alcohol is a highly contentious area of Canada's foreign trade policy. Historically, Canadian provinces maintained monopolies or near monopolies on the sale of alcoholic beverages in order to raise revenue. Provincial liquor boards carefully regulated the sale and importation of all alcohol with a special emphasis on wine and beer. At the completion of the Tokyo Round a Statement of Intent was signed by Canadian provinces that limited regulations on the sale of alcohol. In the years following the agreement a number of European states began to question the commitment of Canadian provinces, especially Ontario. The issue was eventually forwarded to a GATT dispute panel, the Panel on Import, Distribution and Sale of Alcoholic Drinks by Canadian Provincial Marketing Agencies, which reported its findings in October 1987. The ruling favoured the European Community and centred on the GATT's 'federal state clause.'[21] Canada and Europe subsequently negotiated a settlement on 20 December 1988 that focused primarily on EC concerns regarding wine. Beer was included, but only in terms of confirming language related to price mark-up differentials and extending national treatment to listing practices.[22]

This dispute involved the legitimate interests of grape growers and wineries in Ontario and British Columbia, which justified provincial practices based on European agricultural subsidies. Other provinces, especially those with limited wine production, wanted to settle the dispute because of potential disruptions of beer sales. Following the October GATT panel decision, the federal government invited the provinces to observe but not fully participate in three separate negotiating sessions with the EC, which resulted in an agreement 'made with the knowledge and tacit consent of the majority of the provinces[, although Ontario ... reserved its support until a final settlement was reached on wine adjustment measures in March 1989.]'[23]

In the early 1990s there were few official complaints from Europe related to wine and the Canadian provinces. In the late 1990s, however, the European Community began to call for a further review of provincial distribution practices in exchange for concessions allowing greater market access for Canadian ice wines. In December 2000 the EC initiated a dialogue with Ottawa, and several months later the federal government contacted the provinces regarding participation in these discussions. Individual bilateral meetings were also arranged between the EC and Ontario, Quebec, and British Columbia. Although federal officials were present, they were simply observers. Provincial governments were also involved in similar sectoral discussions with the United States regarding market access, although these meetings were with American commercial groups, as opposed to U.S. officials.[24]

The sale and marketing of agricultural products represents another key sectoral issue for Canadian provinces. There are distinct differences in terms of the way different agricultural sectors are sheltered from international competition. Canada's dairy industry, for example, is protected by a combination of import tariffs, pricing programs, and production quotas. In contrast, export-competitive commodities, such as grain, oilseed, and red meat, typically do not support supply management practices.[25] Not surprisingly, these tensions create challenges for the negotiation and implementation of international trade agreements. According to Grace Skogstad, however, the WTO's Agreement on Agriculture is notably restricted in its intrusiveness. Although the previous quota system for dairy, poultry, and eggs was replaced with tariffs, new measures were set at higher levels than previous barriers.[26] In addition, Canada 'had already reduced its domestic aggregate support by the amounts stipulated ... and the process of redesigning agricultural income safety nets for the grains sector to meet the exempt criteria' were well under way.[27] One policy area that did have a direct impact on Canadian producers was export subsidies. Specifically, the Agreement on Agriculture made it clear that these practices were to be reduced, especially in relation to grain and dairy products. As Skogstad points out, however, the Canadian government, driven by a deficit-reduction agenda during the 1990s, exceeded these targets. Finally, compared to Europe and the United States, Canada has one of the lowest transfers as a percentage of total value of production, especially in terms of wheat.[28] As Éric Montpetit has argued, agricultural protection remains, but it will not return to previous levels, despite pressure from lobby groups.[29]

The WTO Agreement on Subsidies and Countervailing Measures (SCM) provides the clearest example of the impact of Canadian provinces during the Uruguay Round negotiations. Specifically, there was considerable pressure from the United States to alter article 2.2 of the SCM, which states explicitly that 'the setting or change of generally applicable tax rates by all levels of government entitled to do so shall not be deemed to be a specific subsidy for the purposes of this Agreement.'[30] During the negotiations, Washington made it clear it wanted to remove, or dilute, this clause in order to stop the practice of state subsidies, which creates considerable competition between non-central governments in the American market. Not surprisingly, Canada opposed this position owing to the threat it posed to regional subsidy programs, especially those of Canadian provinces. As one official pointed out, 'The U.S. proposal would have made provincial programs countervailable and all provinces, not simply Ontario and Quebec, opposed it. The simple reason is that regional subsidies extend beyond agriculture in Canada and provinces did not want other programs targeted.' The other important factor, he suggested, was that 'regional subsidies in the U.S. are primarily state-driven programs, whereas in Canada the provinces rely almost exclusively on funding from the federal government.'[31] Therefore, as a result of provincial pressure Canada did not endorse changes to article 2.2 and the language of the clause was not altered, despite ongoing American pressure during the negotiations.

Another sectoral issue that demonstrates the capacity of provincial governments to at least partially define Canadian foreign trade policy, and contribute to outcomes at the international level, is softwood lumber. In the modern era the Canada-U.S. softwood lumber dispute dates back to the early 1980s. In the case formally referred to among trade law experts as Lumber I (1981–3), the U.S. Department of Commerce (DOC) denied accusations by domestic producers that Canadian lumber was subsidized.

It was not until Lumber II (1986–91), however, that provincial governments became increasingly involved in this bilateral policy area. Not only was the U.S. industry targeting provincial stumpage practices but it became clear that significant differences existed among provinces on the softwood issue: Ontario was opposed to ongoing FTA negotiations and used lumber to draw attention to the agreement's perceived shortcomings; Quebec feared the potential economic costs of new U.S. countervailing duties; and British Columbia began making public statements that openly disagreed with Ottawa's position on softwood lumber.[32] Despite the lack of consensus between provinces, Ottawa and Washington negotiated the November 1986 Memorandum of Understanding (MOU) to end this phase of the dispute. Under the MOU, Canada agreed to collect a 15 per cent export tax on all lumber shipped to the United States, but in response to provincial concerns, individual provinces were allowed to alter stumpage fees in exchange for a reduction of the export charge. In British Columbia, the export tax was eventually eliminated and in Quebec it was reduced in various stages before stabilizing at 3.1 per cent. Subsequent stumpage increases, however, resulted in increased costs for both producers and consumers, and not surprisingly there was considerable pressure from industry and the provinces to terminate the MOU after its five-year term expired in 1991.

A series of GATT and FTA dispute panels were initiated in the aftermath of the MOU and eventually both countries re-established a dialogue on softwood lumber. The result was the five-year Canada–United States Softwood Lumber Agreement (SLA) negotiated in 1996. Once again, provinces mobilized to protect specific interests during Lumber III, but sub-federal activity became especially intense following the end of the SLA in 2001. It was during this period, Lumber IV (2001–6), that Canada and the United States launched numerous NAFTA and WTO dispute settlement cases. Once again, however, several provinces had different priorities related to this policy area. Quebec, for example, refused to accept DOC reforms aimed at making lumber practices more 'market-driven,' something already accepted by a number of provincial governments. Other provinces expressed a willingness to accept a 'sliding-scale export tax' that reflected Canada's share of the U.S. lumber market, but this was rejected by Ottawa. Saskatchewan tied Canadian acceptance of a negotiated settlement to the cancellation of WTO and NAFTA challenges, and Alberta raised concerns related to its proposed allocation of quota. Atlantic Canada, on the other hand, with its large areas of privately owned land and high stumpage fees, sided with the Americans.[33] British Columbia, however, started to consider a separate bilateral agreement with the United States.[34] In this instance, provincial disagreement in addition to a low Canadian dollar, high demand for lumber exports in the U.S. market, and a highly politicized American lumber lobby contributed to a five-year delay in replacing the SLA.

By April 2005, however, it was becoming clear that Canada and the United States were approaching a potential softwood lumber agreement. A key part of the new deal was a provision allowing the United States to withhold approximately $1 billion in duties already collected from Canadian companies. Almost immediately the proposed agreement was condemned by British Columbia, Ontario, and Quebec. British Columbia was especially critical given that approximately 50 per cent of all duties paid to the United States were from BC producers. Despite these concerns the outline of a new softwood lumber agreement was announced on 27 April 2006. Although Ontario and Quebec eventually supported the terms of the deal, opposition began to solidify in British Columbia. The BC Lumber Trade Council, the major industry group within the province, openly condemned the agreement's 'anti-circumvention' clause, which would prevent British Columbia from adopting market-based pricing in the interior of the province. U.S. negotiators called for stumpage prices based on U.S. timber prices, whereas British Columbia wanted pricing to be determined by the declining value of the province's beetle-infested timber. The possibility of higher U.S. import taxes on value-added lumber was also criticized. American negotiators also pushed for a definition of 'independent producers' that would exclude almost all BC re-manufacturers from tax concessions. Finally, west-coast suppliers were concerned about ongoing issues related to U.S. market access.[35]

Despite these concerns, Ottawa signed the legal text of a new Softwood Lumber Agreement (SLA 2006) on 1 July 2006. The length of the agreement was seven years although a termination clause was included that would allow the United States to end the SLA on one month's notice after two years. The terms of the new SLA also allowed Washington to keep nearly $1 billion in collected duties. Of greater concern to British Columbia and other provinces, however, were provisions setting border taxes and quotas on the basis of shipments as opposed to sales. Quotas would also not be transferable from month to month, and if monthly shipments from Canada exceeded historic export levels additional export charges would apply. As a result, provincial opposition to the agreement continued following the release of the legal text. In fact, British Columbia, Quebec, Ontario, and Alberta continued to push Ottawa for additional changes to the SLA. Ultimately, the BC government was successful in getting both Ottawa and Washington to accept several provincial specific revisions to the SLA. Specifically, the province's market-based pricing system was accepted, a bi-national panel would review lumber harvested on private land, and 'running rules,' which detailed Canada's application of taxes and capacity limits to lumber shipments, would also be reviewed to ensure commercial viability. As a result, British Columbia announced its support of the SLA on 16 August 2006. Rapidly declining prices in the months following the SLA, and a growing realization that the Americans would not consider further revisions, encouraged other industry and provincial critics to support the agreement. Bill C-24, the Softwood Lumber Products Export Charge Act, 2006, received royal assent in Parliament on 14 December 2006.[36]

A final non-governmental consideration, distinct from business, is pressure from domestic societal interests. For the most part, these actors have a limited impact on provincial foreign trade policy. Individual provinces also have different approaches to non-governmental actors based on history, sectoral priorities, and bureaucratic resources. In Ontario, linkages tend to be driven by business, although First Nations groups have established a role in the forestry sector. Quebec has attempted to initiate formal consultative frameworks in the past, consistent with provincial corporatist traditions, but the Liberals have returned to a more elite-driven process of interaction. Alberta, on the other hand, faces negligible demands from societal considerations and continues to focus on the concerns of industry. Although the NDP in British Columbia improved access during the 1990s, the role of these interests has diminished considerably in recent years. At the same time, however, there are similar characteristics that define government–societal relations in this policy area. Contact is often ad hoc, reactive, and directed at specific line departments. Much of the consultation that does occur is also done simultaneously with federal initiatives, especially in smaller provinces. Regardless, there is a tendency by provincial officials to question the input of these sources owing to a perceived lack of knowledge and the anti-globalization rhetoric adopted by many of these interests. Societal groups also contribute to this marginalization owing to a failure to direct attention at relevant provincial officials, a lack of resources, and consultation fatigue. There is also the fact that 'influence' is often difficult to determine if non-governmental priorities share similarities with provincial policy agendas. As a result, societal pressures exist in Canada but, for the most part, these factors do not significantly contribute to the foreign trade policy of Canadian provinces.[37]

The Autonomy Question

This brief discussion of provincial trade policy points to several conclusions regarding sub-federal autonomy and the ability of provinces to
alter Canadian trade policy and international norms and standards.
First, it is clear that foreign trade commitments have intruded into areas
of provincial jurisdiction. At the same time, however, these realities do
not place profound limitations on the autonomy of Canadian provinces. In international agreements where specific 'federal state' clauses
exist, there are only a small number of dispute panels focusing on this
issue. Even in cases such as Canada's dispute with the EU on provincial
wine practices, long-term outcomes actually facilitated greater provincial involvement and autonomy. Canadian federalism's ability to
respond to international intrusiveness also points to the ongoing capacity of provinces to pursue independent policy initiatives. In its current
manifestation, CTrade serves as a forum on trade policy that meets four
times annually. The key, however, is that these linkages are primarily
informative. While dialogue between federal and provincial officials
takes place at these meetings, it tends to lack substance. In fact, most
detailed conversations occur on an ad hoc basis between specific
officials, provincial trade policy bureaus or line departments. In the
post-NAFTA/WTO era, federal officials understand that provincial priorities must be addressed in order to implement international trade
commitments. Therefore, linkages between Ottawa and the provinces
typically place minimal or partial limitations on the foreign trade policy
of Canadian provinces. In fact, provincial input during this process can
actually lead to tangible outcomes in which sub-federal interests shape
Canada's global trade relations, as well as the final legal text of international agreements.

Questions of autonomy are also relevant in the evaluation of provincial institutional, sectoral, and societal considerations. In terms of institutional factors it is necessary to distinguish between executive and
bureaucratic interests. Provincial political executives, for example, have
a surprisingly limited role on matters of foreign trade policy. As noted
earlier, executive involvement in the area of trade policy is ad hoc, and
focuses on international negotiations, specific trade disputes, crisis situations, or trade and investment promotion. The ability to selectively
engage the policy process is due primarily to the complexity of this
issue area, but also to the apolitical nature of these concerns. This pattern of involvement, however, indicates a high level of autonomy for

the political executive as it picks and chooses its level of engagement. In cases where direct involvement has occurred, such as with Ontario, these institutional considerations had an obvious impact on provincial foreign policy. There is little evidence to suggest, however, that this influence extended to Canada's foreign trade relations or the codification of external rules and norms. Therefore, provincial political executives have substantial autonomy on matters of process, but limited or partial control over policy outcomes at the federal or international level.

Instead, bureaucratic interests are typically the most significant institutional actors within provincial governments. The reasons for this are tied directly to the technical and legal nature of this policy area. Therefore, provincial bureaucratic actors have extensive autonomy in determining provincial responses to international developments. In many cases, the bureaucracy will also attempt to directly pursue sub-federal priorities in various sectors. Trade officials within provincial bureaucracies also reach autonomous decisions regarding cooperation with representatives in other provinces. At the same time, however, this influence does not always directly correspond with specific outcomes at the federal level. Provincial officials have also pointed to budget and staffing issues, and the legalization of trade policy, as problems contributing to a level of marginalization. This suggests that provincial bureaucracies have considerable influence on process issues, much like the political executive. The difference, however, is that bureaucratic actors have partial, and in some cases substantial, influence that is consistent at the sub-federal level.

In this examination of sectoral interests, however, it is clear that provincial institutional and industry actors are able to influence both Canadian foreign trade policy and international trade rules. As noted, long-term disputes over alcohol contributed to an expanded global presence for Canadian provinces. This discussion also highlighted federal and provincial autonomy in the agricultural sector. Most notably, Ottawa and the provinces were not adversely affected by the WTO's Agreement on Agriculture owing to previous autonomous decisions made prior to the negotiation of the agreement. In some cases, this was driven by federal concerns regarding the cost of ongoing agricultural support. In other examples, however, provinces were dominant, such as in the WTO's SCM and the practice of regional subsidies. Similar outcomes were also evident in terms of softwood lumber, where some provinces, such as British Columbia, had a direct impact on both Canadian foreign trade policy and international outcomes. Therefore, in any evaluation of sectoral concerns it is clear that institutional actors are responding to international developments, but in a way that demonstrates both autonomy and the protection of sub-federal interests. Finally, this discussion has also indicated that provincial societal pressures have only a minimal impact on the foreign trade policy of Canadian provinces, which raises legitimate questions related to transparency, access, and legitimacy.

This being stated, it is important to keep these developments in perspective. While it is true that provinces place limitations on federal autonomy, and have influenced international norms and standards, sub-federal governments are not dictating results at either level of analysis. Media attention has recently homed in on the opening of provincial foreign offices, especially those opened by the Quebec and Alberta governments. The reality, however, is that these initiatives have traditionally concentrated on trade *promotion*, as opposed to trade *policy*. In the case of Alberta it should also be recalled that the Liberal government of Paul Martin offered all provinces a similar presence within the Canadian embassy in Washington to lobby U.S. officials. While Alberta was the only province to formally accept the invitation, Quebec had already established a diplomatic presence in the American capital with the historic 1978 establishment of its 'tourism' office in Washington.[38] Although Alberta did gain some access to U.S. officials, the province's greatest symbolic moment arguably occurred when a large truck from the oil sands was parked in front of the Smithsonian to remind Americans where their automotive fuel originated. These are not insignificant developments, but they do not seriously threaten Canada's capacity to form an independent foreign trade policy, except in selective areas of provincial interest.

NOTES

1 Andrew Coyne, 'Dismembering Canada,' *Ottawa Citizen*, 30 May 2006, A14.
2 Ibid.
3 Louis Sabourin, 'Special International Status for Quebec?' in *An Independent Foreign Policy for Canada?* ed. Stephen Clarkson (Toronto: McClelland & Stewart, 1968).
4 Kim Richard Nossal, *The Patterns of World Politics* (Scarborough, ON: Prentice-Hall Canada, 1997), 279–80.
5 Peter Gourevitch, 'The Second Image Reversed: The International Sources

of Domestic Politics,' *International Organization* 32, no. 4 (Autumn 1978): 881–912; and Robert D. Putnam, 'Diplomacy and Domestic Politics: The Logic of Two-Level Games,' *International Organization* 42, no. 3 (Summer 1988): 427–60.

6 Robert Wolfe, 'Transparency and Public Participation in the Canadian Trade Policy Process,' paper presented at the annual meeting of the Canadian Political Science Association, London, Ontario, 2 June 2005, 14.

7 Gerhard Von Glahn, *Law among Nations: An Introduction to Public International Law,* 2nd ed. (Boston: Allyn and Bacon, 1996), 43–5; Douglas M. Brown, 'The Evolving Role of the Provinces in Canadian Trade Policy,' in *Canadian Federalism: Meeting Global Economic Challenges?* ed: Douglas M. Brown and Murray G. Smith (Kingston: Queen's University Institute of Intergovernmental Relations, 1991), 90; Robert G. Richards, 'The Canadian Constitution and International Economic Relations,' in *Canadian Federalism,* 58–9; and Christopher J. Kukucha, 'From Kyoto to the WTO: Evaluating the Constitutional Legitimacy of the Provinces in Canadian Foreign Trade and Environmental Policy,' *Canadian Journal of Political Science* 38, no. 1 (March 2005).

8 Personal interviews, 11 February, 21 February, and 23 February 1994; G. Bruce Doern and Brian Tomlin, *Faith and Fear: The Free Trade Story* (Toronto: Stoddart Publishing, 1991), 128–30; Brown, 'The Evolving Role of the Provinces in Canadian Trade Policy,' 94–5; and Douglas M. Brown, 'The Evolving Role of the Provinces in Canada-US Trade Relations,' in *Canadian Federalism: Meeting Global Economic Challenges?* ed. Douglas M. Brown and Murray G. Smith (Kingston: Queen's University Institute of Intergovernmental Relations, 1991), 114.

9 Personal interviews, 28 August and 9 October 2001.

10 Grace Skogstad, 'International Trade Policy and Canadian Federalism: A Constructive Tension?' in *Canadian Federalism: Performance, Effectiveness, and Legitimacy,* ed. Herman Bakvis and Grace Skogstad (Don Mills: Oxford University Press, 2002), 171.

11 Doern and Tomlin, *Faith and Fear,* 145–6.

12 Donald E. Abelson and Michael Lusztig, 'The Consistency of Inconsistency: Tracing Ontario's Opposition to the North American Free Trade Agreement,' *Canadian Journal of Political Science* 29, no. 4 (1996): 686–8.

13 Ibid., 691.

14 Personal interview, 9 February 1994.

15 Personal interview, 8 February 1994.

16 Personal interview, 31 August 2005.

17 Personal interview, 12 May 2004.

18 Personal interview, 19 July 2004.

19 Ibid.
20 Provincial legislatures also play a minor role, outside of ratifying some international agreements and enacting institutional reform. For the most part, this limited role is due to party discipline, a lack of legislative activity in this issue area, and the failure of most voters to identify with international trade at the constituency level.
21 As a signatory to the GATT in 1947 Canada bound itself to the agreement's 'federal state clause.' In article XXIV:12 of this section, which was later incorporated into the WTO, there is a statement decreeing that '[e]ach contracting party shall take such *reasonable* measures as may be available to it to ensure observance of the provisions of this Agreement by the regional and local governments and authorities within its territory.'
22 Brown, 'The Evolving Role of the Provinces in Canadian Trade Policy,' 101.
23 Ibid., 106.
24 Personal interview, 28 August 2001. Another example of this engagement was Canada's successful negotiation of the New World Wine Accord with the United States, Australia, Chile, and New Zealand, in December 2001. This pact was a Mutual Recognition Agreement (MRA) dealing with technical oenological (winemaking) practices. Provinces were also involved in a 2003 agreement between Canada and the EU related to labelling and market access. The text of the accord is available at World Wine Trade Group, *Agreement on Mutual Acceptance of Oenological Practices*, at http://www .ita.doc.gov/td/ocg/eng_agreement.htm (accessed 13 January 2007).
25 There is some debate regarding the role of the Canadian Wheat Board. Although the Wheat Board is a Crown corporation that sets prices for the export of wheat from Western producers, these figures are dependent on successfully acquiring foreign markets. This often is beneficial to Canadian producers owing to Canada's comparative advantage in this sector. Opponents of the Wheat Board, however, argue that prices would rise for Canadian exports if wheat were sold directly to American consumers. The province of Alberta has become a vocal advocate for these market-based reforms.
26 Grace Skogstad, 'Canadian Agricultural Trade Policy: Continuity amidst Change,' in *Canada Among Nations 1999: A Big League Player?* ed. Fen Osler Hampson, Martin Rudner, and Michael M. Hart (Don Mills: Oxford University Press, 1999), 76.
27 Ibid.
28 Ibid.
29 Éric Montpetit, *Misplaced Distrust: Policy Networks and the Environment in France, the United States, and Canada* (Vancouver: UBC Press, 2003), 98.

30 World Trade Organization, *Article 2 Agreement on Subsidies and Countervailing Measures*, at http://www.wto.org/english/docs_e/legal_e/24-scm _01_e.htm (accessed 10 June 2005).

31 Personal interview, 9 February 1994.

32 T.M. Apsey and J.C. Thomas, *The Lessons of the Softwood Lumber Dispute: Politics, Protectionism and the Panel Process*, at http://www.acah.org/aspey.htm (accessed 5 April 2003), 12–33. This discussion paper was written in April 1997 by Apsey during his tenure as CEO of the Council of Forest Industries. Thomas was a litigator with the firm Thomas and Davis. It was originally circulated as a backgrounder on the Canada-U.S. lumber dispute and was later posted on the web-site of the American Consumers for Affordable Homes, a pro-Canadian U.S. lumber lobby.

33 Gordon Hamilton and Peter O'Neil, 'Ottawa, B.C. at Odds on U.S. Offer,' *Vancouver Sun*, 17 May 2003, F3; Steven Chase and Peter Kennedy, 'Provinces Reject Softwood Proposal: Trade Minister Will Attempt to Win More Concessions from Washington Next Week,' *Globe and Mail*, 9 January 2004, B3; personal interviews, 2 June and 20 May 2003.

34 John Greenwood, 'BC Tries to Cut Own Deal with U.S. over Softwood: Preference Still for Country-Wide Solution,' *National Post*, 2 April 2004, FP6.

35 Karen Howlett, 'Reduction in Quotas Blindsides Ontario,' *Globe and Mail*, 27 April 2006, A14; Barrie McKenna et al., 'Furious Provinces Aim to Sink Softwood Deal,' *Globe and Mail*, 27 April 2006, A1; Gordon Hamilton, 'Softwood Deal Unacceptable: U.S. Offer to End Dispute Ignores Critical B.C. Demands, Trade Council Says,' *Vancouver Sun*, 1 June 2006, C1; Gordon Hamilton, 'Softwood Deal Worries Coastal Producers: Current Draft Not Addressing B.C.'s Need for Autonomy to Implement Domestic Policies, Group Says,' *Vancouver Sun*, 7 June 2006, D1; and Gordon Hamilton and Peter O'Neil, 'U.S. Must Give on Softwood Deal, B.C. Says: Province's Market-Based Timber Pricing System Has to Be Recognized,' *Vancouver Sun*, 14 June 2006, D1.

36 Steven Chase et al., 'Softwood Deal under Attack: B.C. Government Lobbies Ottawa to Reopen Agreement and Fix 23-Month Escape Clause,' *Globe and Mail*, 5 July 2006, A1; and Wendy Leung, 'B.C. OK's Amended Softwood Agreement,' *Vancouver Sun*, 17 August 2006, A1.

37 Personal interviews, 31 August 2005, 29 May 2003, and 30 May 2002.

38 The Quebec government has also established 'offices' for the promotion of Quebec culture, industry, and political interests at the state level in the major American cities of New York, Atlanta, Boston, Los Angeles, Chicago, and Washington.

PART FIVE

New Frontiers of Independence

The essays in this part of the volume explore two issues – culture and environment – that are 'new,' not in the sense that the policy challenges themselves are new, but rather in the sense that they were not considered in the original *IFPC?* volume, and have been relatively marginal in subsequent debates over the question of independence. Each of these policy areas represents a layer of the larger phenomenon of globalization, and each has grown rapidly in importance within the foreign policy agenda over the last forty years. The very nature of these challenges raises difficult questions about whether any country can exercise a genuinely 'independent' policy in these areas.

In chapter 9 Patricia Goff considers both the foreign policy aspects of cultural policy (e.g., trade disputes) and the cultural aspects of foreign policy (e.g., the promotion of Canadian values abroad). She maintains that an independent cultural policy is possible for Canada, despite significant constraints imposed by regional and international trade regimes, but that domestic factors – such as the divide between the cultural and foreign policy communities in Canada – have gotten in the way. American 'soft power' might be succeeding in depleting the distinctiveness of Canadian culture – making it a faint carbon copy of American culture – but Goff makes the argument that we have only ourselves to blame for this.

In chapter 10 Heather Smith focuses her analysis on Canada's paradoxical approach to climate change issues. The Canadian government ratified the Kyoto Protocol in 2002, but it has since done next to nothing to implement its requirements for emission cuts. More recently it has directly challenged the core premises of the Kyoto regime, and attempted to develop a controversial 'made-in-Canada' policy to address climate change, provoking frustration and disapproval both at home and abroad. Smith unravels some of the contradictions built into recent Canadian policies, and reflects on the implications for Canada's capacity to pursue an environmental policy independent from that of the United States.

The arguments by Goff and Smith highlight the way that the meaning of independence, and the policy instruments that might be used to achieve it, can vary markedly from one issue area to another. They also echo a broader theme running through the volume in making the case that the absence of an effective, autonomous Canadian policy is often best traced back to Ottawa, and not, as we might expect, to Washington.

9 Imagining Independence: At the Intersection of Cultural and Foreign Policies

PATRICIA M. GOFF

Forty years after Stephen Clarkson's volume *An Independent Foreign Policy for Canada?*, a discussion of Canadian international policy-making would be incomplete without analysis of its cultural dimension. Cultural policy figured anecdotally in the earlier volume. However, in a world defined by globalization, where flows of people, ideas, and images cross borders with increasing speed and regularity; where governments seek to project their distinctiveness abroad; where ideas form the basis of the information and services economy, culture, broadly construed, is a crucial element of the discussion of Canadian foreign policy independence. My chapter, therefore, explores two mirror images at the intersection of culture and foreign policy: the cultural dimension of foreign policy and the international dimension of cultural policy.

Clarkson and his colleagues looked to domestic political and structural factors alongside Canada's relationship with the United States to understand Canadian foreign policy choices in the 1960s. These influences remain relevant in my discussion with the caveat that measuring independence in policy-making where culture is concerned requires different indicators than we might invoke in other areas of foreign policy.

If independence means unconstrained policy choice, then Canada can be independent in the cultural domain of foreign policy, though to date it has chosen not to maximize the potential for action. Where domestic cultural policy is concerned, independence is waning. If independence means striking a policy path that is unlike what others do, independence in the cultural aspects of foreign policy may not be laudable. Many of Canada's peers spend significant amounts of money to project their cultural accomplishments on the world stage, while Canada lags behind. Jumping on this bandwagon and imitating this approach would be in Canada's interest. In the domain of domestic cultural policy, on the other hand, where independence is indeed desirable, both as unconstrained choice and as a unique policy path, we face new challenges. In particular, we face a shortening list of domestic cultural policy choices, largely as an unintended consequence of commitments we ourselves have made to international organizations and treaties.

Our relationship with the United States informs our view in both policy areas, but it does not determine policy choice. Ultimately, I argue that international developments are constraining the range of motion of cultural policy-makers at home while our own domestic choices are limiting the effectiveness of cultural diplomacy abroad.

The Cultural Component of Foreign Policy

Foreign policy has a cultural component, which has been known by different names over the years, including cultural diplomacy, international cultural relations, and the 'third pillar'[1] of foreign policy. These are not necessarily synonymous with each other, though all arguably fall under the broader umbrella of public diplomacy. 'Public diplomacy is undertaken by official bodies of one state to target publics of another state for the purpose of persuading these foreign publics to regard favourably the national policies, ideals and ideas of the targeting state.'[2] This approach can be distinguished from conventional diplomatic efforts that tend only to engage another country's leadership.[3] Canada's 2005 International Policy Statement goes further than this, suggesting that Canadian citizens themselves are public diplomats, thus articulating how the projection of Canadian culture abroad can serve foreign policy goals.

> Canada's credibility and influence abroad will be built not only by Government action but by Canadians themselves – artists, teachers, students, travelers, researchers, experts and young people – interacting with people abroad. Public diplomacy includes cultural events, conferences, trade shows, youth travel, foreign students in Canada, Canadian studies abroad and visits of opinion leaders. All this cultivates long-term relationships, dialogue and understanding abroad, underpins our advocacy and increases our influence.[4]

Projecting a country's cultural achievements is part of a longer-term strategy, which helps 'develop a three-dimensional image of a country, leading to a more complete and balanced perception of the country's economic, political and social development.'[5] As John Ralston Saul puts it, 'Canada's profile abroad is, for the most part, its culture. It is our image. That is what Canada becomes in people's imaginations around the world.' He goes onto note that 'we are more dependent on that cultural projection than the handful of larger countries who are our allies and our competitors and who have other ways of projecting their image.'[6] Overall, mobilizing Canadian culture in the service of foreign policy provides a way Canada can be made known to the world, arguably making commercial and political relations with us more appealing.

Andrew Cooper traces the origins of this stream of Canadian foreign policy back to the Royal Commission on National Development in the Arts, Letters and Sciences (Massey Commission), whose report was published in 1951.[7] Canada was not alone in making use of this tool. Cultural resources were being used by all the postwar powers as a means of earning prestige and friendship – what we think of today as 'soft power'[8] or, more recently, 'branding.'[9]

Even though cultural diplomacy has long figured in Canadian debates, 1995 is generally regarded as a high-water mark. Pierre Trudeau's Liberal government used cultural relations as part of 'Third Option' efforts to reorient Canada's focus away from the United States and toward Europe.[10] This included the development of Canadian studies programs, among other things. The emphasis later shifted to cultural diplomacy in the service of a broader export strategy, not just to Europe and not just of cultural products. Nonetheless, Kirton[11] and Hay[12] argue that culture was never a priority in Canadian foreign policy statements before 1995. Similarly, Bélanger observes that 'cultural questions received unprecedented attention'[13] in the run-up to the 1995 foreign policy review.

Analysts explain this shift towards identification of a 'third pillar' of foreign policy in various ways, from the onset of globalization to the strength of cultural lobbies. All agree, however, that the potential for international cultural relations has not been fully realized. Even though culture figured prominently in Canadian foreign policy discussions in the 1990s, its rhetorical importance may have eclipsed its actual implementation. It received only glancing attention in the subsequent 2005 foreign policy review.

Indeed, other countries have larger budgets given over to public diplomacy than Canada does and do more in the area of cultural diplomacy. 'Whereas the Canadian investment on its public diplomacy instruments can be counted in the tens of millions of dollars annually, the U.K. devotes several hundred million dollars and France, Germany and Japan each spend well above one billion dollars.'[14] Some blame this disparity on federal budget cuts, adopted in the late 1990s to put the country on a stronger fiscal footing. However, in discussing Canadian expenditure on the export of culture, Ralston Saul notes that 'even at its highest it was seven times less than the French; four times less than the British.'[15]

Why, then, does the cultural element of our foreign policy appear to be underutilized, despite its potential as an effective and important policy tool? No force seems to be preventing its use; rather, the choice to develop our substantial capacity in this area has not been made. This is at least partially due to the fact that cultural and public diplomacy requires a longer-term strategy that may not produce immediate, tangible results. This can diminish its appeal, as can the cost of doing it well. For example, Potter points to the central role that broadcasting can play in projecting one's presence abroad. Yet, 'Canada does not have a dedicated government-funded international television presence such as the BBC World Service.'[16] Canadian programming is heard and seen abroad in French as part of Radio Canada International and TV5. Nonetheless, augmenting Canada's international broadcasting presence so as to make a significant contribution to foreign policy goals would require a substantial investment on the part of the federal government.

In addition to cost concerns, there is a lack of agreement within and across the various constituencies that participate in these discussions about how culture can or should be projected. The goals of the cultural policy community are not necessarily the goals of the foreign policy community. The former seeks to promote and develop Canadian culture because of its intrinsic value; the latter sees culture through the lens of foreign policy objectives. This difference is exacerbated by the natural fragmentation of government that places culture in one ministry and foreign policy in another. Foreign Affairs is arguably on safe ground arguing that its core mandate is trade, security, and diplomacy, while Canadian Heritage exists to promote Canadian culture.

Conversations with Foreign Affairs officials suggest that the foreign policy component of cultural diplomacy programs is never far from view. At the end of the day, if Foreign Affairs promotes Canadian culture, it does so because it will serve foreign policy goals. It is one tool among many and it may be expendable in an era of fiscal conservatism.

However, even inside the Department of Foreign Affairs and International Trade, where security and prosperity are pursued along parallel tracks, certain officials may understand 'the promotion of culture' as a component of a public diplomacy strategy while others understand it to mean exporting cultural industries for economic return.[17]

In addition to disagreement among principal contributors to the debate, Arnold points to a long-standing, deep conceptual ambiguity.[18] She argues that the link between domestic and foreign policy agendas with regard to the projection of culture has never been adequately defined. Furthermore, she notes that 'culture,' 'arts,' 'cultural industries,' and 'values' can all be present, simultaneously and confusingly, in a discussion about the projection of culture. The 1995 International Policy Statement bears this out. In the section entitled 'Projecting Canadian Values and Culture,' the heart of the case for culture as a 'third pillar' of foreign policy, the Canadian respect for human rights, democracy, and sustainable development is articulated just before a reference to the economic importance of cultural industries. All this is followed by the claim that 'only Canadian culture can express the uniqueness of our country, which is bilingual, multicultural, and deeply influenced by its Aboriginal roots, the North, the oceans, and its own vastness.'[19] We may support all these statements. Nonetheless, even at a moment when there was great support for developing the cultural component of foreign policy, there is persuasive evidence of what Arnold identifies as a lack of conceptual coherence.

If Canadian governments have not maximized the effectiveness of cultural components of foreign policy, it is not because of a lack of independent choice. The United States in no way prevents us from taking such action. In fact, the prominence of American ideas and images internationally arguably necessitates that we do so. To the degree that the message we project includes the embrace of certain liberal values, we may earn points in the eyes of our southern neighbour, simultaneously promoting our image abroad and good relations with our key ally.

Projecting a Canadian voice on an increasingly cluttered international stage does require a departure from familiar foreign policy activities. This might include an express effort to bridge the distance between the cultural and foreign policy communities, a significant investment of resources, and a concerted effort to debate and define the role of culture in an increasingly interconnected world. It may be costly and uncomfortable at first to make this shift, but the return may be enormous.

Internationalizing Cultural Policy

By its very nature, cultural policy appears primarily as a domestic policy category. Its main constituency is domestic and its objectives mostly local or national in scope. In recent years, however, it has become 'internationalized,' so as to create new circumstances that may limit Canadian cultural policy-makers' independence by circumscribing the range of measures they can implement to achieve domestic cultural policy goals. This is largely a function of developments in international trade agreements, which conceptualize long-standing cultural policy measures as discriminatory trade practices.

Craik et al. identify four critical components of cultural policy: arts and culture (libraries, museums, performing arts, etc.); communications and media (public and commercial publishing, broadcasting, film, etc.); citizenship and identity (language policy, multiculturalism, tourism, etc.); and spatial culture (urban regeneration, regional cultural heritage, etc.).[20] The main body charged with overseeing cultural policy in Canada is the Department of Canadian Heritage. According to its website, 'Canadian Heritage is responsible for national policies and programs that promote Canadian content, foster cultural participation, active citizenship and participation in Canada's civic life, and strengthen connections among Canadians.' Its mission is to work towards 'a more cohesive and creative Canada.' In terms of strategic outcomes sought, its aim is that 'Canadians express and share their diverse cultural experiences with each other and the world' and that 'Canadians live in an inclusive society built on intercultural understanding and citizen participation.'

Canadian Heritage is complemented by a range of arm's-length agencies, including the Canada Council for the Arts, the Canadian Radio-Television and Telecommunications Commission, the CBC, and the National Film Board, as well as provincial- and municipal-level agencies and programs. Policy measures range from Canadian content regulations to Canadian ownership requirements, grants, and tax incentives.

These measures are primarily concerned with promoting domestic artists and cultivating a domestic collective identity within national territorial confines. There has been an evolution over the years, but the link between cultural industries and national identity was made early. The 1929 Royal Commission on Broadcasting (Aird Commission) noted that it was in the national interest for Canada's identity to be reflected in radio programming. This led to the creation of what was to become the Canadian Broadcasting Corporation and later included the evolving range of cultural industries. Successive Canadian governments since that time have used policy governing cultural industries to contribute to the related goals of collective identity formation, nation-building, and, more recently, the promotion of cultural diversity.

Mirroring the European approach to cultural policy, Canadian approaches carry a heavy dose of state support for cultural activity. There are numerous reasons for this, including a historical policy legacy and a track record of positive outcomes as a result of government measures. Perhaps most significant, though, is the perceived need for state-led policy owing to the distinctive political economy of the (Canadian) cultural sector.[21]

The Canadian market is relatively small, with a population hovering near thirty million, though made up of at least two linguistic communities. These are unimpressive numbers compared to the economies of scale that U.S. competitors enjoy. Indeed, even with a population nearer to 300 million, American filmmakers are increasingly seeking an international audience to be economically viable.[22] Many countries have markets that are comparable to Canada's in size. Nevertheless, the challenges posed by Canada's small domestic market are intensified by Canada's close proximity to the United States and by the similarity of the two cultures. Canada has long been an easy market for American cultural products to penetrate because the majority of Canadians speak English and are familiar with, even share many elements of, American culture and society, an experience many other countries are now sharing.

The periodical industry provides an example of the difficulties associated with close proximity to the United States. Periodicals depend, to a large degree, on advertising revenues. Many American publications are imported into Canada. Consequently, subsidiaries of American companies operating within Canada do not always use the domestic Canadian media as advertising outlets because they can feel reasonably confident that advertising dollars spent in American publications also reach Canadian consumers. Canadian periodicals lose out on the advertising dollars that could be provided by businesses operating domestically. Therefore, Canada's geographical location compounds the degree to which its small domestic market leaves its cultural industries at a disadvantage.

Private investment has not been significant as compensation for these market disadvantages, since cultural industries are high risk ventures. Industry concentration is one international trend that may make Canadian cultural producers more competitive. But while this strategy makes good business sense, there is resistance to it in Canada because of the accompanying loss of heterogeneity. The publishing industry is especially concerned with this issue.

> The Canadian-controlled industry has gone to significant lengths in trying to avoid industry concentration in market share and location. In general, there is a commitment to the notion that the industry can contribute the most to society, in the generation of ideas, information and development of authors, when numerous firms across the country are all seeking titles and authors ... As a cultural policy, the encouragement of heterogeneity in the industry is a powerful device.[23]

The inference in the above quotation is that heterogeneity is a good *cultural* policy and not a good *economic* policy. Lorimer and O'Donnell report that, in Canada, 'the primary contributors to the publication of domestic fiction and poetry, especially by first-time authors, are the myriad of small to medium-sized, heterogeneously oriented publishing firms scattered all over the country.'[24] This cultural benefit would be lost if firms were encouraged to streamline their operations through mergers. Therefore, in Canada there is little finance capital available from mainstream institutions for risky cultural products. In addition, there is resistance in government and cultural circles to economically logical steps that might make Canadian companies less risky because they are thought to limit opportunities for domestic producers.

Given this set of circumstances, there is a sense that government support measures are needed to ensure that the Canadian cultural sector thrives. Without them, cultural industries would become nothing more than conduits for foreign producers of cultural goods. This impulse is unique to this sector because of the important socio-cultural contribution cultural products can make to nation-building and to the promotion of cultural diversity.

Compare this approach to attitudes towards the domestic automotive industry, where the Canadian government is content to have parts and assembly plants for foreign automakers. At no time has there been an effort to design a 'Canadian' car. Instead, over forty years ago, the automobile industry was the first to be continentalized under the Auto

Pact. Former Prime Minister Mulroney's words confirm the different way in which the car industry is perceived.

> Under the Auto Pact, we have developed an industry in which 130,000 Canadians are directly employed, which accounts for 15 per cent of all our manufacturing, and more than one third, some $35 billion, of all our trade with the United States. That's more trade than we do with all the rest of the world. Since 1979, there's been seven billion dollars in direct new investment in the automotive and parts industry in Canada, mostly in Ontario for reasons of geography and proximity to US markets. That was a tremendous boost for Ontario and Canada. And with that economic strength, our confidence in ourselves as a people has grown accordingly. *We're not any less Canadian because of it.*[25]

In contrast to the automobile sector, public- and private-sector communities across Canada continue to support state-led policy in the cultural sector because of the clear contribution it makes to Canadian identity.

How has this support come to be threatened as a result of the internationalization of cultural policy? It is important to note that cultural policy has had an international dimension in the past. Canadian cultural policy has always been made against an international backdrop and has been informed by international developments. As early as the 1920s, Canadian radio policy sprang from concerns about American radio signals filling Canadian airwaves. Druick traces the influence of UNESCO policies on both the rationale for and the output of the Massey Commission, struck in the late 1940s. She argues that, 'well before cultural-policy discourse in Canada came to be dominated by the notion of trade and cultural industries, it was nonetheless clearly imbricated with international politics.'[26] Along the way, other royal commissions have acknowledged that 'Canadian culture [is] rooted in the global context.'[27]

Nonetheless, it is fair to say that this international dimension has become much more significant in recent decades as the cultural sector has found its way onto the multilateral trade agenda.[28] There are elements of cultural policy that remain firmly domestic – protection of national heritage buildings, for example. However, international forces began to weigh heavily on cultural policy-making with Canada–United States Free Trade Agreement (CUSFTA) negotiations and continued with the North American Free Trade Agreement (NAFTA). In both of these efforts, Canadian negotiators recognized that government support measures to cultural producers might be viewed as discriminatory trade practices. They sought to preserve domestic cultural policy-making independence by excluding the cultural sector from trade agreement provisions. By doing so, it was assumed, the Canadian government could continue state-led cultural policies without being accused of contravening national treatment provisions in NAFTA.

Canada's American trading partners were not pleased with this outcome and later sought to influence Canadian cultural policy by side-stepping the protections negotiated in NAFTA. In 1997 the United States launched a dispute at the World Trade Organization to protest Canadian magazine industry policy. They were able to do this because, in contrast to NAFTA, the exemptions for the cultural sector in the General Agreement on Tariffs and Trade (GATT) only extend to audiovisual industries. The film and television industries are exempted from GATT trade provisions; however, other cultural industries, like magazine and book publishing, are not. The WTO dispute was prompted by an excise tax levied on American split-run magazines. Split-run magazines recycle much of the content used in the American edition of the magazine, making the Canadian edition considerably cheaper to produce, much to the consternation of Canadian magazine publishers who must compete with them.

The tax was designed to deter American publishers from using electronic transmission of text to skirt the ban on bringing split-run magazines across the border, as Time Warner did with *Sports Illustrated* in 1995. Worried that other companies might follow suit, the Canadian government introduced a tax in the amount of 80 per cent of the advertising contained in the issue imposed on split-runs containing less than 80 per cent original content. The tax prompted Time Warner to shut down the Canadian edition of *Sports Illustrated*. It was also the last straw for the United States government, which objected not only to the excise tax, but also to postal subsidies provided to Canadian publishers and incentives to Canadian business to advertise in Canadian publications. The WTO panel reviewing the three Canadian measures ruled that none was in compliance with Canada's trade commitments. As of 1 June 2000, in response to the WTO ruling, new measures govern the periodical industry in Canada. These new measures resulted not from internal debate, but from the need to bring cultural measures into alignment with Canada's obligations as a member of the WTO.

Why does it make sense to understand this drag on Canadian cultural policy-making as a function of internationalization as opposed to our relationship with the United States? After all, it was American objections to Canadian periodicals policy that ultimately led to the introduction of new measures. Such a conclusion would seem to be more in line with the debate sparked by the Clarkson volume forty years ago, which highlighted the potential for our relationship with the United States to constrain our foreign policy independence.

To be sure, opposition from the United States, expressed in various guises, has influenced our cultural policy choices over the years. Washington has registered its displeasure with individual policies in bilateral talks with Canadian government officials. For example, Bill C-58, which prohibited the deduction of expenses for advertising placed in foreign broadcast media but aimed at Canadian audiences, thus encouraging Canadian advertisers to support its national media, elicited responses from American officials at the highest levels.[29] Occasionally, the American government has retaliated against Canada. Indeed, it is interesting to note that, in the original Clarkson volume, in a discussion of how rare American threats of retaliation actually are, more than one contributor points to cultural policy examples to illustrate what retaliation might look like. For example, Plumptre distinguishes between retaliation and pressure. Ironically, he uses a cultural policy example to illustrate his point. 'If Canada adopts a measure like the magazine tax that is clearly unwelcome in various quarters in the United States, we may be reasonably sure that certain identifiable forces will be set in motion against us.'[30] Jewett also comes back to the magazine tax example in discussing retaliation.[31]

Nonetheless, the outcome we witnessed in the magazine policy case is a function of commitments our government made as a member of the World Trade Organization. The binding nature of dispute settlement body decisions, not American power, necessitated a change in Canadian cultural policy. That the United States used these commitments to their benefit is their right. Other countries, including Canada, may do so in the future. As a result, domestic cultural policy-makers must keep one eye on evolving trade commitments as state-led cultural policy measures are reconceptualized as trade impediments and effectively removed from the cultural policy-maker's toolkit. Canada's experience with the WTO dispute points up a new influence on cultural policy-making, one that is unlikely to go away. It illuminates the new ways in which cultural policy has become internationalized, with real consequences for domestic choice.

As Ted Magder puts it, 'What sovereign states can do to regulate the flow of media across their borders and what they can do to regulate media activities within those borders is increasingly influenced by a web of international agreements.'[32] World Trade Organization provisions governing goods trade are not the only international-level influences on domestic cultural policy-making. Evolving international rules for telecommunications and intellectual property may also eventually have similar effects. It is through our participation in these international forums that we sometimes inadvertently tie our own hands.

There is a certain irony in this, especially as pertains to foreign policy. Canada has traditionally sought out multilateral instruments and forums as a way of expanding its reach. However, it is multilateral trade arrangements that are now threatening to limit in significant ways what the government can implement in the realm of domestic cultural policy. Magder argues that the impact of these agreements is hard to judge. 'There is nothing like a co-ordinated global regime for the governance of media and communication. No widely accepted hierarchy of principles exists and the administrative application of most agreements is characterized by inconsistency.'[33] Magder's caution against overstating the degree to which the state's regulatory capacity has been hollowed out by international agreements is important, especially given the fact that the same governments that are limited by this development were complicit in bringing it about by actively negotiating international agreements. To be sure, participation in multilateral arrangements still allows more room for shaping these matters, especially as compared to negotiations of bilateral and regional arrangements to which we are not a party.

Since the Doha Round of international trade talks stalled, the United States has been actively pursuing bilateral trade agreements with governments in Latin America, Asia, and elsewhere. In almost all instances, there is a binding provision pertaining to cultural sector regulation. For example, in current negotiations between the United States and Korea, communities in Korea and abroad are protesting the prospect of a final agreement that greatly circumscribes the Korean government's ability to continue its policy of screen quotas for local content. Azzi quotes the International Liaison Committee of Coalitions for Cultural Diversity:

The clear objective of the US is to establish enough bilateral precedents – 10, 12 or more – in which countries agree to liberalize their cultural sectors, and then attempt to impose this model as a fait accompli when broader WTO talks and larger regional negotiations eventually resume.[34]

As Azzi explains, these agreements are all quite similar. 'They allow subsidies, limit quotas on traditional media (such as broadcasting and cinema), and prevent the imposition of quotas on new forms of content distribution.'[35] Australia and Chile are notable examples of countries with significant cultural policy-making limits now in place as a result of bilateral trade agreements. The long-term effect of this American strategy is unclear. Nonetheless, it is clear that, to the degree that domestic cultural policy choices are constrained by these bilateral agreements, it is more directly due to the exercise of American influence than to obligations associated with participation in international organizations.

At the same time, just as global-level initiatives can have a limiting effect on cultural policy-making, so might international agreements create new possibilities. In response to the outcome of the periodicals case, the Canadian government, in concert with several other national governments and civil society groups, started in motion a process that culminated in 2007 in the ratification of the UNESCO Convention on the Protection and Promotion of the Diversity of Cultural Expressions. This treaty seeks to preserve the domestic cultural policy space that the periodicals dispute and bilateral trade arrangements threaten to reduce. Its ability to do so is a subject of debate.[36] Perhaps most important for this discussion, however, is the fact that the Canadian government led the charge for the creation of this multilateral instrument against strong and continuing American opposition. In many respects, this effort incarnates an ideal of independent Canadian foreign policy-making. In alliance with civil society and a coalition of countries from around the world; convinced that multilateral, rules-based arrangements produce the most just and enduring outcomes; and unbowed before American opposition, the Canadian government led a movement that, in record time, created a widely supported and innovative multilateral solution to a pressing global governance challenge.

An Independent Cultural Policy for Canada

In the Clarkson volume, the contributing authors defined independence against its alternatives. These alternatives include quiet diplomacy or cultivating a closer relationship with the United States, strongly suggesting that the most significant brake on independent foreign policy in Canada is the opposition we may face from our southern neighbour.

> The title, *An Independent Foreign Policy for Canada?* raises two distinct issues – the possibility of independence, and the purposes of an independent foreign policy. Whether Canada *can* be independent depends first of all on our external position, particularly on our relationship with the USA ... Is there a utilitarian justification for an independent approach to our foreign policy or does *raison d'état* argue for Quiet Diplomacy that gives cultivating American friendship higher priority than autonomy?[37]

Though the original volume also argues that structural issues – federalism, distinct modes of decision-making – influence policy choices, the emphasis seems to be on our relationship with the United States. As Clarkson put it in 1968, 'independence, most Canadians seem to feel, begins in Washington. To raise the issue of independence is to conjure up the spectre of American domination, whether economic control, cultural penetration, military absorption or political hegemony.'[38] He goes on to ask, 'Do we really have the freedom to choose an "independent" over a "quiet" diplomacy, or does not the preponderance of American power deter Canadian leaders from adopting policies out of line with those of Washington?'[39] He worries about acts of retaliation by the United States, implying that the price we may pay for independence will be charged in Washington.

There is an implied value judgment that independence is desirable and that independent policy is in the national interest. The introductory chapter implies that independence maps onto an effectual policy, while quiet diplomacy corresponds to comfortable and safe policy. 'If it can be established that Canada is not necessarily dependent on American policy, we then have to ask whether the reasons for our sorry international performance are not internal rather than external.'[40] The author goes on to suggest that 'our sorry international performance' equates a lack of independence with poor performance, political weakness, and lack of effectiveness internationally.

> If our Canadian-American relationship is compatible with greater independence and if our foreign policy's ineffectiveness can be traced to domestic conditions that are in our power to change, we can raise the next issue: Independence, for what purpose? ... The thread running through these sections is that Canada does have a choice. We can choose the comfortable, safe path of a quiet, gentlemanly but less effectual foreign policy

or we can choose the more dynamic, more demanding path of an effective, independent role.[41]

Hanly captures this notion of independence from a different angle, arguing that

> Canada can choose between two basic strategies for its foreign policy: affiliation or independence. Canada is not alone in being confronted by these alternatives ... The affiliation strategy requires a small power to adopt a great power as its leader in international affairs. The small power will then seek to acquire some measure of influence over the course of events through its relation to a great power – an influence which it believes it could not have on the same events if acting independently.[42]

There may be a danger here in overstating the degree to which independence must mean pursuing a policy that is at odds with American policy. There is also a danger in valuing a policy precisely because it is distinct from American policy. It is worth noting Baldwin's caution that 'rational evaluation of independence as a policy-alternative requires more explicit recognition that there are degrees of independence and that the maximum degree may not be the optimum one from every standpoint.'[43]

In domestic cultural policy, only in limited instances are we working to influence actors internationally or influence the United States to act in a foreign arena. Canadian leadership in the campaign to create a global treaty promoting cultural diversity is exceptional in this regard. More commonly, cultural policy seeks to create room in our own domestic environment to make policy choices that suit our interests. For this reason, the notion of quiet diplomacy has less purchase in the cultural policy domain.

While independence likely should not be a goal in itself, it is true that cultural policy is at least partially about demarcating difference. Ensuring 'shelf-space' for Canadian cultural products such that the Canadian public has the choice to purchase domestic or international cultural products is one component of this effort. In addition, certain traditions have come to be associated with certain national contexts, such that differences are prominent and valued in terms not only of *outcomes* – diversity of cultural products and achievement of policy objectives – but also of policy *processes*. In other words, not only does it matter to have *Maclean's* on the shelf next to *Time* magazine, *the measures mobilized* to support Maclean's themselves have meaning. This is especially true when comparing Canadian policy approaches to American ones. Canada cleaves to a more state-led model of cultural policy, while the United States has long opted for greater private participation in the promotion of arts and culture.

Of course, it is not always the case that the course of action we favour is at odds with American preferences. Nonetheless, the very nature of cultural policy may inform our evaluation of independence in unique ways. Difference is prized from the outset to the degree that many Canadians are sceptical that cultural goals can be achieved via an American-style system. As a result, notions of independence like Peyton Lyon's advocacy of 'quiet diplomacy' in the original *IFPC?* volume, 'seeking to influence world affairs through a close alliance with Washington,'[44] seem precluded from the start in a conversation about cultural policy.

That we have maintained a distinct domestic cultural policy and that we have pursued multilateral initiatives germane to preserving that domestic approach suggests that we have been independent, with a few notable exceptions. In some direct ways, cultural policy teaches us a lot about the possibility of independent policy. Canada prefers approaches that are not favoured by the United State. The American government has threatened retaliation. But, ironically, the United States has been most effective in influencing Canadian cultural policy choices via a multilateral mechanism voluntarily embraced by Canadians.

Recognizing the ways in which cultural policy may or may not intersect with foreign policy influences how we assess whether cultural policy can or should be independent, and from what. Ironically, where cultural policy least resembles foreign policy, where it is most concerned with achieving domestic goals, where independence is highly prized, it seems most constrained. Where it is most closely related to foreign policy and where it seeks influence beyond national shores, it seems less constrained, though not fully realized.

Future Considerations

Technology

As Klinenberg and Benzecry point out, both cultural producers and consumers have new opportunities thanks to new technologies. Artists have new outlets for their work with lower entry costs. Consumers can individualize their experience of cultural products, thanks to iPods, home movie rentals, and media available through personal computers and handheld devices.[45] That is not to say that we cannot regulate these technologies in ways that serve long-standing cultural goals. However, the approaches we have used in the past likely will not be sufficient. Furthermore, it is clear that this debate stands not only at the intersection of culture and economics, but also of creativity, innovation, and technology. We have yet to see vibrant public debate about how to ensure that shifts in regulation are purposive and not reactive.

Feigenbaum has argued that the influence of technology on the achievement of the traditional goals of cultural policy will likely be a mixed bag, both enabling and constraining governments. The relationship between technology and culture is a long-standing one, as Benedict Anderson's analysis of how the printing press enabled the creation of national cultures attests.[46] In the current moment, Feigenbaum argues, that 'changes in technology have affected the intensity with which people interact, and the extensiveness of that interaction.'[47] Technology also threatens the ways in which governments can implement cultural policy. For example, Feigenbaum notes that technological innovations in the delivery systems for cultural products render some policy measures obsolete. In particular, he argues that direct satellite broadcasting, video on demand, and Internet streaming make it nearly impossible for governments to employ local content quotas. He suggests a shift towards direct subsidies.

On the other hand, Feigenbaum asserts that some new technologies can strengthen the hand of governments inclined towards cultural policy and cultural diplomacy. The proliferation of channels that has accompanied cable and satellite technologies creates new outlets for diversified content. And, of course, the ease with which individuals can upload content onto the Internet also suggests that corporate gatekeepers (especially distributors), the target of many state-led cultural policies, are themselves weakened by technological innovations. Technology does not make traditional cultural policy obsolete and it does not disempower the state.[48] But it does require new thinking and a shift in approach. It has opened up new areas of regulation where states can be active, including intellectual property, although not necessarily in ways that will produce the sorts of outcomes that traditional cultural policy does.[49]

Culture and Economy

In the past, it was not unusual to find cultural policy debates in Canada framed in terms of two opposing camps – those who promoted culture for culture's sake or those who viewed culture as a public good versus those who viewed cultural industries and products as commercially significant. In recent years this relationship has become greatly complicated. As Terry Flew puts it, the logic of cultural policy is changing.

> Traditional cultural policy models typically placed a largely non-commercial arts sphere at the centre of creative processes, and saw its influence permeating out to broadcast media and other services sectors. By contrast, more recent contributions to creative industries literature have placed creativity at the core of the 'new economy,' where wealth creation is increasingly driven by ideas, intangibles and the creative application of information and communication technologies (ICTs), presenting creativity as an 'axial principle' of the new economy as labour, organization and information have been in previous epochs.[50]

Flew goes on to note that this new logic interrupts assumptions about whether the emphasis should be on public versus private funding, or production versus consumption, as well as whether industries are national as opposed to global, local, or regional.

These debates are taking place alongside efforts at the municipal level to mobilize the arts and culture in the service of urban economic development.[51] Clearly, the fluid relationship between culture and the economy is once again shifting in ways that have consequences for policy. These consequences may go well beyond weighing one familiar measure against another to a significant rethinking of the purpose and best practices of cultural policy and cultural diplomacy in the twenty-first century.

Conclusion

A discussion of the nexus of culture and foreign policy points to a number of observations about the potential for independence in Canadian foreign policy. There is certainly continuity over the last forty years in terms of the objectives of cultural policy. However, the terrain on which we pursue them is shifting. New influences, like international organizations whose reach increasingly extends to culture, have taken their place alongside long-standing participants in the debate, like our American neighbours. New actors have stepped onto the public diplomacy stage. Conceptually, whereas in the past cultural policies were justified in terms of nation-building and protection of tradition, we are more likely now to invoke the need for cultural diversity, branding, and the contribution culture can make to economic development. As Shalini Venturelli has argued, 'The challenge for every nation is not how to prescribe an environment of protection for a received body of art and tradition, but how to construct one of creative explosion and innovation in all areas of the arts and sciences.'[52]

These shifts arguably necessitate a more significant international presence for Canada. They also still require governments to adopt regulatory mechanisms to promote local artists, measures that cannot be hollowed out by global-level commitments, though perhaps not the same measures we have relied on in the past. The good news is that we should not underestimate the enormous potential governments and publics have to shape policy outcomes. Stephen Clarkson was right to demand effective foreign policy in 1968. Forty years later, this call resonates even more loudly. My discussion of culture and foreign policy suggests that if we do not answer it, we will have no one to blame but ourselves.

NOTES

1 Canada, *Canada in the World: Government Statement* (Ottawa: Government of Canada, 1995).
2 Evan Potter, 'Canada and the New Public Diplomacy,' in *Discussions in Public Diplomacy* (The Hague: Netherlands Institute of International Relations, 2001), 3.
3 Commonwealth of Australia (2007), *Australia's Public Diplomacy: Building Our Image*, Report of the Senate Standing Committee on Foreign Affairs, Defence, and Trade, 8. Available at http://www.aph.gov.au/Senate/committee/fadt_ctte/public_diplomacy/report/index.htm.
4 Canada, *Canada's International Policy Statement: A Role of Pride and Influence in the World* (Ottawa: Government of Canada, 2005).
5 Potter, 'Canada and the New Public Diplomacy,' 4.
6 John Ralston Saul, 'Culture and Foreign Policy,' paper prepared for the Government of Canada International Policy Review, 1995, 2. Available at http://www.media-awareness.ca/english/resources/articles/sovereignty_identity /culture_policy.cfm.
7 Andrew Cooper, ed., *Canadian Culture: International Dimensions* (Toronto: Canadian Institute of International Affairs, 1985).
8 Joseph Nye, *Bound to Lead* (New York: Basic Books, 1990).

204 Patricia M. Goff

9 See, for example, Peter van Ham, 'The Rise of the Brand State,' *Foreign Affairs*, September–October 2001.
10 Cooper, *Canadian Culture*, 15.
11 John Kirton, 'Une ouverture sur le monde,' *Études Internationales* 27 (1996): 257–79.
12 John Hay, 'Projecting Canadian Values and Culture,' *Canadian Foreign Policy* 3, no. 2 (Fall 1995): 21–32.
13 Louis Bélanger, 'Redefining Cultural Diplomacy,' *Political Psychology* 20, no. 4 (1999): 680.
14 Potter, 'Canada and the New Public Diplomacy,' 11.
15 Ralston Saul, 'Culture and Foreign Policy,' 2.
16 Potter, 'Canada and the New Public Diplomacy,' 10.
17 For more on this distinction, see Robert J. Williams, 'International Cultural Programmes: Canada and Australia Compared,' in *Canadian Culture: International Dimensions*, ed. Andrew Cooper (Toronto: Canadian Institute of International Affairs, 1985).
18 Samantha Arnold, 'From "Third Pillar" to "Public Diplomacy": Culture and Canadian Foreign Policy,' unpublished paper prepared for NPSIA New Scholars Conference, Waterloo, 2005.
19 Canada. 'Projecting Canadian Values and Culture,' in *Canada in the World* (Ottawa: Queen's Printer, 1995), 4.
20 Jennifer Craik, Glyn Davis, and Naomi Sunderland, 'Cultural Policy and National Identity,' in *The Future of Governance*, ed. Michael Keating and Glyn Davis (Sydney: Allen and Unwin, 2000), 159.
21 Peter S. Grant and Chris Wood, *Blockbusters and Trade Wars*, (Toronto: Douglas and McIntyre, 2004).
22 'Movie Biz Enjoys Global Warming,' *Variety*, 7 April 1997, 1.
23 Rowland Lorimer, 'Book Publishing,' in *The Cultural Industries in Canada*, ed. Michael Dorland (Toronto: J. Lorimer and Co., 1996), 17.
24 Rowland Lorimer and Eleanor O'Donnell, 'Globalization and Internationalization in Publishing,' *Canadian Journal of Communication* 17 (1992): 508.
25 'Notes for an Address to the Nation on the Trade Initiative by the Right Honourable Brian Mulroney, P.C., M.P., Prime Minister of Canada,' Ottawa, 16 June 1986, 3. Archival records of the Canadian Trade Negotiations Office, file 5420–1. Emphasis added.
26 Zoe Druick, 'International Cultural Relations as a Factor in Postwar Canadian Cultural Policy: The Relevance of UNESCO for the Massey Commission,' *Canadian Journal of Communication* 31, no. 1 (2006): 190.
27 Cooper, 'International Cultural Programs,' 147.
28 See Patricia Goff, Invisible Borders: Economic Liberalization and National

Identity,' *International Studies Quarterly* 44, no. 4 (December 2000): 533–62; and Patricia Goff, *Limits to Liberalization: Local Culture in a Global Marketplace* (Ithaca: Cornell University Press, 2007).

29 Congress retaliated by passing legislation that restricted the tax deductions allowed to Americans who attend conventions in Canada. The legislation was later repealed, but not before it reportedly cost Canada hundreds of millions of dollars in lost tourist income.

30 A.F.W. Plumptre, A.E. Safarian, Abraham Rotstein, and Pauline Jewett, 'Retaliation: The Price of Independence?' in *An Independent Foreign Policy for Canada?* ed. Stephen Clarkson (Toronto: University of Toronto Press, 1968): 164.

31 Ibid., 52.

32 Ted Madger, 'International Agreements and the Regulation of World Communication,' in *Media and Cultural Theory*, ed. James Curran and David Morley (Routledge: New York, 2006), 164.

33 Ibid., 165

34 Stephen Azzi, 'Negotiating Cultural Space in the Global Economy,' *International Journal* 60, no. 3 (Summer 2005): 772.

35 Ibid.

36 J.P. Singh, 'Culture or Commerce? A Comparative Assessment of International Interactions and Developing Countries at UNESCO, WTO, and Beyond,' *International Studies Perspectives* 8, no. 1 (February 2007): 36–53. Joost Pauwelyn, 'The UNESCO Convention on Cultural Diversity, and the WTO: Diversity in International Law-Making?' *ASIL Insights* (Washington: American Society of International Law, 2005); available at http://www .asil.org/insights/2005/11/insights051115.html.

37 *An Independent Foreign Policy for Canada?* xiii.

38 Ibid., 3.

39 Ibid., 4.

40 Ibid., xiii.

41 Ibid., xiv

42 Charles Hanly, 'The Ethics of Independence,' ibid., 22.

43 David Baldwin, 'The Myth of the Special Relationship,' ibid., 15.

44 Peyton Lyon, 'Quiet Diplomacy Revisited,' ibid., 31.

45 Eric Klinenberg and Claudio Benzecry, 'Cultural Production in a Digital Age,' *Annals of the American Academy of Political and Social Science* 597 (January 2005): 6–18.

46 Benedict Anderson, *Imagined Communities* (New York: Verso, 1991).

47 Harvey Feigenbaum, 'Is Technology the Enemy of Culture?' *International Journal of Cultural Policy* 10, no. 3 (November 2004): 252.

48 Ibid. See also Grant and Wood, *Blockbusters*; and Madger, 'International Agreements.'
49 Patricia Goff and Barbara Jenkins, 'The "New World" of Culture: Reexamining Canadian Cultural Policy,' *Journal of Arts, Management, Law and Society* 36, no. 3 (Fall 2007): 181–96.
50 Terry Flew, 'Sovereignty and Software,' *International Journal of Cultural Policy* 11, no. 3 (November 2005): 248.
51 See, for example, Richard Florida, *The Rise of the Creative Class* (New York: Basic Books, 2004).
52 Shalini Venturelli. *From the Information Economy to the Creative Economy: Moving Culture to the Center of International Public Policy* (Washington: Center for Arts and Culture, 2002), 212; available at http://www.culturalpolicy.org/pdf/venturelli.pdf.

10 Canada and Kyoto: Independence or Indifference?

HEATHER A. SMITH

Published in 1968, *An Independent Foreign Policy for Canada?*, edited by Stephen Clarkson, is both time-bound and timeless. The volume is time-bound insofar as the introduction refers to the radical intent of the volume, but when read through the eyes of a critical feminist scholar, the radical nature of the volume is not so obvious. Diplomats and bureaucrats are referred to as 'he,' Canada is a 'she,' there is one female contributor, and the environment is not mentioned in the volume. More-over, the world constructed throughout the text is one dominated by states that have the ability to make choices based on national interests. There are indeed challenges to the elitist nature of Canadian diplomacy, chapters on domestic determinants of Canadian foreign policy, calls for an ethical and more democratic foreign policy, but these themes do not seem so radical in 2008. Perhaps it is because Clarkson and his colleagues asked those questions in 1968 that they now seem common-place and for that we must acknowledge their contribution. Without the 'radical' of 1968 we would have no place for the 'radical' of 2008.

And while there are ways in which the volume feels time-bound, it also has a timeless quality because the analytical questions raised throughout the respective chapters continue to have pertinence. Key questions include: How do we understand the world in which Canada operates? What is and should be Canada's role in the world? How do we understand and assess Canada's relationship with the United States? Should and can Canada pursue an independent foreign policy?[1] These questions have been and are central to the study of Canadian foreign policy and it is the timeless nature of these questions that supports the aim of this volume to inquire into the relevance of notions of an independent foreign policy for Canada in the early twenty-first century.

This chapter contributes to the volume through an examination of Canadian climate change policy and, in particular, through an assessment of what appears to be a moment of independence: Canadian ratification of the Kyoto Protocol in 2002. The ratification of the Kyoto Protocol by Canada does differentiate Canada from the United States and thus may be cast as 'independent.' However, a long history of collaboration with the United States on climate change in the international arena, coupled with Canadian policies that have not fundamentally contributed to change in our emissions policies, lead us to ask: independence to what end? Symbolic gestures of independence that are not followed by long-term, substantive environment-centred policy implementation simply exacerbate the commitment-credibility gap with both domestic and international audiences. The potential long-term value in the symbolic gesture is lost in the contradiction.

Canada and the Ratification of the Kyoto Protocol

The international political life of climate change began in 1988, when the Toronto Conference – entitled 'Changing Atmosphere: Implications for Global Security' – was held. Brian Mulroney and the experts housed in the Department of Environment were regarded as early leaders on the issue of climate change and were key architects of the subsequent Framework Convention on Climate Change (FCCC), which was signed in 1992 at the United Nations Conference on Environment and Development.

The FCCC, which came into force in March 1994, called for stabilization of greenhouse gases at 1990 levels by the year 2000. In early 1995 the first Conference of Parties (COP) was held in Berlin. At the Berlin meeting it became obvious that, largely because of perceived economic costs, emissions reductions had proved difficult to achieve for many states, including the United States, most of the members of the European Union (EU), and Canada. It was concluded that progress was inadequate and therefore parties to the convention adopted the Berlin Mandate, which called on states to aim for a legally binding protocol by COP 3 in Kyoto, Japan, in 1997.

At the time of COP 3, in Kyoto, Canada was embedded in a coalition of states known as JUSSCANZ (Japan, US, Canada, Australia, New Zealand, sometimes including Switzerland, Norway, and Iceland).[2] At Kyoto, the EU, frequently in tandem with developing states, faced off against the United States and its partners in the JUSSCANZ coalition.

The division was initially over emissions-reductions commitments. The EU aimed for more ambitious targets than the JUSSCANZ coalition. To break this deadlock, individual-state specific targets for industrialized states were proposed. But in order for states such as Canada and the United States to accept these targets they expected 'maximum flexibility' in implementation. Ultimately, individual targets for Annex I[3] states were adopted and market-based flexibility mechanisms[4] for emissions reductions were included in the Kyoto Protocol.

The Kyoto Protocol requires Annex I states to reduce their greenhouse gas emissions collectively by at least 5 per cent below 1990 levels by 2008–12. Canada agreed to reduce its national emissions to 6 per cent below 1990 levels by 2008–12. The United States agreed to a 7 per cent reduction in spite of a recalcitrant Senate that refused to ratify any treaty that would have adverse economic impacts on the United States. The Kyoto Protocol would enter into force after no 'less than 55 Parties to the Convention, incorporating Parties included in Annex I which accounted in total for at least 55 percent of the total carbon emissions for 1990 of the Parties included in Annex I, [had] deposited their instruments of ratification, acceptance, approval or accession.'[5]

It is interesting to note that at the time of the Kyoto Conference of Parties, Canada was in no position to meet its FCCC commitment and had moved into a coalition of those perceived to be laggards. As well, the Canadian commitment made at Kyoto was different from the 'national' position it had agreed to prior to arriving at the Kyoto negotiations.

Through federal-provincial negotiations a 'national' position of stabilization of greenhouse gases at 1990 levels between 2008 and 2012 was negotiated, but this target was even weaker than the FCCC stabilization commitment and much weaker than the commitment that the Canadian federal government ultimately accepted. The federal government broke from the federal-provincial target just before the Kyoto meeting and stated that Canada's position was for industrialized states to seek a 3 per cent reduction of greenhouse gas emissions from 1990 levels by 2010, with further reductions of 5 per cent by 2015, but the position was modified by the vague statement that 'domestically, Canada will seek to reduce its emissions to 1990 levels by 2007.'[6] This position changed over the course of the negotiations and the Canadian commitment made at Kyoto was to reductions deeper than either previously negotiated with the provinces or identified as the initial Canadian position going into Kyoto.

The reason for the break with the provinces and the even deeper cut at Kyoto is explained, in part, by a combination of pressures. First, the politics of international reputation had an impact on Prime Minister Chrétien, who was mindful of Canada's past image of leadership associated with climate change and aware of public attention to the issue. The politics of reputation was sufficiently significant that, in the months leading up to the Kyoto meetings, there was an impression held by some that Canada would 'beat' the United States in term of its emissions-reductions commitment.[7] Adopting the position advocated by the provinces would severely undermine any attempts to claim leadership on the issue of climate change. Ultimately, Canada did not 'beat' the United States, but the 6 per cent reductions adopted at Kyoto were superior, in terms of the politics of reputation, to the 3 per cent reductions negotiated with the provinces.

Second, U.S. President Clinton sought support for deeper cuts as a means by which to avoid an impasse with the Europeans (who were seeking 15 per cent cuts).[8] And third, Canadian negotiators required support from the United States for flexibility mechanisms, noted above, because these were regarded as a means to offset the need to make domestic emissions reductions. Canada received this support from the United States, the flexibility mechanisms were included in Kyoto, and Canada was thus able to commit to deeper reductions.

Even after the Kyoto Protocol was successfully negotiated, there remained divisions on a host of issues. Matters came to a head at the Sixth Conference of Parties meeting in The Hague in November 2000. Regarding flexibility mechanisms, for example, the EU negotiators remained concerned that the mechanisms would be used to avoid domestic activities. They wanted limits on the use of the mechanisms, which use they regarded as undermining the integrity of the Kyoto Protocol. The American-led coalition (which included Canada), now called the 'Umbrella Group,' remained resistant to caps and committed to flexibility mechanisms. Negotiations at The Hague were eventually suspended, and the Umbrella Group – including Canada – was accused of sabotaging the talks.

In March 2001 the United States pulled out of the Kyoto Protocol negotiations, but stated it would remain a member of the FCCC. The new American President, George W. Bush, believed Kyoto would have severe negative economic implications for his country, and committed to drafting a 'Made-in-America' plan for dealing with climate change.

There was concern that this would be a fatal blow to the Kyoto Protocol because the United States represented '36% of greenhouse gas emissions from Annex I countries,'[9] and many believed that without U.S. participation the requirements for the Kyoto Protocol to come into force would not be met.

Canada stayed in the negotiations after the U.S. withdrawal. To understand this decision, several factors must be considered: First, consistent with Canada's predilection for a rules-based international system, its continued participation was motivated by the desire to ensure the rules being designed would be in Canada's interest. Second, continuing participation reflected concerns for Canada's reputation in the international community; it allowed Canada to present the image of a good and independent international environmental leader, and thereby challenge accusations of having sabotaged past negotiations in tandem with the United States. Third, at this stage Canada had little to gain by withdrawing from the talks. If negotiations failed because of the absence of the United States, Canada would still look like an environmental team player, both internationally and domestically. If the negotiations proceeded, then the threat of withdrawal could be Canada's leverage to gain further advantage in the negotiations. Fourth, the domestic audience, while perhaps not understanding the intricacies of the agreement, clearly supported Canadian participation in the Kyoto Protocol.

While Canada stayed in the negotiations, it would be incorrect to assume that this was a reflection of optimism about the future of the Kyoto Protocol. The minister of environment, David Anderson, expressed the prevailing pessimism in May 2001: 'There's a certain amount of brave face about "Well, let's proceed, let's ratify, let's just proceed as though nothing has happened." That's not realistic.'[10]

The Sixth Conference of Parties (Part 2) met in Bonn in July 2001, without the United States, and, through a difficult series of negotiations, reached the Bonn Agreements. It was, however, well recognized that the agreement had been reached because the EU gave in on key issues. It was about striking a deal – any deal, according to academic Thomas Legge.[11] Failure in the face of the American withdrawal was unacceptable to the Europeans, and Canada, Japan, Australia, and Russia – the so-called Gang of Four[12] – took the opportunity to play hardball. John Drexhage, a former Canadian climate change negotiator, noted of the Bonn 2001 meeting that the current deal contains a number of elements that, from the perspective of the global environment, are weaker than what could have been agreed to at the failed round of negotiations in The Hague last November. For example, Canada received substantially more credits for 'sinks' ... than it would have received in The Hague, thereby easing the pressure to make direct emissions reductions at home.[13]

As implied above in the derogatory reference to Canada as a member of the Gang of Four, there was criticism of Canada's behaviour. However, there were other observers who were more generous. Former executive director of the Sierra Club of Canada Elizabeth May maintained that Canada was committed to the Kyoto Protocol and had worked to keep Japan in the negotiations. While Canada did gain more concessions, she argued, it also played a pivotal role in the survival of the Kyoto Protocol.[14] Looking at these claims from another angle, it is worth noting that while the Kyoto Protocol may have survived, it was certainly weakened, and while Canada worked to keep Japan involved, it also worked to ensure its interests were met in terms of opportunities to undertake activities, or count activities (such as 'sinks'), that did not have a deleterious impact on the Canadian economy.

With the Bonn Agreements in place, the focus turned to fine-tuning the technical details and waiting to see if Kyoto would come into force. After a very tempestuous domestic debate, Canada ratified the protocol in December 2002. With Russia's ratification in November 2004, the requirements for the protocol's entry into force were met, and the Kyoto regime was formally activated in February 2005. The United States has not ratified the treaty, and the Bush administration has maintained that it has no intention of doing so.

Canadian Ratification of the Kyoto Protocol: A Case of Independent Foreign Policy?

At first glance, one could argue that Canada's ratification of the Kyoto Protocol is an example of foreign policy independence from the United States, but that would be too simplistic. To equate a decision that differentiates Canada from the United States as a marker of independence may serve some political agenda, but the argument lacks substance and denies the history and complexity of the climate change issue. Instead, we might begin with the characteristics of an independent foreign policy identified by Stephen Clarkson in 1968. These are not meant to 'test' the independence of a particular decision, but rather to serve as a general guide to policy-making and to provoke reflection on what constitutes 'independence.' Ultimately, this section shows that the ratification of the Kyoto Protocol is nothing more than a hollow, symbolic gesture, and raises questions about the value and logic of independence as such.

First, according to Clarkson, pursuing an independent foreign policy does not mean opting out of collective diplomacy. In the case of the ratification of the Kyoto Protocol, the signal sent by Canada was in support of multilateral endeavours, in spite of the American decisions to withdraw from the Kyoto negotiations and ultimately not to ratify the protocol.

How do we square Canada's apparent commitment to collective or multilateral diplomacy with the details of its participation in the negotiations? In the early stages, prior to 1994, Canada was seen as a leader, but as the negotiations evolved they were increasingly driven by contending coalitions. For practical, geographic, and political reasons, Canada became embedded in the American-led coalition (i.e., JUSSCANZ, the Umbrella Group). Canada changed its commitment at Kyoto in support of President Clinton, according to Elizabeth May, and worked with the coalition partners to achieve outcomes at the Bonn 2001 meeting that were consistent with American goals, even after the United States left the negotiations. It was a commonality of interests, in particular related to reducing the domestic economic impacts of emissions reductions, that bound this coalition together. In addition, the fact that the EU also worked as a coalition reinforced the need for other states to work that way, and coalitions imply constraints.

Second, Clarkson suggests that an independent foreign policy is not necessarily an anti-American one. Was the decision to ratify the Kyoto Protocol inspired by anti-Americanism? During the very public debate leading up to the ratification of the protocol, federal government proponents of ratification framed the decision as one where Canada was showing leadership on a crucial international environmental issue. It was not cast as an anti-American decision. In the domestic debate, consideration of the United States did loom as those who were not in favour of ratification regularly stated that by ratifying Kyoto we would be 'out of step' with our largest trading partner, and there was concern that Canada would penalize itself by adopting targets while the United States did not. However, in this instance the argument was not framed in anti-American terms.

There were arguments made by members of the Bloq Québécois, who were very pro-Kyoto during the House of Commons debate on the protocol that could be interpreted as anti-American. For example, Mario Laframboise, Member of Parliament for Argenteuil-Papineau-Mirabel, argued: 'Countries that signed on have not been given unrealistic targets. They are reachable. What is irresponsible is to do what the United States, among others, is doing, and not care about global warming. That is totally irresponsible. One day, the Americans will understand the harm they will have caused our planet ... Why follow them blindly, like some parties in this House want to do? Why say "if the Americans are not signing, we are not signing either"?'[15] Odina Desrochers, BQ member from Lotbinière-L'Érable, also spoke about the American decision to not sign Kyoto: 'When I hear that the Bush administration does not want to sign Kyoto, I know exactly why. As we know, President Bush is from Texas. We know what this means in the United States. This is the state where oil companies are concentrated. These companies could not care less whether the atmosphere is polluted or not. What they care about is making money.'[16]

As well, there was an intervention – or perceived intervention – by U.S. ambassador Paul Cellucci, in early 2002, where he was accused of encouraging Canada to not ratify Kyoto and instead focus on a bilateral approach to climate change. According to the *Globe and Mail*, Cellucci stated: 'We just think Kyoto is not in the interests of the United States or its economy and we don't think it's in the interests of the Canadian economy either ... we ought to have a North American strategy.'[17] Cellucci responded to this report, saying it was a 'fanciful interpretation of my responses to questions from a *Globe and Mail* reporter,' and that 'whether Canada will ratify the Kyoto Convention or chose another route to address climate change is a choice that clearly will be made by Canada's elected representatives based on Canada's best interests.'[18]

Pro- or anti-Americanism were peripheral to the Kyoto ratification debate in Canada; the dominant discourse instead emphasized questions about whether or not the regime was consistent with Canadian interests and values. This relates to Clarkson's third point, that an independent foreign policy is more assertive in the articulation of Canadian interests. Not surprisingly, the debate was characterized by sharply conflicting views about what constituted Canada's interests.

During the months leading up to ratification there emerged a common set of anti-Kyoto claims coming from the Province of Alberta, the oil and gas–led coalition, and the Alliance Party.[19] The anti-Kyoto argument typically hinged on presenting a 'Made-in-Canada' approach to climate change. The 'Made-in-Canada' approach had a bit of a different spin depending on who was talking, but all variations shared the common theme that Kyoto was somehow imposed from the outside and did not truly represent 'Canadian' interests.

In contrast, the proponents of Kyoto, including the prime minister, minister of environment, and various environmental groups, pointed to countless consultative mechanisms that had been in place, and argued that the decision to ratify was a reflection of Canadian interests. The National Change Secretariat, created in 1998 to be an integral part of the federal-provincial consultative process after Canada's Kyoto commitment, established sixteen issues tables, which included 450 individuals representing all sectors and levels of government. Following the work of the issues tables, there were cross-country stakeholder sessions held in every province in 2000, with another round of cross-country sessions in 2002. In addition, Canada's international delegations to the COPs have included stakeholders. Ultimately, the Kyoto Protocol did not dictate how states were to meet their targets, and so Canada had to develop its own implementation plans. These plans, while seriously lacking in substance, were certainly made in Canada.

An interesting twist on the 'Made-in-Canada' argument articulated by the Alliance Party and the anti-Kyoto industry coalition was that the Kyoto Protocol did not address critical issues related to air quality and consequently did not deal with 'real' Canadian environmental issues. While not designed to positively impact local air quality, measures to reduce greenhouse gas emissions such as driving one's car less to save on energy consumption do have the side benefit of having a positive impact on local air quality, because we are consequently reducing exhaust emissions that contribute to air quality problems. Thus, the 'Made-in-Canada' coalition are critical of international attempts to address a global problem because it is global, while denying the positive local impacts that they say are not sufficiently covered in the agreement. Kyoto was never designed specifically to deal with local air quality, but benefits accrue nonetheless.

Competing visions of economic interests also emerged during the debate. In discussions around the impacts of climate change the anti-Kyoto alliance typically spoke in terms of trade and competitiveness, and suggested that the Canadian economy would be gravely undermined if Kyoto was ratified. The province of Alberta, the industry coalition, and the leader of the Canadian Alliance Party, Stephen Harper, all stated that the protocol could cost Canadians anywhere between $23 billion and \$40 billion a year. In contrast, nongovernmental organizations such as the David Suzuki Foundation and the Pembina Institute painted a different economic future under the Kyoto Accord. Both suggested Canada could afford to meet its Kyoto commitments and that efforts to meet those commitments would result in increased competitiveness and new opportunities for firms working in areas related to greenhouse gas technologies.[20]

So was the ratification of the Kyoto Protocol a reflection of Canada's interests? In the view of the federal government of the day, it was a sound decision that reflected the interests of Canadians, but in the view of anti-Kyoto forces it was directly contrary to Canadian interests. Clearly, it is not enough to say that Kyoto ratification reflected our interests to conclude in any way that the decision was somehow independent.

Fourth, Clarkson also argued that an independent foreign policy is marked by policy decisions made on their own merits, based on a 'socially concerned view of the world that shows that Canada's interests coincide more with general progress than with the maintenance of the USA's super-power status' and informed by international objectives that focus on 'international equality and socio-economic modernization.'[21]

At the level of policy statements and federal government explanations for ratification, Canada did make an independent decision based on the perceived merits of the protocol and on Canadian interests. As noted above, the decision to ratify signalled support for multilateral endeavours and indeed for environmental well-being. The public statements by then minister of environment David Anderson are rife with sentences that would lead one to think that the decision was based on a concern for general progress. For example, in the House of Commons debate on the ratification of the Kyoto Protocol Anderson stated: 'This House is rarely asked to turn its attention to a matter with the impact of climate change. For we are discussing an issue that extends well beyond the normal vision of elected officials. We will be debating what kind of world we want for our children, our grandchildren, and their children as well.'[22] This said, the debate within Canada tended to focus on Canadian environmental and economic well-being. Because it was so focused on Canadian interests, international interests, while still relevant, were nonetheless less central to the public debate. Declaratory policy statements, however, are only part of the equation, and one would be hard pressed to say that the ratification of the Kyoto Protocol was based on a socially concerned view of the world.

Nor does one decision necessarily reflect the life of the issue area. To focus on the point of ratification obfuscates the broader reality of Canadian behaviour over time. Canada was active in the U.S.-led coalition for several years before the American withdrawal from Kyoto negotiations. During that time Canada was regularly accused of being a laggard, and cast as a member of the 'Gang of Four' seeking to gut the Kyoto Protocol. More significantly, Canadian policies designed to tackle climate change have been ineffectual and subsequent governments have consistently been faced with a growing gap between the country's Kyoto targets and actual emissions growth. This gap is now widely acknowledged and has resulted in the Conservative government's public declaration that the Kyoto commitments would not be met.

Unfortunately, one has to wonder if Prime Minister Chrétien's concern with building up his own legacy, rather than any social concern, was the real driving force behind the Kyoto ratification. There were hints in the press at the time that ratification was regarded as separate from implementation, and thus the Liberal government was willing to ratify even if it was not sure how to achieve the domestic emissions-reductions target. In 2002, then minister of natural resources Herb Dhaliwal stated that 'Canada has no intention of meeting the conditions of the Kyoto Protocol on greenhouse gases even though the government hopes to ratify it this fall.'[23] Dhaliwal, according to the same report, was supported in his statement by the prime minister, who said, 'Canada should ratify now and worry about implementation later.'[24]

While the notion of an independent foreign policy characterized as socially concerned is a reflection of the left-nationalist position adopted by Clarkson, and could be rejected by those working from different ideological perspectives, it is nonetheless an idea that pushes us to think about intentionality. The decision to ratify may have supported the multilateral endeavour represented by Kyoto at that time, but it lacked substance and served the interests of the Liberal Party and their green image more than it has the Canadian people, certainly in the long term.

Finally, for Clarkson, there is an additional normative component to an independent foreign policy, insofar as he explicitly points to the need for an ethically just foreign policy: 'an independent approach is necessarily more ethical for it requires an autonomous calculation for every policy of the probable consequences for Canada and for those our policy will affect.' And 'an independent foreign policy also presupposes responsibility.'[25] This final characteristic of an independent foreign policy is as slippery as trying to measure national interest. It is incredibly subjective. Was the decision to ratify the Kyoto Protocol ethical and responsible? On one level it is possible to argue the decision is both ethical and responsible. By ratifying the Kyoto Protocol we signalled a commitment to multilateral processes and environmental well-being, and accepted that Canada had an obligation to reduce emissions. On another level, however, we participated in a coalition that routinely sought to avoid domestic emissions reductions in favour of reductions elsewhere, we threatened to leave the negotiations when they did not meet our interests, and we ratified the protocol knowing our emissions were rising and we were nowhere near our target. Further, if we believe that the Liberal government knowingly ratified the Kyoto Protocol with little intention of meeting the Kyoto commitments, then we must conclude that our actions were both unethical and irresponsible from the perspective of the global good, the environment, and the Canadian people.

Concluding Reflections

Was the Canadian ratification of the Kyoto Protocol an example of an independent foreign policy? Ultimately, using Clarkson's criteria for an independent foreign policy as a guide, and applying them to Canada's ratification of the Kyoto Protocol, leads us to conclude that the decision to ratify was independent based on Canadian interests (as long as we follow the reasoning of the federal government). We opted for multilateral diplomacy. and it was a decision that was pro-Canadian rather than anti-American. In spite of concerns about being out of step with the United States and regardless of calls for a North American pact, Canada ratified Kyoto. But this argument reflects neither the essentially contested nature of the Clarkson criteria nor the shallowness of the decision to ratify.

As argued throughout this chapter, to draw any conclusion that the ratification of the Kyoto Protocol is a wholesale example of independence is to deny the complexities revealed in the application of the Clarkson criteria. It is clear that we need to ask a host of questions: Whose interest? Whose ethics? Responsible to and for whom? Collective diplomacy to what end? Do we consider just one moment in the life of a policy or the evolution of the policy over time?

The ratification of the Kyoto Protocol by the Canadian government did support multilateral diplomacy and it was an action that stands in contrast to the American position. In that sense we have been 'different.' But there is a long history of collaboration with the United States on the issue of climate change that suggests that the Kyoto ratification is but one part of the story. In many regards, Canada and the United States were partners in the laggards' coalition, and decisions to work with the United States were based on a commonality of interests. And indeed, the decision to ratify was not so much anti-American as, rather, driven by domestic politics, legacy-building by Prime Minister Chrétien, and an attempt to prop up Canada's international reputation. The ratification decision can also be seen as a failed attempt to tie the hands of future governments. If we want to use the language of 'independence,' then the decision to ratify Kyoto can be understood as a symbolic gesture of independence that captured our attention but has amounted to little in terms of long-term sustainable environmental policies.

We must, however, wonder if the language of independence and its implied opposite of dependence are even relevant or useful to the discussion of Canadian climate change policy. The language is so inherently state-centric and implies an embedded dichotomy that lacks sophistication. Is it really possible to have a meaningfully 'independent' environmental policy when the point of reference is a set of global environmental issues with multiple sources and world-wide implications? The environment does not respect state boundaries and cares little if one state or another adopts particular policies. If this chapter were to be written from the perspective of the environment, whether or not Canada acted independently would become irrelevant. The questions worth asking would be whether we acted responsibly towards the environment and whether we recognized our dependence on the environment. In the end, Canada's ratification of the Kyoto Protocol may have marked us as different or independent from the United States, but it was a gesture rooted in indifference to the environment.

NOTES

1 Stephen Clarkson, 'The Choice to Be Made,' in *An Independent Foreign Policy for Canada?* ed. Stephen Clarkson (Toronto: McClelland and Stewart, 1968), 253–4.

2 This discussion is drawn from International Institute for Sustainable Development, *Earth Negotiations Bulletin*, 13 December 1997, available at http://www.iisd.ca/linkages/download/asc/end127e.txt (accessed 29 October 2002).

3 The Annex I states include the EU, economies in transition, Canada, the United States, and other states typically considered 'industrialized,' such as Japan, Australia, and New Zealand.

4 The flexibility mechanisms include joint implementation and emissions trading between Annex I parties. The Clean Development Mechanism (CDM) was included in the protocol, thus potentially providing for the flexibility required by the American-led coalition, because it allowed Annex I parties such as Canada and the United States to undertake projects that reduce emissions in non–Annex I parties that could be used to meet Kyoto commitments.

5 United Nations, *Kyoto Protocol* (New York, 1997), art. 25.1.

6 Canada, *News Release: Canada Proposes Targets for Reductions in Global Greenhouse Gas Emissions*, 1 December 1997, 2.

7 Douglas MacDonald and Heather A. Smith, 'Promise Made, Promises Broken: Questioning Canada's Commitments to Climate Change,' in *Readings in Canadian Foreign Policy: Classic Debates and New Ideas*, ed. Duane Bratt and Christopher J. Kukucha (Toronto: Oxford University Press, 2007), 364.

8 Elizabeth May, 'From Montreal to Kyoto, How We Got from Here to There – or Not,' *Policy Options*, 24, no. 1 (December 2002–January 2003): 16.

9 Jon Hovi, Tora Skodvin, and Steinar Andresen, 'The Persistence of the Kyoto Protocol: Why Other Annex I Countries Move on without the United States,' in *Global Environmental Politics* 3, no. 4 (November 2003): 2.

10 Planet Ark, 'US Stance Key to Global Warming Talks – Canada,' 14 May 2001, available at http://www.Planetark.com (accessed 9 October 2001).

11 Thomas Legge, 'The Unexpected Triumph of Optimism over Experience,' *Centre for European Policy Studies Commentary*, 27 July 2001, available at http://www.ceps.bc/Commentary/July01/unexpected.htm (accessed 12 March 2002).

12 For more information on Canada and the 'Gang of Four' see, Hovi, Skodvin, and Andresen, 'The Persistence of the Kyoto Protocol.'

13 International Institute for Sustainable Development, *Commentary: Canada and COP-6*, 23 July 2001, available at http://www.iisd.org/bonnoped.htm (accessed 4 September 2002).

14 May, 'From Montreal to Kyoto,' 17.

15 Canada, House of Commons, 37th Parliament, 2nd Session, *Hansard*, 2 December 2002, available at: http://www2.parl.gc.ca/HousePublications/Publicaion.aspx?Lan guage=E&Mode=1&Parl.

16 Ibid.

17 Steven Chase, 'Canada Shouldn't Ratify Kyoto, U.S. Envoy Says,' *Globe and Mail*, 26 January 2002, A10.

18 Embassy of the United States of America in Canada, 'Kyoto: The U.S. Position,' 2 February 2002, available at http://canada.usembassy.gov/content/content.asp?section=embc onsult&document=cellucc (accessed 25 October 2007).

19 See Canadian Coalition for Responsible Environmental Solutions, 'Coalition Formed to Advance "Made in Canada" Strategy on Climate Change,' 26 September 2002, available at http://www.cpeq.qc.ca/anglais/apropos/ReleaseCCRES.pdf; Canadian Coalition for Responsible Environmental Solutions, 'Backgrounder on Kyoto,' available at http://www.canadiansolution.com/backgrounder.asp; Alberta, *News Release: Kyoto Could Cost Canada up to $40 Billion, Study Shows*, 21 February 2002, available at http://www.gov.ab.ca/acn/200202/11952.html; Alberta, *Potential Consequences of Canada's Kyoto Ratification Highlighted in New Awareness Campaign*, 18 September 2002, available at http://www.gov.ab.ca/acn/200209/13149.html; Alberta, *Alberta's Opposition to Federal Kyoto Plan Still Firm, Minister Says*, 1 November 2002, available at http://www.gov.ab.ca/acn/200211/13445.html; and Canada, House of Commons, *Hansard*, 37th Parliament, 2nd Session, no. 041, 9 December 2002.

20 See Sylvie Boustie et al., *How Ratifying the Kyoto Protocol Will Benefit Canada's Competitiveness* (Ottawa: Pembina Institute, 2002) and David Suzuki Foundation, *Keeping Canada in Kyoto: The Case for Immediate Ratification and Domestic Emissions Trading* (Vancouver: David Suzuki Foundation, 2002), available at: http://davidsuzuki.org/files/ClimateBrief.pdf.

21 Clarkson, 'The Choice to Be Made,' 255–6.

22 Environment Canada, 'Notes for an Address by the Honourable David Anderson, P.C., M.P., Minister of the Environment to Open the Parliamentary Debate on Ratification of the Kyoto Protocol,' 9 December 2002, available at http://www.ec.gc.ca/media_archive/minister/speeches/2002/021209_s_e.htm (accessed 25 October 2007).

23 Bruce Cheadle, 'Canada to Sign Kyoto, but Won't Abide by It,' *Toronto Star*, 5 September 2002, available at http://thestar.com (accessed 29 October 2002).

24 Ibid.

25 Clarkson, 'The Choice to Be Made,' 263.

Conclusions: Beyond 'Independence'

PATRICK LENNOX AND BRIAN BOW

In the introduction to this volume, we argued that the 'quiet diplomacy' versus 'independence' dichotomy drawn in the original 1968 volume captured some of the main lines of debate over Canadian foreign policy at that time, and continues to resonate today. But we believe that the dichotomy has tended to oversimplify the challenges, and obscure some of the choices, before us. Our aim here has thus been to take us (in dialectical fashion) beyond the 'independence' debate towards a mature discussion of Canada's future place in the world that would be grounded in a more fruitful, synthesized middle ground between the two rival camps.

Like the contributors to this volume, those in the original, 1968 volume – both the proponents of 'quiet diplomacy' and the advocates of 'independence' – were ultimately concerned with achieving an *effective* foreign policy for Canada. While they saw different pathways to this goal, neither group would have been content to see a foreign policy that was not actively pursued and intellectually informed by a clear perspective on what the country hoped to achieve in the world.

None of the contributors to the original *IFPC?* volume were interested in independence for its own sake, and the same can certainly be said of our contributors. But here there seems to be a further inclination to move the debate beyond the question of 'independence' itself. A consistent desire to regard autonomy as important and interesting mostly as a means to other ends is evident throughout the chapters of this volume. Consequently, our authors are inclined to think about policy choices not in terms of style, but in terms of results. Each in their own way has sought to shift the focus of Canadian foreign policy analysis to the question of whether or not a given policy can effectively achieve the aims that Canadians want achieved, and do so in a way that is consistent with Canadian values. To the extent that our contributors are interested in autonomy per se, it is generally in terms of the impact that today's policy will have on the range of available options for future policy choices.

Collectively, we are trying to move beyond independence as a question of political status or diplomatic approach. Our attention is accordingly drawn towards recognition of the structural constraints on Canada as an international actor, but also to the enabling features built into our geographic position, our economic capacities, our political institutions, and our cultural values. Our focus, then, in developing and evaluating foreign policy options, turns towards the effort to maximize policy discretion and diplomatic leverage within an increasingly complex, increasingly interdependent international environment – which is of course where it always should have been.

Challenges and Choices

As we have noted more than once already, much has changed over the last forty years. But *plus ça change, plus c'est la même chose*. Many of the core challenges for Canadian policy-makers today are essentially the same as those in the 1960s. Adam Chapnick reminds us in his chapter that there is no such thing as total foreign policy independence, for Canada or for any country. When we think about the scope and nature of Canada's foreign policy independence, then, we may begin by thinking about constraints and the room left for manoeuvring within them. There can be no doubt that Canada is limited by its size and its position within the continental and international orders, and, as Patrick Lennox's chapter explains, accepting the realities of how these structural factors constrain and compel the country towards the performance of an array of specialized roles will be crucial not only to the success of Canadian foreign policy in the future, but also to the future of the relationship with the United States, the stability of the current world order, and the internal unity of Canada itself.

The original volume clearly recognized that the primary source of both the constraints and the opportunities for Canadian foreign policy was the bilateral relationship with the United States. This reality seems ever more pressing in our current context. But while the spectre of American power looms even larger today than in 1968, Brian Bow reminds us that Washington nevertheless rarely if ever engages in direct retaliation for actions out of step with the general direction of American foreign policy. Room for manoeuvre within the evolving continental hierarchy still exists, but the price might be exacted through less direct mechanisms, and Canadians must be willing to weigh the costs of 'grudges' held in Washington when contemplating a foreign policy choice at odds with American goals or strategies.

This theme is picked up on in Christopher Sands's discussion of contemporary security issues. Canada's efforts to pursue independence as 'freedom of action,' he argues, can have the paradoxical effect of lessening its 'freedom from dependency.' Given our close ties to the United States, Canada's best opportunities to make an impact on the world might indeed come through the gentle steering of the American elephant towards a more moderate approach to global leadership. Echoing the original advocates of quiet diplomacy, Sands suggests that when Canada acts in ways that squander its diplomatic capital in Washington, it can find its influence in world affairs significantly diminished. This is a reality that, while uncomfortable, cannot be ignored.

Canada's position within the international order, and its inescapable dependency on the United States, sets limits on the range of choice for Canadian foreign policy. But – as virtually all of the contributors to this new volume have concluded – Canadian governments' repeated failures to build a coherent agenda, and maintain the capabilities to pursue it, have often done more to tie Canada's hands than anything the United States (or other states) might do. This is certainly not a new development, as Chapnick reminds us, but these tendencies do seem to have intensified since the 1960s. An effective foreign policy requires a degree of leadership, strategic vision, and commitment that are often sorely lacking in Canada, with politicians fixed on immediate and tangible domestic political results, and often not really held to account by a public that is generally much more concerned with domestic political questions.

We can see the effects of this lack of foreign policy planning and follow-through most clearly in Rob Huebert's account of the Canadian government's recurring failure over the years to do anything more than talk the talk on the issue of Canada's Arctic sovereignty. When it comes to actually walking the walk, he argues, successive Canadian governments have consistently fallen down. We see similar tendencies in Patricia Goff's chapter on cultural policy, where the government has had difficulty in developing new regulatory instruments to keep pace with new communications technology and new international legal regimes.

Stephanie Golob also provides a striking example of how the lack of a clear strategic vision for the future of North America, in line with traditional Canadian values, has led to a missed opportunity for Ottawa in shaping the agenda of the Security and Prosperity Partnership. And Heather Smith's chapter further highlights the dangers of an ad hoc approach to Canadian foreign policy. By ratifying the Kyoto Protocol with no long-run plan for implementing its requirements, Smith argues, Canada has effectively discredited itself as an advocate in the multilateral struggle against climate change in the eyes of its European allies.

Together, these contributions suggest that a cautious, reactive foreign policy for Canada is doomed to failure. There is more to the chess game of international politics than material capabilities alone. Advanced planning and a clear strategic purpose will become of even greater significance for Canadian foreign policy going forward. We are not advocating the establishment of a grand strategy for Canada of the sort great powers are prone to propound, but as the above examples of Canada's missed foreign policy opportunities and strategic miscalculations suggest, greater effort must go into assessing the national interest and the national ability to pursue that interest across the growing domain of foreign policy issues. As Geoffrey Hale's chapter suggests, there is a great deal of variation across issue areas in the kinds of limits placed on Canadian policy-makers' discretion. Going 'back to basics' and trying to simplify the equation in an increasingly complex international strategic environment might be the best way forward. Preoccupation with the 'independence' of our foreign policy in such circumstances may be a recipe for confusing substance with style, and optics with effects.

Challenges and Choices for the Future

In reflecting on a debate that took place forty years ago, this volume has presented a number of challenges and choices for the future of Canadian foreign policy, which we hope will inspire renewed public and academic attention.

While we have tried to provide a range of analyses on a range of issues currently confronting the country and its foreign policy-makers, we feel that the pivotal issue confronting us today is our relation to the U.S.-led war on terror. On the face of it, our relation to this far-reaching campaign – which has, to a greater or lesser extent, a bearing on all the issues confronted in this volume – seems straightforward: as a Western, liberal democracy, Canada faces (along with other Western states) the asymmetrical threat of suicide bombs and other sorts of terrorist attacks inspired by a militant interpretation of Islam. The neutrality once seriously contemplated in the defence and foreign policy reviews of the early Trudeau era, is even more impossible in the current strategic environment than it was then.

This fundamental reality being acknowledged, Canada's foreign policy choices are nevertheless much more complex than the Bush administration's 'with us or with the terrorists' rhetoric suggests. There is still room for disagreement and policy differentiation within the seemingly more constrictive contours of the war on terror. And while Canada is compelled to find ways to work with the United States (and other traditional allies) in pursuing transnational terrorist groups, responding to state failure in Afghanistan, and (one way or another) trying to clean up the mess created by the war in Iraq, the crucial choices involve decisions on how and when to contribute.

Canadians need to think carefully about the long-term implications of different types of contributions they choose to make to the struggle against Islamic fundamentalism and terrorism. Taking on major military challenges, as we have done in Afghanistan, comes with costs and benefits less immediately tangible than lives and treasure, alone. Canada's reputation abroad and its internal cohesion at home are stressed and strained each time the country commits to a taxing international engagement that is outside the range of its traditional international reputation. While such contributions presumably raise Canada's profile in Washington and overseas in the short term, they also detract from the long-term image that successive Canadian governments have cultivated of Canada as a power focused on the establishment and maintenance of peace and stability in the international system.

Leaving the military challenges to others, and trying to tackle terrorism and other post-Cold War security challenges through efforts to confront the problems of state failure, ethnic conflict, poverty, disease, and environmental change bring forth their own challenges. Canada, however, has an established track record as an important multilateral player on many of these issues, a record it could build on in an effort to raise its diplomatic profile, and could make specialized contributions to the stability and progressive evolution of the current world order. But these issues are also potentially explosive ones which can sometimes pit international priorities against domestic ones. We see this conflict in Canada's climate change policy, where successive governments have failed to find the right balance between Canadians' impulse to multilateral leadership and their short-run economic interests, and the result has been frustration and resentment, both at home and abroad.

These broad strategic choices should be tied into a serious rethinking of Canada's identity as an international player. Critics of Canadian foreign policy often argue that it is all image and no substance,[1] but we haven't really begun to think seriously about what image to cultivate, or more practically how to do so – at least not in this post–Cold War, post-9/11, post-NAFTA, post-SPP world.

There is of course another set of security challenges after 9/11, which blur the distinctions between foreign and domestic policy, and between national security and other issues such as transportation, policing, and immigration. Again, Canada has no choice but to find new understandings with the United States. But Canadians will have difficult choices to make about what changes they are prepared to face when it comes to policies ranging from legal reform to the treatment of refugees. There are two kinds of rationales that have a bearing here: the first centres on actually making Canadians more secure, while the second centres on convincing U.S. policy-makers that Canada is doing all it can to help make *Americans* more secure. These two rationales may actually diverge on some specific policy issues. Accordingly, the challenge is to devise policies that effectively achieve the first objective and still find the best possible balance in terms of the larger bilateral relationship.

When it comes to 'low politics,' the main choice for the future will likely be over the resolution of policy frictions with other states, particularly the United States. Canadian policy-makers have tended to see this in terms of a trade-off, wherein we purchase limits on others states' policy discretion by accepting limits on our own. In the past this was often done informally (particularly vis-à-vis the United States), but over the last twenty years it has increasingly been done through formal international institutions (e.g., CUSFTA/NAFTA, WTO). Canada's autonomy has thus been reduced, in the sense that some policy instruments are ruled 'out of bounds,' but successive governments have found ways to protect valued policy instruments, and to develop alternative instruments that create new forms of policy discretion. The main choices for the future are therefore likely to be over whether to reduce policy frictions with other states through unilateral reforms, negotiated agreements, or cession of decision-making or standard-setting to supranational institutions. The Security and Prosperity Partnership experience shows us that a big part of the challenge for policy-makers is going to be in preventing the negotiating process from being hijacked or derailed by narrow interests, while still finding ways to foster public engagement and create political legitimacy.

Finally (though perhaps first in importance), there is the need to build a post–Cold War, post-NAFTA, post-9/11 consensus on foreign policy. One of the major challenges for the future is likely to be the development of new structures for federal–provincial dialogue that provide for provincial input *before* potential 'ratification' crises, and still maintain Ottawa's capacity to speak 'with one voice' on the international stage. But the major challenge in building a national consensus on foreign policy is still likely to be in developing a meaningful dialogue with the general public. Canada's isolated geographic position and its highly centralized political institutions make it possible for the public to forget about foreign policy most of the time, and for the government to side-step public pressure when it does take form. Efforts to bring 'public input' into the foreign policy process over the last twenty years have been frustrating, both for the representatives of the public that have participated in the process and for the policy-makers charged with translating the results into concrete policies. But – to echo the call from the original *IFPC?* volume – there must be an effort to keep the process going, and to find new ways to encourage engagement and develop a post–Cold War foreign policy consensus.

Some might argue that the relative absence of meaningful public debate today is actually helpful, in the sense that it creates space for a more effective 'quiet diplomacy.' It is certainly true that there are times when public pressure (or even a vague public awareness of an issue) may tempt the political leadership to put electoral opportunism ahead of good judgment, or otherwise weaken the hand of the Canadian policy-maker or diplomat. But there are also times when public pressure makes a tough bargaining position more credible, and when public interest in an issue prods the government towards effective action. As the contributors to this volume have repeatedly pointed out, Canada has a record of missed foreign policy opportunities that can often be traced back to inertia in Ottawa, rather than to intimidation from Washington. If this inertia is to be broken – if the government is to come up with a supply of effective foreign policies, then there must be a clear demand from the Canadian public.

A fruitful policy debate, however, needs to be anchored in shared concepts and categories that are useful in moving forward to clear prescriptions for action. It needs, moreover, to recognize that there are actually many debates out there. As we have seen in the preceding chapters, there are some essential continuities that seem to run through every facet of Canadian foreign policy, but the kinds of challenges and choices we face vary in important ways from one issue area to another, and from one policy context to another.

The original *IFPC?* debate's success in stirring up interest in foreign policy issues came mostly from the polarizing effects of the 'quiet di- plomacy' versus 'independentist' dichotomy, which provoked readers with veiled accusations of political naivety or disloyalty (respectively). To advance our thinking on Canadian foreign policy and Canada's place in the world, we feel it essential to release ourselves from the bonds of this false dichotomy. Moving beyond the 'independence' debate itself towards a mature discussion of Canada's interests and obligations, and the capabilities it has to pursue them in a complex and changing world, is – we feel – the most promising way forward.

NOTE

1 This is effectively captured in the title of a recent article by Bill Dymond and Michael Hart: 'The Potemkin Village of Canadian Foreign Policy,' *Policy Options* 25 (December 2003–January 2004): 39–45.

Bibliography

Ackelson, Jason, and Justin Kastner. 'The Security and Prosperity Partnership of North America.' *American Review of Canadian Studies* 36, no. 2 (Summer 2006): 207–32.

Aitken, Hugh G.L. *American Capital and Canadian Resources.* Cambridge, MA: Harvard University Press, 1961.

Alberta. *Alberta's Opposition to Federal Kyoto Plan Still Firm, Minister Says.* 1 November 2002. Available at http://www.gov.ab.ca/acn/200211/13445.html (accessed 2 October 2007).

– *News Release: Kyoto Could Cost Canada up to $40 Billion, Study Shows.* 21 February 2002. Available at http://www.gov.ab.ca/acn/200202/11952.html (accessed 2 October 2007).

– *Potential Consequences of Canada's Kyoto Ratification Highlighted in New Awareness Campaign.* 18 September 2002. Available at http://www.gov.ab.ca/acn/200209/13149.html (accessed 2 October 2007).

Alberta Securities Commission. The *Alberta Capital Market: A Comparative Overview.* Calgary: Alberta Securities Commission, 2006.

– *The Alberta Capital Market: A Comparative Overview. 2007 Report.* Calgary: Alberta Securities Commission, 2007.

Alberts, Sheldon. 'Saddam Should Have Weeks, Not Months.' *National Post,* 25 February 2003, A11.

Alper, Donald K., and Robert L. Monahan. 'Bill C-58 and the American Congress: The Politics of Retaliation.' *Canadian Public Policy* 4 (Spring 1978): 184–92.

Anderson, Benedict. *Imagined Communities.* New York: Verso, 1991.

Anderson, Greg, and Christopher Sands. 'Negotiating North America: The Security and Prosperity Partnership.' *Hudson Institute White Paper,* Fall 2007.

Andreas, Peter. 'A Tale of Two Borders: The US-Mexico and US-Canada Lines after 9/11.' In *The Rebordering of North America*, ed. Peter Andreas and Thomas J. Biersteker, 1–23. New York: Routledge, 2003.

Apsey, T.M., and J.C. Thomas. *The Lessons of the Softwood Lumber Dispute: Politics, Protectionism and the Panel Process*. Available at http://www.acah.org/aspey.htm (accessed 5 April 2003).

Arnold, Samantha. 'From "Third Pillar" to "Public Diplomacy": Culture and Canadian Foreign Policy.' Unpublished paper prepared for NPSIA New Scholars Conference, Waterloo, September 2005.

Australia. 'Australia's Public Diplomacy: Building Our Image (Report of the Senate Standing Committee on Foreign Affairs, Defence, and Trade).' Canberra: Commonwealth of Australia, 2007. Available at http://www.aph.gov.au/Senate/committee/fadt_ctte/public_diplomacy/report/index.htm (accessed 1 October 2007).

Ayres, Jeffrey, and Laura Macdonald. 'Deep Integration and Shallow Governance: The Limits of Civil Society Engagement across North America.' *Policy and Society* 25, no. 3 (2006): 23–42.

Azzi, Stephen. 'Magazines and the Canadian Dream: The Struggle to Protect Canadian Periodicals, 1956–65.' *International Journal* 54, no. 3 (Summer 1999): 502–23.

– 'Negotiating Cultural Space in the Global Economy.' *International Journal* 60, no. 3 (Summer 2005): 765–84.

– *Walter Gordon and the Rise of Canadian Nationalism*. Montreal and Kingston: McGill-Queen's University Press, 1999.

Bacevich, Andrew J. 'No Disrespect to Canada ...' *The National Interest* no. 90 (July/August 2007): 12–13.

Baldwin, David. 'The Myth of the Special Relationship.' In *An Independent Foreign Policy for Canada?* ed. Stephen Clarkson, 5–17. Toronto: McClelland & Stewart, 1968.

Beaton, Leonard. 'Declaration of Independence.' *Canadian Forum* 48 (April 1968): 1–3.

Barry, Donald. 'Chretien, Bush, and the War in Iraq.' *American Review of Canadian Studies* 35, no. 2 (Summer 2005): 215–45.

'Being Independent Doesn't Mean Being Rude.' *Maclean's* 67 (1 April 1954): 2.

Bélanger, Louis. 'Redefining Cultural Diplomacy.' *Political Psychology* 20, no. 4 (1999).

Benjamin, Daniel, and Steven Simon. *The Age of Sacred Terror: Radical Islam's War against America*. New York: Randon House, 2002.

Bourassa, Henri. 'Future Anglo-Canadian Relations: Independence or Imperial Partnership.' In *Henri Bourassa on Imperialism and Biculturalism, 1900–1918*, ed. Joseph Levitt, 94–5. Toronto: Copp Clark, 1970.

Boustie, Sylvie, et al. *How Ratifying the Kyoto Protocol Will Benefit Canada's Competitiveness*. Ottawa: Pembina Institute, 2002.

Bow, Brian. 'Anti-Americanism in Canada, before and after Iraq.' *American Review of Canadian Studies* 38, no. 3 (Fall 2008): 141–59.

– *The Politics of Linkage: Power, Interdependence, and Ideas in Canada-US Relations.* Vancouver: UBC Press, forthcoming.

– 'Out of Ideas?: Models and Strategies for Canada–US Relations.' *International Journal* 62, no. 1 (Winter 2006–7): 123–44.

Brown, Douglas M. 'The Evolving Role of the Provinces in Canadian Trade Policy.' In *Canadian Federalism: Meeting Global Economic Challenges?* ed. Douglas M. Brown and Murray G. Smith, 81–128. Kingston: Queen's University Institute of Intergovernmental Relations, 1991.

Campbell, Robert M. *Grand Illusions: The Politics of the Keynesian Experience in Canada, 1945–1975*. Peterborough, ON: Broadview Press, 1987.

Canada. *Agenda: Jobs and Growth – A New Framework for Economic Policy.* Ottawa: Department of Finance, 1994.

– *Canada's International Policy Statement: A Role of Pride and Influence in the World.* Ottawa: Government of Canada, 2005.

– *Canada in the World: Government Statement.* Ottawa: Government of Canada, 1995.

– 'Creating a Canadian Advantage in Global Capital Markets.' In *Budget 2007.* Ottawa: Department of Finance, 19 March 2007. Available at http://www.budget.gc.ca/2007/pdf/bkcmae.pdf (accessed 1 October 2007).

– *Hansard*, 37th Parliament, 2nd Session, no. 041, 2 and 9 December 2002.

– *News Release: Canada Proposes Targets for Reductions in Global Greenhouse Gas Emissions.* 1 December 1997.

– 'Projecting Canadian Values and Culture.' In *Canada in the World*. Ottawa: Queen's Printer, 1995.

– 'Table 13: Goods by Georgraphic Area, Annual.' In *Canada's Balance of International Payments: System of National Accounts Second Quarter 2007*. Statistics Canada Catalog no. 67-001. Available at http://www.statcan.ca/english/freepub/67-001-XIE/2007002/t017_en. htm (accessed 10 September 2007).

Canada, House of Commons Standing Committee on Foreign Affairs and International Trade. *Partners in North America: Advancing Canada's Relations with the United States and Mexico.* Tabled 12 December 2002. Available at http://cmte.parl.gc.ca/Content/HOC/committee/372/fait/reports/rp1 032319/faitrp03/faitrp03-e.pdf (accessed 28 September 2007).

Canadian Coalition for Responsible Environmental Solutions. 'Coalition Formed to Advance "Made in Canada" Strategy on Climate Change.' 26 September 2002. Available at http://www.cpeq.qc.ca/anglais/apropos/ReleaseCCRES.pdf (accessed 1 October 2007).

– 'Backgrounder on Kyoto.' 3 October 2002. Available at http://www
    .canadiansolution.com/backgrounder.asp (accessed 1 October 2007).
Canadian Institute of Public Opinion. Survey, 20 November 1943. In *Public
    Opinion Quarterly* 8, no. 1 (Spring 1944): 124–61.
Canadian Labour Congress. 'Deep Integration in North America: Security and
    Prosperity for Whom?' Accessed 22 March 2007, at http://canadianlabour
    .ca/index.php/Deep_Integration/Deep_Integration_in.
Carpentier, Cecile, Jean-François L'Her, and Jean-Marc Suret. 'How Healthy Is
    the Canadian Stock Market?' 28 August 2005. Available at http://www
    .fsa.ulaval.ca/personnel/suretjm/documents/Carpentier_How%20
    Healthy%20is%20the%20Canadian%20Stock%20Market.pdf (accessed 1
    October 2007).
CBC News. 'Chretien Government Rejected Military's Advice on Afghan
    Deployment: Ex-Army Chief.' *CBC News*, 18 October 2006. Available at
    http://www.cbc.ca/canada/story/2006/10/18/afghan-military-advice
    .html (accessed 18 October 2006).
Chapnick, Adam. *The Middle Power Project: Canada and the Founding of the United
    Nations*. Vancouver and Toronto: UBC Press, 2005.
Chase, Steven. 'Canada Shouldn't Ratify Kyoto, U.S. Envoy Says.' *Globe and
    Mail*, 26 January 2002, A10.
Chase, Steven, and Peter Kennedy. 'Provinces Reject Softwood Proposal: Trade
    Minister Will Attempt to Win More Concessions from Washington Next
    Week.' *Globe and Mail*, 9 January 2004, B3.
Chase, Steven, et al. 'Softwood Deal under Attack: B.C. Government Lobbies
    Ottawa to Reopen Agreement and Fix 23–Month Escape Clause.' *Globe and
    Mail*, 5 July 2006, A1.
Cheadle, Bruce. 'Canada to Sign Kyoto, but Won't Abide by It.' *Toronto Star*, 5
    September 2002. Available at http://www.thestar.com/ (accessed 29 October
    2002).
Chen, Duanjie, and Jack M. Mintz. 'Federal-provincial combined marginal
    effective tax rates on capital: 1997–2006, 2010.' Toronto: C.D. Howe Institute,
    20 June 2006. Available at http://www.cdhowe.org/pdf/ebrief_31_SI.pdf
    (accessed 1 October 2007).
Clark, Joe. *Canada's International Relations: Response of the Government of Canada
    to the Report of the Special Joint Committee of the Senate and the House of Com-
    mons*. Ottawa: Minister of Supply and Services Canada, 1986.
Clarkson, Stephen. *Canada and the Reagan Challenge: Crisis and Adjustment, 1981–
    85*. Updated edition. Toronto: James Lorimer & Company, 1985.
– 'The Choice to Be Made.' In *An Independent Foreign Policy for Canada?* ed.
    Stephen Clarkson, 253–69. Toronto: McClelland & Stewart, 1968.

– 'The Choices to Be Made.' In *Readings in Canadian Foreign Policy*, ed. Duane Bratt and Christopher Kukucha, 46–61. Toronto: Oxford University Press, 2007.

– *Uncle Sam and Us: Globalization, Neoconservatism, and the Canadian State*. Toronto: University of Toronto Press, 2002.

Clarkson, Stephen, Sarah Davidson Ladly, Megan Merwart, and Carleton Thorne. 'The Primitive Realities of North America's Transnational Governance.' In *Complex Sovereignty: Reconstituting Political Authority in the Twenty-First Century*, ed. Edgar Grande and Louis Pauly, 168–95. Toronto: University of Toronto Press, 2005.

Clarkson, Stephen, Sarah Davidson Ladly, and Carleton Thorne. 'De-Institutionalizing North America: NAFTA's Committees and Working Groups.' Paper presented to Third EnviReform Conference, Toronto, 8 November 2002. Available at http://www.envireform.utoronto.ca/conference/nov2002/clarkson-paper2.pdf (accessed 1 October 2007).

Clarkson, Stephen, and Timothy Lewis. 'The Contested State: Canada in the Post-Cold War, Post-Keynesian, Post-Fordist, Post-National Era.' In *Shape Shifting: Canadian Governance toward the 21st Century – How Ottawa Spends: 1999–2000*, ed. Leslie A. Pal, 293–340. Toronto: Oxford University Press, 1999.

Commonwealth of Australia. *Australia's Public Diplomacy: Building Our Image*. Report of the Senate Standing Committee on Foreign Affairs, Defence, and Trade. Available at http://www.aph.gov.au/Senate/committee/fadt_ctte/public_diplomacy/report/index.htm.

Cooper, Andrew, ed. *Canadian Culture: International Dimensions*. Toronto: Canadian Institute of International Affairs, 1985.

Cooper, Barry, and Mercedes Stephenson. 'Ballistic Missile Defence and the Future of Canada-US Cooperation.' *Fraser Forum*, March 2005. Available at http://www.fraserinstitute.org/commerce.web/product_files/Mar05ff ballistic.pdf, 9–11 (accessed 1 October 2007).

Council of Canadians et al. 'Behind Closed Doors: What They Are Not Telling Us about the SSP.' At http://www.canadians.org/integratethis/backgrounders/guide/index.

Courchene, Thomas J., and Richard G. Harris. 'From Fixing to Monetary Union: Options for North American Currency Integration.' *Commentary* 127. Toronto: C.D. Howe Institute, 1999.

Coyne, Andrew. 'Dismembering Canada.' *Ottawa Citizen*, 30 May 2006, A14.

Coyne, J.H. 'Loyalty and Empire, II.' In *The United Empire Loyalists*, ed. Leslie Upton, 137–9. Toronto: Copp Clark, 1967.

Craik, Jennifer, Glyn Davis, and Naomi Sunderland. 'Cultural Policy and

National Identity.' In *The Future of Governance*, ed. Michael Keating and Glyn Davis, 158–81. Sydney: Allen and Unwin, 2000.

Crawford Panel on a Single Canadian Securities Regulator. *Blueprint for a Canadian Securities Commission – Final Report*. Toronto, 2006. Available at http://www.crawfordpanel.ca/Crawford_Panel_ final_paper.pdf (accessed 1. October 2007).

Crow, John. *Making Money: An Insider's Perspective on Finance, Politics and Canada's Central Bank*. Toronto: Wiley, 2002.

Cuff, Robert, and J.L. Granatstein. 'The Rise and Fall of Canadian-American Free Trade, 1947–8.' *Canadian Historical Review* 58 (December 1977): 459–82.

D'Aquino, Thomas. 'Security and Prosperity: The Dynamics of a New Canada–United States Partnership in North America.' Presentation to the annual general meeting of the Canadian Council of Chief Executives, Toronto, 14 January 2003.

David Suzuki Foundation. *Keeping Canada in Kyoto: The Case for Immediate Ratification and Domestic Emissions Trading*. Vancouver: David Suzuki Foundation, 2002. Available at http://davidsuzuki.org/files/ClimateBrief.pdf (accessed 14 October 2007).

Dobson, Wendy. 'Shaping the Future of the North American Economic Space.' *Commentary* [C.D.Howe Institute], *The Border Papers* 162 (April 2002).

Dodge, David A. 'The Interaction between Monetary and Fiscal Policies.' *Canadian Public Policy* 28, no. 2 (June 2002): 187–201.

Doern, G. Bruce, and Monica Gattinger. *Power Switch: Energy Regulatory Governance in the Twenty-First Century*. Toronto: University of Toronto Press, 2003.

Doern, G. Bruce, and Brian Tomlin. *Faith and Fear: The Free Trade Story*. Toronto: Stoddart Publishing, 1991.

Donaghy, Greg. *Tolerant Allies: Canada and the United States, 1963–68*. Montreal and Kingston: McGill-Queen's University Press, 2003.

Donnelly, Jack. 'Sovereign Inequalities and Hierarchy in Anarchy: American Power and International Society.' *European Journal of International Relations* 12, no. 2 (2006): 139–70.

Dosman, Edgar J. *The National Interest: The Politics of Northern Development, 1968–75*. Toronto: McClelland & Stewart, 1975.

– 'The Northern Sovereignty Crisis 1968–70.' In *The Arctic in Question*, ed. Edgar Dosman. Toronto: Oxford University Press, 1976.

Druick, Zoe. 'International Cultural Relations as a Factor in Postwar Canadian Cultural Policy: The Relevance of UNESCO for the Massey Commission.' *Canadian Journal of Communication* 31, no. 1 (2006): 177–95.

Dymond, Bill, and Michael Hart. 'The Potemkin Village of Canadian Foreign Policy.' *Policy Options* 25 (December 2003–January 2004): 39–45.

Embassy of the United States of America in Canada. 'Kyoto: The U.S. Position.'
    2 February 2002. Available at http://canada.usembassy.gov/content/
    content.asp?section=embconsul t&document=cellucc (accessed 25 October
    2007).
Environment Canada. 'Notes for an Address by the Honourable David Ander-
    son, P.C., M.P, Minister of the Environment to Open the Parliamentary
    Debate on Ratification of the Kyoto Protocol.' 9 December 2002. Available at
    http://www.ec.gc.ca/media_archive/minister/speeches/2002/021209_s
    _e.htm (accessed 25 October 2007).
Ewart, J.S. 'The Kingdom of Canada.' In *Imperialism and Nationalism, 1884–1914:
    A Conflict in Canadian Thought*, ed. Carl Berger, 82–4. Toronto: Copp Clark,
    1969.
Eyre, K. 'Forty Years of Defence Activity in the Canadian North, 1947–87.'
    Arctic 40, no. 4 (1987): 292–9.
Farrell, D.K. 'The Canada First Movement and Canadian Political Thought.'
    Journal of Canadian Studies 4, no. 4 (November 1969): 16–26.
Feigenbaum, Harvey. 'Is Technology the Enemy of Culture?' *International Jour-
    nal of Cultural Policy* 10, no. 3 (November 2004): 251–63.
Fisher, Devin. 'Canada's New Chief of Defence Staff Visits NORAD,
    USNORTHCOM.' *USNORTHCOM News*, 25 April 2005.
Flew, Terry. 'Sovereignty and Software.' *International Journal of Cultural Policy*
    11, no. 3 (November 2005): 243–60.
Florida, Richard. The *Rise of the Creative Class*. New York: Basic Books,
    2004.
Foreign Affairs and International Trade Canada. 'Canada and Mexico: A Pro-
    ductive Partnership.' At http://www.dfait-maeci.gc.ca/mexico-city/extra/
    60/menu-en.asp.
– 'Key Border Documents, and What's New.' Available at http://geo
    .international.gc.ca/can-am/main/border/key_border-en.asp (accessed
    18 October 2007).
Gaddis, John Lewis. *Surprise, Security, and the American Experience*. Cambridge:
    Harvard University Press, 2004.
Gibson, Douglas J. 'Canada's Declaration of Less Independence.' *Harvard Busi-
    ness Review* 51 (September–October 1973): 69–79.
Gillespie, W. Irwin. *Tax, Borrow and Spend*. Toronto: Oxford University Press,
    1991.
Girard, Charlotte S.M. *Canada in World Affairs*. Vol. 13: *1963–65*. Toronto: Cana-
    dian Institute for International Affairs, 1980.
Goff, Patricia. 'Invisible Borders: Economic Liberalization and National Iden-
    tity.' *International Studies Quarterly* 44, no. 4 (December 2000): 533–62.

– *Limits to Liberalization: Local Culture in a Global Marketplace.* Ithaca: Cornell University Press, 2007.

Goff, Patricia, and Barbara Jenkins. 'The "New World" of Culture: Reexamining Canadian Cultural Policy.' *Journal of Arts, Management, Law and Society* 36, no. 3 (Fall 2006): 181–96.

Goldfarb, Danielle. 'The Canada-Mexico Conundrum: Finding Common Ground.' The *Border Papers*, CD. Howe Institute, no. 91 (July 2005), 8.

Gordon, Walter L. *A Choice for Canada: Independence or Colonial Status.* Toronto and Montreal: McClelland & Stewart, 1966.

Gotlieb, Allan E. 'Canada–US Relations: The Rules of the Game.' *SAIS Review* 2 (Summer 1982): 177–87.

Gourevitch, Peter. 'The Second Image Reversed: The International Sources of Domestic Politics.' *International Organization* 32, no. 4 (Autumn 1978): 881–912.

Governments of Yukon, Northwest Territories, and Nunavut. *Developing a New Framework for Sovereignty and Security in the North: A Discussion Paper.* April 2005.

Granatstein, J.L. *Whose War Is It? How Canada Can Survive in the Post 9/11 World.* Toronto: HarperCollins Publishers Ltd, 2007.

– *Yankee Go Home? Canadians and Anti-Americanism.* Toronto: HarperCollins, 1996.

Grant, Peter S., and Chris Wood. *Blockbusters and Trade Wars.* Toronto: Douglas and McIntyre, 2004.

Grant, Shelagh. *Sovereignty or Security: Government Policy in the Canadian North 1936–1950.* Vancouver: UBC Press, 1988.

Grant, William L. 'The Impossibility of Isolationism.' In *Imperialism and Nationalism, 1884–1914*, ed. Carl Berger, 20–42. Toronto: Copp Clark, 1989.

Greene, J.J. '"Canada Can't Moan over Oil Cuts" – Greene.' *Ottawa Citizen*, 11 March 1970, A1, A21.

Greenspon, Edward, and Anthony Wilson-Smith. *Double Vision.* Toronto: Doubleday, 1996.

Greenwood, John. 'BC Tries to Cut Own Deal with U.S. over softwood: Preference Still for Country-Wide Solution.' *National Post*, 2 April 2004, FP6.

Griffiths, Franklyn. 'Opening up the Policy Process.' In *An Independent Foreign Policy for Canada?* ed. Stephen Clarkson, 110–18. Toronto: McClelland & Stewart, 1968.

Grubel, Herbert G. *The Case for the Amero: The Economics and Politics of a North American Monetary Union.* Vancouver: Fraser Institute, 1999.

Guillemette, Yvan, and Jack M. Mintz. 'A Capital Story: Exploding the Myths around Foreign Investment in Canada.' *Commentary* 201. Toronto: C.D. Howe Institute, August 2004.

Gwyn, Richard. *Nationalism without Walls: The Incredible Lightness of Being Canadian*. Toronto: McClelland & Stewart, 1995.

Hale, Geoffrey. 'Canadian Federalism and North American Integration: Managing Multi-Level Games.' Paper presented to conference on 'Different Perspectives on Canadian Federalism: Retrospective and Prospective.' University of Waterloo, 27 April 2007.

– 'The Dog That Hasn't Barked: The Political Economy of Contemporary Debates on Canadian Foreign Investment Policies.' *Canadian Journal of Political Science* 41, no. 3 (September 2008): 1–29.

– 'Getting Down to Business: Rebuilding Canada–US Relations.' In *How Ottawa Spends: 2007–2008*, ed. G. Bruce Doern, 63–86. Montreal: McGill-Queen's University Press, 2007.

– 'International Capital and Domestic Politics: Stumbling towards Tax Reform?' In *How Ottawa Spends: 2008–2009*, ed. Allan M. Maslove. Montreal: McGill-Queen's University Press, forthcoming.

– *The Politics of Taxation in Canada*. Toronto: Broadview Press, 2001.

– 'WHTI: Now for the Hard Part.' *Fraser Forum*, December–January 2007: 14–17.

Hamilton, Gordon. 'Softwood Deal Unacceptable: U.S. Offer to End Dispute Ignores Critical B.C. Demands, Trade Council Says.' *Vancouver Sun*, 1 June 2006, C1.

– 'Softwood Deal Worries Coastal Producers: Current Draft Not Addressing B.C.'s Need for Autonomy to Implement Domestic Policies, Group Says.' *Vancouver Sun*, 7 June 2006, D1.

Hamilton, Gordon, and Peter O'Neil. 'Ottawa, B.C. at Odds on U.S. Offer.' *Vancouver Sun*, 17 May 2003, F3.

– 'U.S. Must Give on Softwood Deal, B.C. Says: Province's Market-Based Timber Pricing System Has to Be Recognized.' *Vancouver Sun*, 14 June 2006, D1.

Hamre, John J. 'Address to the Calgary Chamber of Commerce.' Remarks as delvered by the Deputy Secretary of Defense. Washington, 18 February 2000. Available at http://www.defenselink.mil/speeches/speech.aspx?speechid=531 (accessed 3 March 2008).

Hanly, Charles. 'The Ethics of Independence.' In *An Independent Foreign Policy for Canada?* ed. Stephen Clarkson, 17–29. Toronto: McClelland & Stewart, 1968.

Hart, Michael. 'Almost but Not Quite: The 1947–48 Bilateral Canada-US Negotiations.' *American Review of Canadian Studies* 19 (Spring 1989): 25–58.

240   Bibliography

Harvey, Frank P. 'Canada's Addiction to American Security: The Illusion of Choice in the War on Terrorism.' *American Review of Canadian Studies* 35, no. 1 (Summer 2005): 265–94.

Hay, John. 'Projecting Canadian Values and Culture.' *Canadian Foreign Policy* 3, no. 2 (Fall 1995): 21–32.

Head, Ivan, and Pierre Trudeau. The *Canadian Way: Shaping Canada's Foreign Policy, 1968–1984.* Toronto: McClelland & Stewart Inc., 1995.

Heeney, A.D.P. 'Independence and Partnership: The Search for Principles.' *International Journal* 27, no. 2 (Spring 1972): 159–71.

Helliwell, John F. 'Globalization: Myths, Facts, and Consequences.' Benefactors Lecture, 23 October 2000. Toronto: C.D. Howe Institute, 2000.

Hobbes, Thomas. *Leviathan.* New York: Penguin, 1981.

Hoffman, Stanley. *Gulliver's Troubles.* New York: McGraw-Hill, 1968.

Holmes, John W. *The Better Part of Valour: Essays on Canadian Diplomacy.* Toronto: McClelland & Stewart, 1970.

– 'Interdependence: Political Aspects.' *Canadian Forum* 48 (February 1969): 245–6.

Holsti, K.J. 'Canada and the United States.' In *Conflict in World Politics*, ed. Steven Spiegel and Kenneth Waltz, 375–96. Cambridge, MA: Winthrop, 1971.

Holsti, K.J., and Thomas Allen Levy. 'Bilateral Institutions and Transgovernmental Relations between Canada and the United States.' *International Organization* 28 (Autumn 1974): 875–901.

Hovi, Jon, Tora Skodvin, and Steinar Andresen. 'The Persistence of the Kyoto Protocol: Why Other Annex I Countries Move on Without the United States.' *Global Environmental Politics* 3, no. 4 (November 2003): 1–23.

Howlett, Karen. 'Reduction in Quotas Blindsides Ontario.' *Globe and Mail*, 27 April 2006, A14.

Huebert, Rob. 'Steel, Ice and Decision-Making: The Voyage of the *Polar Sea* and Its Aftermath: The Making of Canadian Foreign Policy.' Unpublished MA thesis, Dalhousie University, 1993.

Huntington, Samuel J. 'American Ideals vs. American Institutions.' *Political Science Quarterly* 97 (Spring 1982): 1–37.

Ikenberry, G. John. 'Liberalism and Empire: Logics of Order in the American Unipolar Age.' *Review of International Studies* 30 (2004): 609–30.

– 'The Myth of Post–Cold War Chaos.' *Foreign Affairs* 75, no. 3 (May/June 1996): 79–91.

Independent Panel on Canada's Future Role in Afghanistan. January 2008: 38. Available at http://www.independent-panel-independant.ca/pdf/Afghan_Report_web_e.pdf (accessed 6 February 2008).

International Institute for Sustainable Development. *Commentary: Canada and COP-6.* 23 July 2001. Available at http://www.iisd.org/bonnoped.htm (accessed 4 September 2002).

– *Earth Negotiations Bulletin*, 13 December 1997. Available at http://www.iisd.ca/linkages/download/asc/end127e.txt (accessed 29 October 2002).

Jockel, Joseph T., and Joel J. Sokolsky. 'The End of the Canada–U.S. Defense Relationship.' CSIS Policy Papers on the Americas, 1996.

Kant, Immanuel. 'Perpetual Peace: A Philosophical Sketch.' In *Kant's Political Writings*, ed. H.B. Nisbet, 93–130. Cambridge: Cambridge University Press, 1970.

Keohane, Robert O., and Joseph S. Nye, Jr. *Power and Interdependence: World Politics in Transition.* Boston: Little Brown & Co., 1977.

Kirkey, Chris. 'Delineating Maritime Boundaries: The 1977–78 Canada-U.S. Beaufort Sea Continental Shelf Delimitation Boundary Negotiations.' *Canadian Review of American Studies* 95, no. 2 (Spring 1995).

Kirton, John. 'Une ouverture sur le monde.' *Études Internationales* 27 (1996): 257–79.

Kirton, John, and Don Munton. 'The Manhattan Voyages and Their Aftermath.' In *Politics of the Northwest Passage*, ed. Franklyn Griffiths. Kingston and Montreal: McGill-Queen's University Press, 1987.

Klinenberg, Eric, and Claudio Benzecry. 'Cultural Production in a Digital Age.' *Annals of the American Academy of Political and Social Science* 597 (January 2005): 6–18.

Kukucha, Christopher J. 'From Kyoto to the WTO: Evaluating the Constitutional Legitimacy of the Provinces in Canadian Foreign Trade and Environmental Policy.' *Canadian Journal of Political Science* 38, no. 1 (March 2005):1–24.

Lackenbauer, Whitney, and Matthew Farish. 'The Cold War on Canadian Soil: Militarizing a Northern Environment.' *Environmental History* 12, no. 3 (October 2007).

Lajeunesse, Adam. 'The Distant Early Warning Line and the Canadian Battle for Public Perception.' *Canadian Military Journal* 8, no. 2 (Summer 2007). Available at http://www.journal.forces.gc.ca/engraph/Vol8/no2/09-lajeunesse_e.asp.

Lake, David A. 'Escape from the State of Nature: Authority and Hierarchy in World Politics.' *International Security* 32, no. 1 (Summer 2007): 47–79.

Leacock, Stephen. *Greater Canada: An Appeal – Let Us No Longer Be a Colony.* Montreal: Montreal News Co. Ltd, 1907.

Legere, Laurence J., to McGeorge Bundy. 'Subject: Follow-up with Canadians on Hyannis Port.' White House Staff Files, Myer Feldman, John F. Kennedy Library.

Legge, Thomas. 'The Unexpected Triumph of Optimism over Experience.' *Centre for European Policy Studies Commentary*, 27 July 2001. Available at http://www.ceps.bc/Commentary/July01/unexpected.htm (accessed 12 March 2002).

Lennox, Patrick. 'Defence against Help': Canada and Transnational Security after 9/11.' In *Revolution or Evolution? Emerging Threats to Security in the 21st Century*, ed. Riley Hennessey and Alexandre S. Wilner. Halifax: Centre for Foreign Policy Studies, Dalhousie University, 2005.

– 'From Golden Straightjacket to Kevlar Vest: Canada's Transformation to a Security State.' *Canadian Journal of Political Science* 40, no. 4 (December 2007): 1017–38.

Leung, Wendy. 'B.C. OK's Amended Softwood Agreement.' *Vancouver Sun*, 17 August 2006, A1.

Lorimer, Rowland. 'Book Publishing.' In *The Cultural Industries in Canada*, ed. Michael Dorland, 3–34. Toronto: J. Lorimer and Co., 1996.

Lorimer, Rowland, and Eleanor O'Donnell. 'Globalization and Internationalization in Publishing.' *Canadian Journal of Communication* 17 (1992): 493–510.

Lyon, Peyton V. 'Problems of Canadian Independence.' *International Journal* 16, no. 3 (Summer 1961): 250–9.

– 'Quiet Diplomacy Revisited.' In *An Independent Foreign Policy for Canada?* ed. Stephen Clarkson, 29–43. Toronto: McClelland & Stewart, 1968.

McCall, Christina, and Stephen Clarkson. *Trudeau and Our Times*. Vol. 2: *The Heroic Delusion*. Toronto: McClelland & Stewart, 1994.

McCallum, John. *Engaging the Debate: Costs and Benefits of a North American Currency*. Toronto: Royal Bank Economics, 2000.

MacDonald, Douglas, and Heather A. Smith. 'Promises Made, Promises Broken: Questioning Canada's Commitment to Climate Change.' In *Readings in Canadian Foreign Policy: Classic Debates and New Ideas*, ed. Duane Bratt and Christopher J. Kukucha. Toronto: Oxford University Press, 2007.

McDorman, Ted. 'In the Wake of the *Polar Sea*: Canadian Jurisdiction and the Northwest Passage.' *Marine Policy* 10 (1986): 243–6.

McDonough, David S. 'The Paradox of Afghanistan: Stability Operations and the Renewal of Canada's International Security Policy?' *International Journal* 62 (Summer 2007): 620–41.

McKenna, Barrie, et al. 'Furious Provinces Aim to Sink Softwood Deal.' *Globe and Mail*, 27 April 2006, A1.

Mackenzie, Hector. 'Canada's Nationalist Internationalism: From League of Nations to the United Nations.' In *Canadas of the Mind: The Making and Unmaking of Canadian Nationalisms in the Twentieth Century*, ed. Norman Hillmer and Adam Chapnick, 89–109. Montreal and Kingston: McGill-Queen's University Press, 2007.

McKinney, Joseph. *Created from NAFTA: The Structure, Function and Significance of the Treaty's Related Institutions*. Armonk, NY: M.E. Sharpe, 2000.

McKinnon, Janice. *Minding the Public Purse*. Montreal and Kingston: McGill-Queen's University Press, 2003.

McLeod, Lori. 'Pension Funds on Steroids.' *Globe and Mail*, 7 July 2007, B4.

McRae, Don. 'The Negotiation of Article 234.' In *Politics of the Northwest Passage*, ed. Franklyn Griffiths. Kingston and Montreal: McGill-Queen's University Press, 1987.

Magder, Ted. 'International Agreements and the Regulation of World Communication.' In *Media and Cultural Theory*, ed. James Curran and David Morley, 164–76. Routledge: New York, 2006.

Martin, Lawrence. *Iron Man: The Defiant Reign of Jean Chrétien*. Vol. 2. Toronto: Viking, 2003.

Martin, Paul. 'An Independent Foreign Policy.' In *Statements and Speeches* 66, no. 3. Ottawa: Department of External Affairs Information Division, 1966.

Mason, Dwight N. 'Canada Alert: Canada and the U.S. Missile Defense System.' *CSIS Hemisphere Focus*, 9 January 2004.

– 'Canada and the Future of Continental Defense: A View from Washington.' *CSIS Policy Papers on the Americas* 14 (September 2003). Available at http://www.csis.org/index.php?option=com_csis_pubs&task=view&id=724 (accessed 1 November 2007).

May, Elizabeth. 'From Montreal to Kyoto, How We Got From Here to There – or Not.' *Policy Options* 24, no. 1 (December 2002–January 2003): 14–19.

Mintz, Jack M. *The 2006 Tax Competitiveness Report: Proposals for Pro-Growth Tax Reform*. Toronto: C.D. Howe Institute, 2006.

Montpetit, Éric. *Misplaced Distrust: Policy Networks and the Environment in France, the United States, and Canada*. Vancouver: UBC Press, 2003.

Morton, Desmond. 'Independence: It Won't Be Easy.' *Canadian Forum* 52 (April 1972): 3–13.

Moseley, Lt. Gen. T. Michael. *Operation Iraqi Freedom – By the Numbers*. 30 April 2003. Available at http://www.globalsecurity.org/military/library/report/2003/uscent af_oif_report_30apr2003.pdf (accessed 1 October 2007).

'Movie Biz Enjoys Global Warming.' *Variety*, 7 April 1997, 1.

Mulroney, Brian. 'Notes for an Address to the Nation on the Trade Initiative by the Right Honourable Brian Mulroney, P.C., M.P., Prime Minister of Canada.' Ottawa, 16 June 1986. Archival records of the Canadian Trade Negotiations Office, file 5420-1.

Munton, Don, and Don Page. 'Planning in the East Block: The Post-Hostilities

Problems Committees in Canada, 1943–5.' *International Journal* 32, no. 4 (Autumn 1977): 677–726.

Naftali, Timothy, and Philip Zelikow, eds. *The Presidential Recordings, John F. Kennedy: The Great Crises*, vol. 2. New York: Norton, 2001.

Nash, Knowlton. *Kennedy and Diefenbaker: Fear and Loathing across the Undefended Border.* Toronto: McClelland & Stewart, 1990.

Nicholls, Christopher. 'The Characteristics of Canada's Capital Markets and the Illustrative Case of Canada's Legislative Regulatory Response to Sarbanes-Oxley.' Research Report for Task Force to Modernize Securities Legislation in Canada. Toronto: Government of Ontario, 15 June 2006. Available at http://www.tfmsl.ca/docs/V4(3A)%20Nicholls.pdf (accessed 1 October 2007).

Noble, Paul C. 'Problems of Canadian Independence.' *CIIA Notes* 2, no. 2 (August 1961): 1–4.

North American Competitiveness Council. 'Enhancing Competitiveness in Canada, Mexico, and the United States: Private Sector Priorities for the Security and Prosperity Partnership of North America – Initial Recommendations of the NACC.' February 2007. Available at http://www.as-coa.org/files/PDF/grp_10_4.pdf (accessed 28 October 2007).

Nossal, Kim Richard. 'Defense Policy and the Atmospherics of Canada-U.S. Relations: The Case of the Harper Conservatives.' *American Review of Canadian Studies* 37, no. 1 (Spring 2007): 23–34.

– *The Patterns of World Politics.* Scarborough, ON: Prentice-Hall Canada, 1997.

Nye, Joseph. *Bound to Lead.* New York: Basic Books, 1990.

Olliver, Maurice. *Problems of Canadian Sovereignty from the British North America Act, 1867 to the Statute of Westminster.* Toronto: Canadian Law Book Co., 1945.

Osberg, Lars, and Pierre Fortin, eds. *Hard Money, Hard Times.* Toronto: James Lorimer, 1998.

Parkinson, David. 'Bank of Canada Seen Setting Own Course.' *Globe and Mail*, 22 August 2007, B1.

Patterson, Kelly. 'Integrating North America "By Stealth."' *Ottawa Citizen*, February 7, 2007, A7.

Pauwelyn, Joost. 'The UNESCO Convention on Cultural Diversity, and the WTO: Diversity in International Law-Making?' *ASIL Insights.* Washington: The American Society of International Law, 2005. Available at http://www.asil.org/insights/2005/11/insights051115.html (accessed 15 October 2007).

Peacock, Nina. 'New Lessons from the Old World: Side-Payments and Regional Development Funds.' *Norteamérica* 1, no. 2 (July–December 2006): 99–125.

Pentand, Charles. 'Mandarins and Manicheans: The "Independence" Debate on Canadian Foreign Policy.' *Queen's Quarterly* 77 (Spring 1970): 99–103.

Pharand, Donat. *Canada's Arctic Waters in International Law.* Cambridge: Cambridge University Press, 1988.

Planet Ark. 'US Stance Key to Global Warming Talks – Canada.' 14 May 2001. Available at http://www.Planetark.com (accessed 9 October 2001).

Plourde, André. 'The Changing Nature of National and Continental Energy Markets.' In *Canadian Energy Policy and the Struggle for Sustainable Development*, ed. G. Bruce Doern, 51–82. Toronto: University of Toronto Press, 2005.

Plumptre, A.F.W., A.E. Safarian, Abraham Rotstein, and Pauline Jewett. 'Retaliation: The Price of Independence?' In *An Independent Foreign Policy for Canada?* ed. Stephen Clarkson, 43–56. Toronto: McClelland & Stewart, 1968.

Podhoretz, Norman. *World War IV: The Long Struggle against Islamofascism.* New York: Doubleday, 2007.

'Polar Vision or Tunnel Vision: The Making of Canadian Arctic Waters Policy: *Marine Policy* 19, no. 4 (July 1995): 343–63.

Potter, Evan. 'Canada and the New Public Diplomacy.' In *Discussions in Public Diplomacy.* The Hague: Netherlands Institute of International Relations, 2001.

David Pratt. 'Is There a Grand Strategy in Canadian Foreign Policy?' *Policy Options* (September 2007): 6–11.

Purver, Ron. 'The Arctic in Canadian Security Policy, 1945 to the Present.' In *Canada's International Security Policy*, ed. David Hewitt and David Leyton-Brown. Scarborough: Prentice Hall, 1995.

Putnam, Robert D. 'Diplomacy and Domestic Politics: The Logic of Two-Level Games.' *International Organization* 42, no. 3 (Summer 1988): 427–60.

Reber, Grant L. 'Canadian Independence in an Asymmetrical World Community: A National Riddle.' *International Journal* 29, no. 4 (Autumn 1974): 535–56.

Reid, Escott. 'The United States and Canada: Dominion, Co-operation, Absorption.' 12 January 1942. Library and Archives Canada, Escott Reid Papers, MG31 E46, vol. 30, United States and Canada, 1942–1945.

'Report on Business 1000.' *Globe and Mail: Report on Business*, July–August 2007.

Richards, Robert G. 'The Canadian Constitution and International Economic Relations.' In *Canadian Federalism: Meeting Global Economic Challenges?* ed. Douglas M. Brown and Murray G. Smith. Aldershot, UK: Ashgate, 1991.

Robinson, H. Basil. *Diefenbaker's World: A Populist in Foreign Affairs.* Toronto: University of Toronto Press, 1988.

Robson, William B.P. 'No Small Change: The Awkward Economics and Politics of North American Monetary Integration.' *Commentary* 167 (Toronto: C.D. Howe Institute, July 2002).

Rosenau, James N. *Distant Proximities: Dynamics beyond Globalization.* Princeton, NJ: Princeton University Press, 2003.

Rotstein, Abraham, and Gary Lax, eds. *Independence: The Canadian Challenge.* Toronto: Committee for an Independent Canada, 1972.

Rousseau, Jean-Jacques. *Project of Perpetual Peace: Rousseau's Essay.* Trans. Edith M. Nuttall, intro. G. Lowes Dickinson. London: Richard Cobden-Sanderson, 1927.

Rubin, Jeff, Peter Buchanan, and Avery Shenfeld. 'A Merger Driven Market.' Toronto: CIBC World Markets, 1 June 2007.

Sabourin, Louis. 'Special International Status for Quebec?' In *An Independent Foreign Policy for Canada?* ed. Stephen Clarkson, 97–109. Toronto: McClelland & Stewart, 1968.

Samyn, Paul. 'Planners in Mideast a Prelude to War?' *Winnipeg Free Press*, 12 February 2003, A12.

Sands, Christopher. 'Canadian National Security after 9/11: What Does the United States Expect?' *Canadian American Strategic Review* (Simon Fraser University) 1 (August 2002).

Saul, John Ralston. 'Culture and Foreign Policy.' Paper prepared for the Government of Canada International Policy Review, 1995. Available at http://www.media-awareness.ca/english/resources/articles/sovereignty_identity/culture_policy.cfm.

Schmidt, Brian C. *The Political Discourse of Anarchy: A Disciplinary History of International Relations.* Albany: SUNY Press, 1998.

Scoffield, Heather, Andrew Willis, and Tara Perkins. 'A Deal That Was 10 Hours in the Making.' *Globe and Mail*, 17 August 2007, B5.

Seaborn, J. Blair. 'Mission to Hanoi: The Canadian Channel, May 1964–November 1965.' In *Canadian Peacekeepers in Indochina, 1954–1973*, ed. Arthur E. Blanchette, 89–99. Ottawa: Golden Dog, 2002.

Security and Prosperity Partnership (SPP). '2005 Launch of SPP.' Available at http://www.spp.gov/2005_launch.asp (accessed 12 December 2005).

– 'SPP Prosperity Working Groups.' Available at http://www.spp.gov/prosperity_working/index.asp?dName=prosperity_ working (accessed 12 December 2005).

– 'Report to Leaders.' 27 June 2005. Available at http://www.spp.gov/report_to_leaders/index.asp?dName=report_to_leaders (accessed 12 December 2005).

– 'Report to Leaders (Cancún Summit).' August 2006. Available at http://www.spp.gov/2006_report_to_leaders/index.asp?dName=2006_report_to_leaders (accessed 1 May 2007).

Singh, J.P. 'Culture or Commerce? A Comparative Assessment of International Interactions and Developing Countries at UNESCO, WTO, and Beyond.' *International Studies Perspectives* 8, no. 1 (February 2007): 36–53.

Skogstad, Grace. 'Canadian Agricultural Trade Policy: Continuity amidst Change.' In *Canada among Nations 1999: A Big League Player?* ed. Fen Osler

Hampson, Martin Rudner, and Michael M. Hart, 73–90. Don Mills: Oxford University Press, 1999.

- 'International Trade Policy and Canadian Federalism: A Constructive Tension?' In *Canadian Federalism: Performance, Effectiveness, and Legitimacy*, ed. Herman Bakvis and Grace Skogstad, 159–77. Don Mills: Oxford University Press, 2002.

Soward, F.H., and Edgar McInnis, 'Forming the United Nations, 1945.' In *Canadian Foreign Policy: Selected Cases*, ed. Don Munton and John Kirton, 4–19. Scarborough: Prentice-Hall, 1992.

Stacey, C.P. *Canada and the Age of Conflict*. Vol. 1: *1867–1921*. Toronto: University of Toronto Press, [1977] 1984.

Stairs, Denis. *The Diplomacy of Constraint: Canada, the Korean War, and the United States*. Toronto: University of Toronto Press, 1974.

- 'Myths, Morals and Reality in Canadian Foreign Policy.' *International Journal* 57 (Spring 2003): 239–56.

- 'Will and Circumstance in the Postwar Study of Canadian Foreign Policy.' *International Journal* 50 (1994–5): 9–39.

Stein, Janice, and Eugene Lang. *The Unexpected War: Canada in Kandahar*. Toronto: Viking, 2007.

Studin, Irvin. 'Revisiting the Democratic Deficit: The Case for Political Party Think Tanks.' *Policy Options*, February 2007, available at http://www.irpp.org/po.

Sutherland, R.J. 'A Defence Strategist Examines the Realities.' In *Canadian Foreign Policy since 1945: Middle Power or Satellite?* ed. J.L. Granatstein, 21–9. Toronto: Copp Clark Publishing, 1969.

- 'The Strategic Significance of the Canadian Arctic.' In *The Arctic Frontier*, ed. R. St. J. MacDonald. Toronto: University of Toronto Press, 1966.

Tremblay, Col. Alain. 'The Canadian Experience in Afghanistan.' In *The New World of Robust International Peacekeeping Operations: What Roles for NATO and Canada?* ed. Brian S. MacDonald and David S. McDonough, 64–82. Toronto: Royal Canadian Military Institute, 2005.

United States. 'Integrated Border Enforcement Teams Now Cover Canada-U.S. Border from Coast to Coast.' Press release. Washington: U.S. Department of Justice, 19 November 2003.

- International Trade Administration. Work Reference (Organizational) Chart. Available at http://www.ita.doc.gov/ooms/MACCHART.pdf (accessed 14 October 2007).

- The National Security Strategy of the United States of America. Washington: The White House, 2006.

- The National Strategy for Homeland Security. Washington: Office of Homeland Security, 2002.

United Nations. *Kyoto Protocol*. New York: United Nations, 1997.

Upton, L.S.F., ed., *The United Empire Loyalists: Men and Myths*. Toronto: Copp Clark Publishing, 1967.

van Ham, Peter. 'The Rise of the Brand State.' *Foreign Affairs*, September–October 2001.

Venturelli, Shalini. *From the Information Economy to the Creative Economy: Moving Culture to the Center of International Public Policy*. Washington: Center for Arts and Culture, 2007. Available at http://www.culturalpolicy.org/pdf/venturelli.pdf (accessed 10 September 2007).

Vieira, Paul. 'Flaherty Flip Sparks Confusion.' *Financial Post*, 15 May 2007, FP4.

Von Glahn, Gerhard. *Law among Nations: An Introduction to Public International Law*. 2nd ed. Boston: Allyn and Bacon, 1996.

Waltz, Kenneth N. *Man, the State, and War: A Theoretical Analysis*. New York: Columbia University Press, 1954.

– *Theory of International Politics*. Don Mills: Addison-Wesley, 1979.

Wartime Information Board. Survey 7. 27 March 1943. Library and Archives Canada, W.L.M. King Papers, MG26 J2, vol. 379, file W-319-2, War-W.I.B. Surveys, 1943.

Watson, William. *Globalization and the Meaning of Canadian Life*. Toronto: University of Toronto Press, 1998.

Weber, Katja. *Hierarchy amidst Anarchy: Transaction Costs and Institutional Choice*. Albany: State University of New York Press, 2000.

Wendt, Alexander, and Daniel Friedheim. 'Hierarchy under Anarchy: Informal Empire and the East German State.' *International Organization* 49, no. 4 (Autumn 1995): 689–721.

Whitaker, Reg. 'Made in Canada: The New Public Safety Paradigm.' In *How Ottawa Spends: 2005–2006 – Managing the Minority*, ed. G. Bruce Doern, 77–95. Montreal and Kingston: McGill-Queen's University Press, 2005.

Williams, Robert J. 'International Cultural Programmes: Canada and Australia Compared.' In *Canadian Culture: International Dimensions*, ed. Andrew Cooper. Toronto: Canadian Institute of International Affairs, 1985.

Wolfe, Robert. 'Transparency and Public Participation in the Canadian Trade Policy Process.' Paper presented at the annual meeting of the Canadian Political Science Association, London, Ontario, 2 June 2005.

World Trade Organization. *Article 2 Agreement on Subsidies and Countervailing Measures*. Available at http://www.wto.org/english/docs_e/legal_e/24-scm_01_e.htm (accessed 10 June 2005).

Contributors

Brian Bow is Assistant Professor of Political Science at Dalhousie University.

Adam Chapnick is Deputy Director of Education and Assistant Professor of Defence Studies at the Canadian Forces College.

Patricia Goff is Associate Professor of Political Science at Wilfrid Laurier University.

Stephanie R. Golob is Associate Professor of Political Science at Baruch College.

Geoffrey Hale is Associate Professor of Political Science at the University of Lethbridge.

Rob Huebert is Associate Professor of Political Science and Associate Director of the Centre for Military and Strategic Studies, University of Calgary.

Christopher Kukucha is Associate Professor of Political Science at the University of Lethbridge.

Patrick Lennox is a Postdoctoral Fellow at the Centre for Military and Strategic Studies at the University of Calgary.

Christopher Sands is a Senior Fellow at the Hudson Institute, Washington DC.

Heather A. Smith is Associate Professor of International Studies at the University of Northern British Columbia.